Changing the Victorian Subject

This book is available as a free fully-searchable ebook from
www.adelaide.edu.au/press

Changing the Victorian Subject

Edited and Introduction by

Maggie Tonkin, Mandy Treagus, Madeleine Seys
School of Humanities, The University of Adelaide

Sharon Crozier-De Rosa
School of Humanities and Social Inquiry, The University of Wollongong

UNIVERSITY OF
ADELAIDE PRESS

Published in Adelaide by

University of Adelaide Press
The University of Adelaide
Level 14, 115 Grenfell Street
South Australia 5005
press@adelaide.edu.au
www.adelaide.edu.au/press

The University of Adelaide Press publishes externally refereed scholarly books by staff of the University of Adelaide. It aims to maximise access to the University's best research by publishing works through the internet as free downloads and for sale as high quality printed volumes.

© 2014 The Contributors

This work is licenced under the Creative Commons Attribution-NonCommercial-NoDerivatives 4.0 International (CC BY-NC-ND 4.0) License. To view a copy of this licence, visit http://creativecommons.org/licenses/by-nc-nd/4.0 or send a letter to Creative Commons, 444 Castro Street, Suite 900, Mountain View, California, 94041, USA. This licence allows for the copying, distribution, display and performance of this work for non-commercial purposes providing the work is clearly attributed to the copyright holders. Address all inquiries to the Director at the above address.

For the full Cataloguing-in-Publication data please contact the National Library of Australia: cip@nla.gov.au

ISBN (paperback) 978-1-922064-73-8
ISBN (ebook: pdf) 978-1-922064-74-5
ISBN (ebook: epub) 978-1-922064-75-2
ISBN (ebook: mobi) 978-1-922064-76-9

Editors: Patrick Allington and Rebecca Burton
Book design: Zoë Stokes
Cover design: Emma Spoehr
Cover image: Robert Dowling, English 1827-1886, emigrated to Australia 1834. *Masters George, William and Miss Harriet Ware with the Aborigine Jamie Ware 1856*, oil on canvas, 63.7 x 76.4 cm, National Gallery of Victoria, Melbourne. Eleanor M. Borrow Bequest, 2007. Used with permission.

Contents

	Notes on Contributors	vii
1	Re-visiting the Victorian subject *Maggie Tonkin, Mandy Treagus, Madeleine Seys and Sharon Crozier-De Rosa*	1
2	Queen Victoria's Aboriginal subjects: a late colonial Australian case study *Amanda Nettelbeck*	21
3	Identifying with the frontier: Federation New Woman, Nation and Empire *Sharon Crozier-De Rosa*	37
4	A 'Tigress' in the Paradise of Dissent: *Kooroona* critiques the foundational colonial story *Margaret Allen*	59
5	The making of Barbara Baynton *Rosemary Moore*	83
6	A literary fortune *Megan Brown*	105
7	Olive Schreiner's *From Man to Man* and 'the copy within' *Dorothy Driver*	123
8	Guy Boothby's 'Bid for Fortune': constructing an Anglo-Australian colonial identity for the *fin-de-siècle* London literary marketplace *Ailise Bulfin*	151

9	The scenery and dresses of her dreams: reading and reflecting (on) the Victorian heroine in M.E. Braddon's *The Doctor's Wife*	177
	Madeleine Seys	
10	The woman artist and narrative ends in late-Victorian writing	201
	Mandy Treagus	
11	Miss Wade's torment: the perverse construction of same-sex desire in *Little Dorrit*	217
	Shale Preston	
12	'All the world is blind': unveiling same-sex desire in the poetry of Amy Levy	241
	Carolyn Lake	
13	From 'Peter Panic' to proto-Modernism: the case of J.M. Barrie	259
	Maggie Tonkin	

Notes on Contributors

Margaret Allen is Professor Emerita in Gender Studies, University of Adelaide. She has researched gendered histories for four decades publishing on women writers and Australian cultural history, South Australian women's history and nineteenth century British Quakers. Currently she researches transnational, postcolonial and gendered histories and on whiteness, in particular, on links between India and Australia from c. 1880-1940. She also examines the changes in women's missionary approaches in India consequent upon the Edinburgh conference in 1910. She has published in a number of fields and is a co-editor of *Women's Activism: Global Perspectives from the 1890s to the present* (2012). She is a member of the Fay Gale Centre for Research on Gender.

Megan Brown is an Honorary Post-Doctoral Research Associate at the University of Wollongong. Her PhD thesis 'I Shall Tell Just Stories as I Please' examined Mary Fortune's writing in the *Australian Journal* from 1865-1885. Her publications include an essay on sensational aspects of Fortune's writing in the special edition of Australian Literary Studies in honour of Elizabeth Webby, a chapter on Fortune's life writing in *The Unsociable Sociability of Women's Life Writing* (2010) and, in 2012, an essay in *Australian Literary Studies* titled 'Mary Fortune as Sylphid: "blond, and silk and tulle"'.

Ailise Bulfin has recently been awarded her doctorate from Trinity College Dublin, where she is a teaching assistant in the School of English. Broadly speaking her research examines the fin-de-siècle phenomenon of invasion fiction as written by colonial authors such as M.P. Shiel and Guy Boothby, and has been funded in part by a postgraduate scholarship from the Irish Research Council for the Humanities and Social Sciences. Her publications include articles and book chapters on aspects of the relationship between imperialism and fin-de-siècle popular fiction in *English Literature in Transition* and a number of edited collections.

Sharon Crozier-De Rosa is a Lecturer in History at the University of Wollongong. She has published research on gender and empire (for which she was awarded the Mary Bennett Prize), the New Woman globally, and emotions and popular culture in history. Currently, she is writing a book entitled *Shame and the Anti-Feminist Backlash: Britain, Ireland and Australia, 1890-1920* to be published by Routledge. Sharon is also national co-convenor of the Australian Women's History Network.

Dorothy Driver is Professor of English at the University of Adelaide, and Emerita Professor at the University of Cape Town, where she taught for twenty years. She has also held visiting positions at the University of Chicago and Stanford University. Her major research interests and publications are in South African literature, the constructions and representations of gender and race both under Apartheid and after Apartheid, and writing by women. Her new edition of Olive Schreiner's *From Man to Man* will be published in 2014.

Carolyn Lake is a postgraduate research student in English at the University of Adelaide, South Australia. Her thesis project explores the poetry and prose of Amy Levy, examining narrative strategies of marginal representation in urban space. She is interested in lesbian and proto-lesbian cultures and cultural products from the late-Victorian period. Other research interests include contemporary Australian literature and film and queer film histories.

Rosemary Moore is an Adjunct Senior Lecturer, formerly Senior Lecturer, in English and Creative Writing at the University of Adelaide, where she has taught courses in narrative with emphasis on the influence of gender on women writers of the nineteenth and twentieth centuries. She has published articles in this field and researched into the relations between psychoanalysis and feminist studies.

Amanda Nettelbeck is Professor in the School of Humanities at the University of Adelaide. She is co-author with Robert Foster of *Out of the Silence: the History and Memory of South Australia's Frontier Wars* (2012), *In the Name of the Law: William Willshire and the Policing of the Australian Frontier* (2007), and *Fatal*

Collisions: the South Australian Frontier and the Violence of Memory (with Rick Hosking, 2001). A new collaborative book is in progress titled *Fragile Settlements: Aboriginal peoples, law and resistance in Australia and western Canada*. Her most recent project 'Protection and Punishment', funded by an ARC Discovery grant, deals with how policies of Aboriginal protection in colonial Australia intersected in practice with Aboriginal punishment under the law.

Shale Preston is an Honorary Research Fellow in the English Department at Macquarie University. Her work explores the representation of gender and sexuality in Charles Dickens's fiction and the relationship between Dickens's oeuvre and Contemporary Philosophy. She has published a range of articles and book chapters on Dickens and is the author of *Dickens and the Despised Mother: A Critical Reading of Three Autobiographical Novels* (2013). Currently, she is co-editing an anthology forthcoming from Routledge (2015) titled *Queer Victorian Families: Curious Relations in Literature*.

Madeleine Seys is a postgraduate student in the Discipline of English and Creative Writing and an affiliate member of the Fay Gale Centre for Research on Gender at the University of Adelaide. She teaches Victorian literature and social and cultural history in the Discipline. Her doctoral thesis explores the use of dress to fashion femininity and female sexuality and to tell the woman's story in Victorian popular literature. The project combines her research interests in the narrative and generic conventions of Victorian popular literature, gender and sexuality, fashion and textile history, and material culture. Madeleine is Costume Curator at the National Trust of South Australia's Ayers House Museum. Her research interests also include museology and museum curatorship, in particular, the use of costume and textiles in museum displays.

Maggie Tonkin is a Lecturer in English at the University of Adelaide. She is the author of *Angela Carter and Decadence* (2012) and a number of book chapters and articles on Carter and contemporary women's writing. She regularly writes on dance for the national industry magazine, *Dance Australia*, and is currently working on a book to be co-authored with Garry Stewart, Artistic Director of the Australian Dance Theatre, commemorating the company's 50th anniversary. She is also in the preliminary stages of researching the impact of R.D. Laing and existential psychiatry on late twentieth-century fiction. Maggie is a member of the Adelaide Critics Circle and the J.M. Coetzee Centre for Creative Practice.

Changing the Victorian Subject

Mandy Treagus is Senior Lecturer in English and Creative Writing at the University of Adelaide, where she teaches nineteenth- and twentieth-century literature and culture, and film. She researches Victorian, Australian and Pacific literature, film, and cultural history. Her book *Empire Girls: the colonial heroine comes of age* (2014) examines the female *Bildungsroman* in British colonies. She is the author of numerous articles, most recently appearing in *JASAL*, *Australian Humanities Review* and the *Journal of Postcolonial Writing*. Her current project explores the display of Pacific peoples in colonial exhibitions, especially with regard to the agency of performers, and has appeared in several edited collections, including *Oceania and the Victorian Imagination* (2013). She is a member of the Fay Gale Centre for Research on Gender.

1

Re-visiting the Victorian subject

Maggie Tonkin, Mandy Treagus, Madeleine Seys and Sharon Crozier-De Rosa

Critical Perspectives

In entitling this collection of essays *Changing the Victorian Subject*, we are not supposing that the Victorian subject has ever been singular or monolithic. Indeed, we take Martin Hewitt's caution against just such an assumption to be self-evident. In 2001 Hewitt wrote:

> The denomination 'Victorian' continues to be widely used in the 1990s both denotatively and connotatively, but in ways which make no attempt to interrogate the nature of the 'Victorian.' Where the 'Victorian' is subject to direct critical enquiry, it is almost always as part of a conventional reading against the grain, in which some monolithic 'Victorian' identity is conjured only for the doubtful and unenlightening pleasure of deconstructing it. Taken to its logical conclusion, such a stance leaves Victorian Studies as a label of purely temporal convenience. (143)

As academics based in Australia but working within a field that goes by the name of a British sovereign, we are fully cognisant of the plurality of what might fall under the rubric 'Victorian'. The imagined relationships of colonial subjects to a foreign monarch, and a foreign yet hegemonic culture, need always to be imagined in the plural. For colonial subjects, the 'Victorian', even taken as 'a label of purely temporal convenience', is fraught with complexity and nuance, since in the colonies that very epoch saw the emergence of discourses of nationhood and of anti-colonial rhetoric, alongside strident declarations of allegiance and conformity to metropolitan values. In the colonies, the Victorian and the anti-Victorian co-existed: indeed, the colonies were *the* prime sites of contestation of, and ambivalence about, metropolitan values and social mores.

At the heart of this collection, then, is the intersection of the Victorian with the colonial, and an interrogation of the varied relationships between the colonial Victorian subject and hegemonic British Victorian mores and values. We are interested in exploring the imagined nexus between the culture of the metropolis and that of the colonies, and the multifarious ways in which colonial subjects and authors were positioned, and positioned themselves, in relation to dominant British ideologies and emergent nationalist sentiments. In colonial texts and histories, negotiating Victorian and settler subject positions emerges as a key trope. At the same time, British authors also negotiated Victorian subjects and subjectivities in their work. Essays in this collection explore these changing and developing gendered, national and authorial subjectivities. They also examine the work of British writers, arguing for their repositioning within literary history and for new readings of key Victorian texts. This array of approaches to the 'Victorian' works in concert to expand any understanding of what might fall under the rubric of Victorian studies. Key, then, is how we understand the field, and why we have chosen to retain the term 'Victorian', given the recent pressure it has been under.

Since what is usually taken to be its inception — the 1957 founding of the interdisciplinary journal, *Victorian Studies* — Victorian studies has been constantly changing its subject. This correlates squarely with the expansionist dynamic of the Victorian period itself, with its colonising project that coloured half the world pink, in the process creating new markets, new colonies and new subjects. From its initial focus on English culture and history, Victorian studies has broadened incrementally, firstly to encompass the cultures and histories of Great Britain and secondly to encompass those of the Victorian Empire. The interdisciplinarity that marked the field's foundation has similarly increased. Whereas at first the disciplines were limited to literary studies and history, a bias that this collection largely reflects, the field now includes a broad range of disciplines: art history and criticism, museum studies, the history of costume and textiles, performance and music studies, periodical studies, the history of technology and science, theology and religious history and so forth. The original subjects of inquiry were canonical authors and traditional histories; now marginal voices and topics are more frequently the recipients of scholarly attention.

But perhaps as a result of this radical expansion, the adequacy of the term 'Victorian' to designate such a broad field of scholarship has recently been questioned. In its simplest incarnation, 'Victorian' is a temporal category denoting the reign of the redoubtable queen and empress herself from 1837 to 1901. Yet for some scholars this periodisation is problematic. Kate Flint, for instance, argues that the length of a royal reign is a poor container for the social or cultural movements which spill beyond it, yet she also finds that temporal designations such as 'the nineteenth century' are equally arbitrary (230). Alternatively, Margaret Harris argues for the term 'Long Nineteenth Century' to replace the 'Victorian', positing a range from the French Revolution of 1789 to the outbreak of the Great War in 1914. According to Harris, this moniker makes sense in European history because it marks the transition from feudalism to the emergence of secular, democratic, technological societies (67-8). In the Australian context, she argues, the exact dates could shift slightly to encompass the period from Governor Phillip's landing in 1788, skimming over the historical coincidence of Federation in 1901 with Queen Victoria's death, to the Gallipoli landings in 1915. These dates bracket off the period of colonial settlement from the arrival of white Europeans through to one of the foundational myths of Australian nationhood, Gallipoli (Harris 68). The flexibility of Harris's formulation suggests that the exact dates of the 'Long Nineteenth Century' could be calibrated to the specifics of individual colonial histories.

Another objection to the term 'Victorian' stems from its nationalist connotations. Flint claims that the term 'carries with it an unmistakable national, and nationalist, overtone' which poses issues when discussing the 'dynamics of transnational cultures' (230). This is an important point, but one that can be viewed as enabling rather than necessarily limiting. Whereas in Hewitt's 2001 review of the field, the subjects addressed in Victorian studies were construed as uniformly British, Sharon Marcus points out that 'in recent years Victorian studies has expanded out from the English nation into the United Kingdom and the British Empire' (679). Indeed, Pablo Mukherjee mounts a strong case for considering the Victorian as co-terminous with Empire, arguing that 'the binding of Britain (and within Britain, of the "provinces" to London) to the world through the twin thrusts of capital and Empire was the central feature of Victorian England' (659). In his view, Victorian Britain is indivisible from an Empire in which Australian Aborigines, Chinese labourers, Canadian trappers, Zulu warriors and Kentish cricketers are bound together by a network of trade and transport (646).

If Victorian Britain is inseparable from its Empire, then this necessitates a reconsideration of what can be regarded as Victorian culture or literature, a reconsideration of what could or *should* be the subject of Victorian studies. For Mukherjee, the Victorian Empire was a global system, hence its literature ought to be considered global as well (645). Thus British literature should be read in tandem, indeed *in tension with*, colonial literatures. After all, he argues, colonial texts were

> largely published by English publishing companies, circulated through the imperial communication networks, and reacted to the cultural, political, and material norms of a London-centric England. This is not a claim for the derivative nature of all Victorian English writing, but a suggestion that we read this writing as a system of world or global English — a system that was unevenly developed, just as capital and empire forced an uneven development of the world. We must always pay scrupulous attention to the 'local' historical, material, and aesthetic specificities of texts produced in the disparate parts of the world. But we must also, together with Dickens, Eliot, Tennyson, Kipling, read Marcus Clarke, Olive Schreiner, Flora Annie Steele, Charles Harpur, and Catherine Spence to grasp the true extent of Victorian writing. (659-60)

Patrick Brantlinger similarly argues that Victorian literature is invariably marked by Empire: whether it originates in the colonies or the metropole, Victorian writing is shot through with discourses of imperialism, race and nation. He notes that the colonial encounter was mutually constitutive: 'the colonizers did not simply impose their beliefs and values on the colonized; exchanges across cultural boundaries always involve two-way alterations in individual attitudes and behaviours' (4). Hence, according to Brantlinger, 'rather than jingoist, much nineteenth-century writing about the Empire was ambivalent' (2). The notion advanced by both Mukherjee and Brantlinger that the literature of the Victorian metropolis should be read alongside that of the Victorian colony is one that underpins this collection. Juxtaposing chapters on colonial writers such as Catherine Martin, Barbara Baynton, Iota, Mary Fortune, Sara Jeanette Duncan and Guy Boothby (who are relatively unknown outside local national contexts) with canonical British writer Charles Dickens, and with writers such as Olive Schreiner, Mary Elizabeth Braddon, Amy Levy and J.M. Barrie (who until the last decades were relatively neglected), is a deliberate strategy designed to push the boundaries of what is thought of as Victorian writing.

Priya Joshi affirms Mukherjee's notion of the Victorian as a global system, pointing out that Victorianism has had a far greater global impact than the 'ism' that preceded it chronologically, Romanticism. She elaborates further on the idea of a range of geographically distinct yet interrelated Victorian literatures with her discussion of 'indigenous Victorianisms' (20). However, Joshi argues that whilst over the past two decades postcolonial scholarship has remodelled the previously nationalist focus of Victorian studies, the notion that the metropolis was 'hegemonic and defined the terms of production in the colonial periphery, if not by economic power then by indirect cultural influence' (21) has nevertheless persisted. In her view, 'a new kind of transnational study is now in order, one where the cultural and economic hegemony of the metropolis is no longer dominant, so that other circuits and relations, long-obscured in the centre-dominant model, become evident' (21). A similar shift has been occurring in the realm of historical studies. Transnational and imperial histories proliferate but in the last decade or so, more of these transnational approaches to the past have moved away from 'discrete comparison[s]' of metropole and periphery where metropolitan culture dominates towards more complex and nuanced understandings of metropolitan-colonial relations. Many more histories now recognise, as historian Fiona Paisley puts it, 'the significance of circulating populations and ideas, including from "margin" to "metropolis"' (272).

Joshi's challenge to what she sees as the persistent 'centre-dominated' model of Victorian studies does not mean that she wants to abandon the moniker 'Victorian' (21). Rather, and in contradistinction to Flint, Joshi wants to retain 'Victorian' but to relocate it across the globe and the designated timeframe in order to generate insights that the term's current usage renders opaque (20). She asks whether '"Victorian"' might be a term whose real use lies in *indexing* a set of preoccupations rather than confining those preoccupations to history and geography' (21, emphasis in original). Joshi argues:

> Like globalization, the term 'Victorian' captures the unevenness intrinsic in transnational economic and cultural encounters. A term with a specific origin in nineteenth-century England, 'Victorian' refers today not only to historical boundaries, but more cogently to a set of interrelated cultural, intellectual, and social preoccupations that far outlive the originary moment. 'Victorian' persists as a contact zone: a space of encounter, (mis) recognition, and sometimes, refusal. It makes sense, therefore, to speak in terms of 'half-lives' — a concept originally used in nuclear physics to understand the activity of notable elements over extended if unpredictable periods of time. (39)

Joshi's formulation of the Victorian as a contact zone, and her concept of half-lives, suggests productive ways forward for Victorian studies for both postcolonial critics and historians, and those working on British culture. It is particularly apposite to the Australian context, in which Australian Victorian studies is often subsumed under the rubric of Australian studies.

This has important ramifications: Harris argues that '[a] great deal of work in Australian and New Zealand literature has proceeded in isolation from its connections with British (and other overseas) milieu' (69). Reconsidering Australian cultural products and institutions in terms of the Victorian, reading them in dialogue with British cultural products and institutions rather than in isolation, might throw up entirely new insights into the Victorian reimagined as a contact zone. When Meg Tasker asserts that '[a]ny study of the local literary culture has to acknowledge not only the limited market and infrastructure for publishing within Australia, but also the shared consciousness of being in the colonies, not in England' (1), she is implicitly highlighting the tension — we might even say, the dialectic — between England and 'not England' that suffuses Australian colonial texts. For as Harris points out, Australian history and literary culture is enmeshed in, but not identical to, British history and literary culture, and it is therefore essential to investigate how 'the colony negotiated the cultural imperatives of the imperial centre' (68). Writing in 2003, Harris bemoaned the 'crudely nationalist approaches to Australian culture' which had hitherto elided 'the pervasive and complex interactions of exotic influences such as those of Great Britain' (69).

However, more recently there has been a shift in Australian literary studies away from such a narrowly nationalist focus towards a more globally oriented reading practice that aligns with the broad category of transnational literary studies. In a noteworthy intervention, Ken Gelder has advanced the notion of 'proximate reading', which he describes thus:

> Proximate reading opens up a number of aspects of reading and literary practice that are to do with the way readers negotiate place, position and what can be called literary sociality (that is, relations between readers, texts and the meanings that bind these relations together), where these things are understood and evaluated in terms of degrees of closeness and/ or distance, that is, proximity. (1)

Proximate reading, Gelder argues, enables a way of mediating the transnational connections between texts and readers, 'insofar as it relies on the reader's negotiation of relationships between origin and destination' (4). Applied to Australian literary studies, it enables an understanding of Australia as 'routinely criss-crossed by other literatures, localized in some instances and woven into transnational semantic networks in others' (4). The essays in the 2013 collection, *Scenes of Reading: is Australian Literature a World Literature?*, explore the multifarious ways in which questions and methodologies derived from the disciplines of world and comparative literature are being applied to the study of Australian literature to open up a discipline that in the past, according to the editors, Robert Dixon and Brigid Rooney, has mainly adopted 'a nationally focused approach' (xiv). Recent writing by scholars such as Gelder, Bill Ashcroft, Graham Huggan and Philip Mead have in common, Dixon and Rooney argue, a 'critical analysis of new theoretical vocabularies that would allow Australian literature — as both an academic discipline and a field of cultural production — to be "worlded", or located in relation to world literary space' (xv). Australian exceptionalism is challenged, but this does not mean that understandings of the local epistemologies that inform Australian writing are ignored (xvi). Rather, the national and the transnational interweave, forming part of a global system of circulation and exchange.

Considerations of Victorian literature as world literature or transnational literature are given further credence in Lauren M.E. Goodlad's exploration of the theory she terms 'the Victorian geopolitical aesthetic', an application of Fredric Jameson's 'geopolitical aesthetic' to Victorianism and one that casts light on how Victorian literature engages with past and present 'actually existing cosmopolitanisms' (399). Goodlad posits this model as another useful way of reading Victorian literature, in particular for viewing British literature as 'world literature'. She argues that applying newer transnational perspectives to our reading of Victorian literature allows us to understand how those in the Victorian period were aware of and explored their global connections or geopolitics. Referring to Margaret Cohen and Carolyn Dever's idea of 'the novel's "inter-national" provenance' or Franco Moretti's notion of '"world literature" as a global morphology in which local materialities meet and transfigure novelistic form', Goodlad adds further depth to the realm of transnational Victorian studies, arguing that

> both formulations enable critics to capture literature's globality through the interplay of aesthetic expression and geohistorical process — conceiving form as a medium through which transnational processes are encountered, figured and, to some degree, shaped. (404)

Goodlad's application of theories of geopolitical aesthetics to the study of Victorian literature need not stop at British literature. Such an approach has the potential to reveal further forms of nineteenth-century cosmopolitanism, including those that allow for the exploration of the interconnectedness of metropolitan and colonial literature.

If a broadening of Victorian studies to include the colonial results in a more accurate examination of the two-way traffic of Empire, how might the examination of colonial texts and subjects as Victorian illuminate them? Alongside Amanda Nettelbeck's historical reconsideration of the ambiguous subject position occupied by Australian Aboriginals under Queen Victoria's reign, this collection includes analyses of a range of literary texts, most of which are of colonial origin. Critically, these have predominantly been seen in their national contexts, contributing to the very notion of 'nation' in their home countries. Sometimes, though rarely, they have escaped this perspective and become part of the growing canon of Victorian literature. The most obvious writer in this collection to escape critical confinement due to her origins is Schreiner. Her engagement, and indeed precipitation of, many of the New Woman debates of *fin-de-siècle* Britain, placed her at the heart of London intellectual life. Given that in her novel *The Story of An African Farm* no foot was ever set down in the metropolis, it is even more remarkable that it was as influential as it was. This is the exception, however. Most of the colonial authors featured here have only received critical attention in their home nations, and even then, very little. Some, such as Boothby, have largely slipped out of critical consciousness for over a hundred years. In Boothby's case, he was perhaps too colonial for serious contention in the metropolis, and, having located himself in Britain, too metropolitan for consideration in the national canon.

All of the literary texts addressed in this collection which are of colonial origin are most usefully read as Victorian *and* as part of nascent national literatures. The British Empire had ensured that globalisation, even if it wore a different face to that of the early twenty-first century, was a factor in both colonial and metropolitan life. In many ways, the shared modernity of Victorian cities, whether located in Britain or Australia, ensured that they had more in common than, for example, remote rural areas of Scotland had with London. This shared global cosmopolitanism is apparent in many of these texts, and is especially evident in Duncan's study of a young North American woman artist trying to make her way in the great cities of culture, Paris and London. That it was written while Duncan was resident in Calcutta merely illustrates the traffic, both cultural and literal, that bound the Victorian world.

Boundaries of discipline and field are of necessity artificial. Despite this they remain useful tools for focusing scholarly discussion, allowing debate that is meaningful and deep because of shared knowledge. The problem with boundaries between national literary studies and Victorian ones is that if the emphasis is on the national, the wider context is harder to see. Indeed, texts can be misread without this wider context, in which cultural change, and in particular, literary production, is a result of global, rather than entirely local, flows and influences. The heterogeneity of literary production, and indeed the variety of subjectivities produced by and reflected in it, is a factor in both metropolitan and colonial works. As Susan Magarey, Sue Rowley and Susan Sheridan point out, one does not have to assent to 'a historical unity or *zeitgeist*' to the period under discussion (xv), though one might point to the opposite — the rapidity of change and the variety of subjectivities produced by it — as characteristics which are even more apparent on the outskirts of Empire than in the centre, and which go some way toward describing the era. As this collection shows, the colonies offered a potential for social mobility that was generally unparalleled in the centre; accordingly, the opportunity to remake oneself was both offered and inflicted on individuals in rapidly altering social worlds.

Debates were inflected in different ways in colonial settings as well. Whereas the Woman Question in Britain intensified national anxieties about motherhood, the race and the Empire, in colonies such as those which made up what became the Federation of Australia, women's early enfranchisement took those anxieties in new directions. (For example, many newly enfranchised women, such as the women of the Australian Women's National League, worried about how to carry out their new public responsibilities in the most womanly way possible.) The literature is more concerned, therefore, with women's changing contribution to the developing nation, and whether the masculinist frontier could be figured as a space for women as well as for men. Assertions of Australian national character, which seemed to peak in the 1890s, have been remembered for much of the twentieth century as masculine ones; we are reminded in the re-examination of women's work in this collection that the revisioning of gender and national character which occurred late in the century was an accurate corrective to what had gone before. Marilyn Lake's influential article 'The Politics of Respectability' (1986) reminded scholars that the story of Australia's national character was debated in terms of gender, not just separation from the homeland. This was part of a wider drive in the wake of second-wave academic feminism in which the historical record was re-examined and women's texts from the late nineteenth century were reprinted. These debates around gender have tended to have an international, rather than purely national, focus — demonstrating, as this collection asserts, that identities and identifications are multiple, not just singular, and often in process rather than fixed.

What the inclusion of texts from the colonies can bring to Victorian studies is the sense of a wider conversation, one that takes in the consequences of metropolitan policies, especially where frontiers are concerned. The role of whiteness is rarely stated in studies of this era, but it is the pivotal yet elided factor that underpins almost all of the subjectivities explored in this collection. Nettelbeck's analysis of the problematic legal status of Queen Victoria's Aboriginal subjects addresses this elision directly by demonstrating the gap between benign metropolitan policies and the violence of frontier realities. By focusing on the interaction of Aboriginal subjects with the colonial judicial system, Nettelbeck's chapter — the only purely historical chapter in the collection — speaks to the unease about the treatment of Australia's indigenous peoples that subtends several of the literary texts examined in other chapters. The privilege of whiteness thus emerges in some of these colonial fictions in a way that it rarely does in fictions from the colonial centre. Additionally, as Vron Ware notes in her germinal work *Beyond the Pale: White Women, Racism and History* (1992), 'to be white and female is to occupy a social category that is inescapably racialized as well as gendered' (xii), and this is evident in several of the female-authored colonial works featured here.

The collection also traces various trends in Victorian writing which are central to debates in Victorian studies. Changes in the role of realism are important in this, with the collection addressing a number of instances where it is questioned, unpicked or eventually abandoned in pursuit of newer forms and readerships. For example, Braddon's challenge to realism is highlighted in her self-reflexive literary tactics; in drawing attention to her fictional mechanisms she constructs a new ideal reader, the Victorian woman familiar with the material practices of femininity and resistant to romantic plot devices of more dominant realist modes. Similarly, in characterising her protagonist as female in the *Künstlerroman*, *A Daughter of Today*, Duncan comes up against the incapacity of the form to accommodate her New Woman heroine, thereby demonstrating the limitations of the realism of the late nineteenth century.

In common with many in Victorian studies, we also move beyond the Victorian. Barrie serves to demonstrate the ways in which realism had become irrelevant to children's fiction and indeed to his broader project. In *Peter Pan*, intrusive narrative commentary, coupled with the broaching of boundaries between narrators, characters and readers, marks the move away from the dominant realism of the Victorian era and a shift into proto-Modernism. New critical readings not only enable an identification of queer subjectivities in Barrie's work, but also, even more explicitly, allow the unearthing of queer writerly positions in the poetry of Levy — positions which were apparently unavailable to earlier critics. The chapter on Dickens's *Little Dorrit* outlines a similar incapacity, or indeed resistance, in earlier critics' readings of Miss Wade. Reading her as a lesbian indicates one of the ways in which revisiting canonical texts with new critical practices has the potential to revitalise the field, and illuminate previously suppressed readings.

In this book

The first part of the collection investigates the ways in which the Victorian subject and Victorian subjectivities were changed by historical forces and challenged in colonial texts from Australia and South Africa. Nettelbeck examines the ambiguous subject positions occupied by indigenous Australians *vis-à-vis* the Victorian legal code as administered by the colonial judiciary. Sharon Crozier-De Rosa, Margaret Allen, Rosemary Moore, Megan Brown and Dorothy Driver explore female narratives of nation building: repositioning women on the colonial frontier and on the frontier of newly emerging nations. Examining the traffic between Britain and the colonies, Ailise Bulfin explores Guy Boothby's creation of an Anglo-Australian authorial identity.

In the second part of *Changing the Victorian Subject*, contributors explore Victorian writers' refashioning of authorial and gendered subjectivities. Moving from the colonies to the metropolis, they consider a range of self-conscious, representational, narrative, stylistic and poetic techniques by which authors Braddon, Duncan and Levy write new female and authorial subjectivities in the mid-to-late Victorian period. Carolyn Lake and Shale Preston undertake queer readings of Levy and Dickens respectively, reading against the grain of current critical discourses. In the final chapter in the collection, Maggie Tonkin repositions Barrie within critical discussions regarding the death of the author, literary style and historical and literary temporality.

Drawing on an exceptional legal case from the 1890s, in which an indigenous man accused of the murder of a white settler was acquitted on the grounds of provocation, Nettelbeck's 'Queen Victoria's Aboriginal subjects: a late colonial Australian case study' exposes the gap between the legal status of Australian Aboriginals — who were nominally held to have equal rights with white settlers as Her Majesty's subjects — and the realities of the 'colonial social order that excluded Aboriginal people from those rights'. As Nettelbeck argues, this case is important 'for the ways in which it speaks to the unstable character of Australia's still-evolving frontiers' (23) even as Federation was drawing near, and to the ambiguous subject position forced upon the Aborigines. In the context of the collection as a whole, Nettelbeck's essay is critical in that it demonstrates how the whole colonial edifice rested on the dispossession and disempowerment of the indigenous inhabitants of the continent — a dispossession emblematic of the injustice and violence of the colonising process that underpinned the Victorian Empire as a whole. By foregrounding this often conveniently elided historical reality, Nettelbeck's essay thus speaks explicitly to the readings of colonial texts that follow, several of which are haunted by the displacement and marginalisation of Aboriginal people, while also speaking implicitly to the readings of metropolitan Victorian texts in which the colonised figure by their very absence.

In the second chapter of the collection, 'Identifying with the frontier: Federation New Woman, Nation and Empire', Sharon Crozier-De Rosa changes the critical and historical subject by reinserting women into discussions of *fin-de-siècle* Australian identity. As Crozier-De Rosa argues, the tenacious hold of the mythical Australian bushman on the popular imagination — celebrated in both the metropole and the colonies as the ideal of imperial manhood — resulted in the widespread elision of women from depictions of the colonial frontiers. Through an analysis of Catherine Martin's 1890 novel, *An Australian Girl*, Crozier-De Rosa situates the New Woman both on the bush frontier and on the frontier of the emerging Australian nation. She explores the transition from a colonial past to a new national future. Martin contributes a female voice to 'those that were helping to shape the collective consciousness of a newly emerging nation, a voice that favoured the "Australian" over the "European" and that championed the New World over the Old' (38).

Margaret Allen also explores women's negotiations of an Australian identity in her chapter on Iota (Mrs Mary A. Meredith)'s *Kooroona* (1871). Douglas Pike's influential 1957 study, *Paradise of Dissent: South Australia 1829-57*, champions the role of religious dissenters in South Australia's foundational story. *Kooroona*, on the other hand, portrays South Australia as a chaotic and unruly colony, rather than the paradise that histories such as Pike's record. In

Iota's opinion, religious Dissenters were primary instigators of this disorder. In 'A "Tigress" in the Paradise of Dissent: *Kooroona* critiques the foundational colonial story', Allen argues that Iota's novel challenges South Australia's foundational story, and is critical of South Australia's governance and of its treatment of the indigenous population. This, Allen argues, led to the novel's contemporary unpopularity and subsequent neglect in discussions of South Australian literature. By resurrecting this long-overlooked text, Allen challenges readers to revisit popularly held views of the foundation of the Australian colonies and the development of a colonial identity.

Whilst Iota's *Kooroona* critiques the role played by Dissenters in South Australia's foundational stories, Baynton is herself a dissident writer. However, the critical discussion poses the question: 'What does she dissent from?' In her chapter, 'The making of Barbara Baynton', Rosemary Moore argues that Baynton critiques the nationalism depicted by her literary contemporaries and the representational and narrative styles underpinning it. Like Crozier-De Rosa and Allen, Moore explores feminist challenges to conventional gendered narratives of the Australian bush and Australian identity. In her 1902 collection, *Bush Studies*, and 1907 novel, *Human Toll*, Baynton employs hysterical symbolism to develop a complex and unique narrative style that enables her to write about unmentionable aspects of life in colonial Australia: incest and the abuse and rape of women. Moore argues that Baynton interrogates the conflation of the bush with masculinity, mateship and misogyny. Furthermore, Moore shows that Baynton's dissenting bush stories were integral to the creation of her literary identity: they were the means by which she reshaped her past and her identity and established a lasting literary reputation. In her chapter, Moore continues this process of changing and reshaping by re-reading the significance of the bush in Baynton's *Bush Studies* through Jacque Lacan's theory of hysteria.

Megan Brown also explores the struggle for female writers to establish a literary reputation in Australia in her discussion of the serial writing of Mary Fortune. Like Baynton, Fortune perceived Australia as a 'new land' in which to construct a new gendered and authorial identity. Under a variety of pseudonyms, Fortune wrote for the *Australian Journal* between 1865 and 1908. 'A literary fortune' focuses on her contributions between 1865 and 1885, a time of both fortune and misfortune for this author and the Australian colonies. Fortune's writing reveals her negotiation of the traditionally male spaces of city, bush and goldfields. Fortune acts in, views, analyses and criticises Australian colonial society and the construction of colonial female subjectivities. At the same time, however, she reveals 'the uncertain and contradictory nature of colonial attempts at defining gender' (119). In her writing, Fortune changes the 'Victorian female subject to suit colonial life' (119). Likewise, Brown finds that reading her work 'changes our perspective on the subject of colonial women' (105).

Like Fortune, South African author Olive Schreiner was concerned with redefining Victorian subjectivities in the colonies. In 'Olive Schreiner's *From Man to Man* and "the copy within"', Dorothy Driver explores the ways in which Schreiner problematises *fin-de-siècle* notions of gender and race in her novels. This chapter explores the intersection of discourses of gender and race in *The Story of an African Farm* (1883) and *From Man to Man* (posthumously published in 1926). In these novels, Schreiner presents a newly gendered and raced figure as an image of a new South African nation. This figure is represented by the classical statue of Hercules holding an infant in his arms, a recurring symbol of the African male in eighteenth- and nineteenth-century travel literature and fiction. This 'new' nurturing figure of creative change is juxtaposed with a winged fossil, an evolutionary dead end. Together, these represent the difficulty, as Schreiner perceives it, of realising her vision of a social revolution.

Boothby, born in South Australia and wildly popular in Britain for his Australasian adventure fiction, embodies the movement of people, ideas and texts between the colonies and the metropolis during the Victorian period. In 'Guy Boothby's *Bid for Fortune*: constructing an Anglo-Australian colonial identity for the *fin-de-siècle* London literary marketplace', Ailise Bulfin explores the construction of a hyphenated Anglo-Australian identity. Travelling between Australasia and London, Boothby made a place for himself in the British literary market by constructing an identity as an Anglo-Australian celebrity author. Bulfin argues that Boothby's success as a *fin-de-siècle* novelist was due to his success in establishing himself as the mediator of all things Australian for a metropolitan readership; his 1895 novel, *Bid for Fortune*, took the London literary marketplace by storm and catapulted its author to overnight celebrity status. Boothby's self-conscious performance as an Anglo-Australian produced a double-voice in his writing which reveals the tensions and contradictions of belonging to neither the home colony nor the adopted metropolitan abode. This chapter, and Boothby's journeys, mark the change of subject between the colonies and metropolis in the collection.

British popular novelist Braddon refashioned her authorial subjectivity through changing the subject of her fiction; she fashioned 'a form of highly self-conscious and culturally receptive authorship and readership in the genred literary climate of the mid-nineteenth century' (177). In 'The scenery and dresses of her dreams: reading and reflecting (on) the Victorian heroine in M.E. Braddon's *The Doctor's Wife*', Madeleine Seys explores the significance of the mirror as a tool for reflection, both literal and figurative, in Braddon's 1864 novel, *The Doctor's Wife*. Readings of this novel have long been overshadowed by Braddon's reputation as 'The Sensation Novelist'. Contemporary critics were scathing of the novel's generic instability, and recent critical work has defined it as either self-consciously sensational or unsuccessfully realist. In this chapter, Seys shifts the critical discussion by exploring the self-conscious construction of literary genre and authorial, feminine and readerly subjectivity through metaphors of dressing, reading and reflecting in Braddon's novel.

Mandy Treagus's 'The woman artist and narrative ends in late-Victorian writing' also explores the representation of a new figure in late-Victorian writing: the female artist. Treagus considers the accounts of the female artist's life in *The Journal of Marie Bashkirtseff* (published in English translation in 1890) and Duncan's *A Daughter of Today* (1894). This chapter examines the development of the heroines as artists and women through the *Künstlerroman*. This, Treagus argues, required 'an abandonment of the dominant mode of being' for the nineteenth-century heroine (201). Unlike earlier Victorian fiction where the heroine's sense of duty governs her actions, there is no sense of self-sacrifice in either Bashkirtseff's journal or Duncan's novel; both texts represent a new female subject: the desiring heroine 'whose cultivation of ego is her most defining mode' (202). In this chapter, Treagus explores the ways in which realism in the late nineteenth century fails to accommodate changing ideas about femininity, female subjectivity and women's roles.

In 'Miss Wade's torment: the perverse construction of same-sex desire in *Little Dorrit*', Shale Preston also addresses the 'presence of a new and different kind of subjectivity' (218) in Dickens's novel (1855). Preston argues that Miss

Wade is a lesbian or bisexual woman, a subjectivity that was so 'frightfully new' as to elude Victorian epistemological frameworks (218). As Preston notes, scholars remain reluctant to read Miss Wade as a lesbian, a reluctance she attributes to Dickens's desire to 'figuratively lock [Miss Wade] up and throw away the key'. Dickens 'uses every rhetorical weapon at his disposal to foreclose Miss Wade's identity' and sexuality (232). In this chapter, Preston demonstrates that Dickens's depiction of Miss Wade is framed between sexual voyeurism and discourses of disease and contamination. Rather than the ideal 'angel in the house', Miss Wade is represented as the perverse (or perverted) 'ghost in the house'.

In Levy's 1880s poetry, the lesbian is also represented as a ghost; significantly, though, she is also depicted as an absent or lost love. In '"All the world is blind": unveiling same-sex desire in the poetry of Amy Levy', Carolyn Lake explores the poetics and politics of same-sex desire in Levy's collections, *A Minor Poet and Other Verse* (1884) and *A London Plane-Tree and Other Verse* (1889). Lake departs from an emphasis on Levy's 'triple marginalisation' — on account of her gender, Jewishness and non-heterosexuality — to an analysis of the poetics of her incoherent identities, desires and subjectivities. Lake argues that during the late nineteenth century, female same-sex desire eluded representation. Lake explores the literary tactics allowing Levy to represent desires that have been largely denied by language, noting the ways in which Levy captures the incoherent pleasures of same-sex desire. Lake concludes that Levy's work is valuable for its attempts to negotiate and theorise agency and change, despite, or even through, a poetics of misrecognition.

Changing the subject from the misrecognised to the infamous, the final chapter of the collection reconsiders the author as the subject of Victorian studies. In 'From "Peter Panic" to proto-Modernism: the case of J.M. Barrie', Maggie Tonkin seeks to remove Barrie both from the spectre of psychobiography and from charges of paedophilia in order to reposition *Peter Pan* (1902) in literary history. Drawing on a variety of contemporary sources, both scholarly and popular, this chapter illustrates the public fixation with the author as the ultimate arbiter of textual meaning — a fixation which, in the case of Barrie, is manifested in psychobiographical readings of *Peter Pan*. Tonkin re-reads Barrie's iconic text through the greater historical continuum from Victorianism to Modernism in stylistic terms. Although this chapter touches upon the notion that Barrie himself modelled an emergent queer subjectivity, its primary focus is textuality rather than sexuality. Tonkin argues that *Peter Pan* displays a proto-Modernist experimentation with literary representation and style. This chapter marks the final change of the subject and the collection: from the sexual to the textual, the author to the text, and the Victorian to the Modernist.

Works Cited

Brantlinger, Patrick. *Victorian Literature and Postcolonial Studies.* Edinburgh: Edinburgh UP, 2009.

Dixon, Robert, Brigid Rooney. 'Introduction.' *Scenes of Reading. Is Australian Literature a World Literature?* North Melbourne: Australian Scholarly Publishing, 2013.

Flint, Kate. 'Why Victorian? Response.' *Victorian Studies* 47.2 (2005): 230-9.

Gelder, Ken. 'Proximate Reading: Australian Literature in Transnational Reading Frameworks.' *JASAL: Journal of the Association for the Study of Australian Literature* Special Issue: Common Readers (2010) 1-12.

Goodlad, Lauren M.E. 'Cosmopolitanism's Actually Existing Beyond; Toward A Victorian Geopolitical Aesthetic.' *Victorian Literature and Culture* 38 (2010): 399-411.

Harris, Margaret. 'The Antipodean Anatomy of Victorian Studies.' *AUMLA: The Journal of the Australasian Universities Language and Literature Association* 100 (2003): 61-72.

Hewitt, Martin. 'Victorian Studies: Problems and Prospects?' *Journal of Victorian Culture* 6.1 (Spring 2001): 137-61.

Joshi, Priya. 'Globalizing Victorian Studies.' *Yearbook of English Studies* 41.2 (2011): 20-40.

Lake, Marilyn. 'The Politics of Respectability: Identifying the Masculinist Context.' *Historical Studies* 22.86 (1986): 116-31.

Magarey, Susan, Sue Rowley, Susan Sheridan. 'Introduction.' *Debutante Nation: Feminism Contests the 1890s.* St. Leonards, NSW: Allen & Unwin, 1993.

Marcus, Sharon. 'Same Difference? Transnationalism, Comparative Literature, and Victorian Studies.' *Victorian Studies* 45.4 (June 2003): 667-86.

Mukherjee, Pablo. 'Victorian Empire.' *The Cambridge History of Victorian Literature*. Ed. Kate Flint. Cambridge: Cambridge UP, 2012. 641-61.

Paisley, Fiona. 'Introduction.' *Australian Feminist Studies* 16.36 (2001): 271-7.

Pike, Douglas. *Paradise of Dissent: South Australia, 1829-57*. Melbourne: Melbourne UP, 1957.

Tasker, Meg. 'Introduction.' *Victorian Poetry* 40.1 (Spring 2002): 1-6.

Ware, Vron. *Beyond the Pale: White Women, Racism and History*. London and New York: Verso, 1992.

2

Queen Victoria's Aboriginal subjects: a late colonial Australian case study

Amanda Nettelbeck

In the same year that Queen Victoria came to the throne, the British House of Commons Select Committee on Aboriginal Tribes (British Settlements) issued its much-awaited report. The report was strongly influenced by the mood of evangelical humanitarianism that over the last several years had risen to change the political direction of the Colonial Office, and that had only recently led to the abolition of slavery in Britain's colonies. With imperial governmental attention now turned to the rights of Aboriginal people, the report reflected with dismay on the past colonial practices that had seen Aboriginal people's lands 'usurped', their numbers 'diminished' and their character 'debased' (77). The report's recommendations on future colonial policy were geared around the principles that Aboriginal people must receive the law's protection as British subjects, and that through the protection of these rights they would ultimately be taught the benefits of Christianisation and civilisation.

Until this point in the Australian colonies, the legal status of Aboriginal people had remained profoundly ambiguous. The fictional principle that Australia was settled peaceably rather than taken by force from a sovereign people implied from the outset that Aboriginal people would be treated as subjects of the

Crown. This was embedded in the instructions issued in April 1787 to Captain Arthur Phillip, the first governor of New South Wales, which urged him to 'endeavour by every means in his power' to conciliate the goodwill of Aboriginal people and, if settlers 'should wantonly destroy them', to 'cause such offenders to be brought to punishment'.[1] In reality, fulfilling these instructions was no easy task. Not only did colonial governments have little regulatory control over frontier conflict between settlers and Aboriginal people, but they also doubted that peoples who neither understood nor submitted to British law could come within the jurisdiction of their courts (Kercher 10). For at least the first five decades of British settlement, as Bruce Kercher has put it, the legal protection of Aboriginal people as subjects of the Crown was 'certainly not the general rule' (5).

The 1837 Select Committee Report appeared to clarify a line of imperial policy that henceforth Aboriginal people would be treated as subjects of the Crown, amenable to the protection and punishment of British law. Yet in practice, this status remained ambiguous for decades to come in an environment where the continent had to be won from a people with whom no treaties had been forged. 'It is notorious that not a week passes without the settlers suffering loss from the depredations of the blacks', complained one commentator to the press. The 'erroneous' insistence of the imperial government that Aborigines [*sic*] were to be considered British subjects was a symptom of its 'total ignorance of the circumstances of the colony, the position of the settlers relative to the blacks, and the hardships which such position entails' (*The Australian*, 31 July 1843). Long after the matter appeared settled in policy, the question of whether Aboriginal people could be tried as British subjects when they had no understanding of British law continued to concern colonial judiciaries. In a piece entitled 'Are the Aborigines British Subjects?' an 1858 press editorial expressed this dilemma as a problem of jurisdiction, since the extension of British law over Aboriginal people must remain doubtful 'unless the native chiefs agree by treaty, or are compelled by conquest to submit to the jurisdiction of Parliament'. For as long as there was neither a treaty with Aboriginal people nor their open surrender to

---

1   Instructions for Arthur Phillip Esqu., 25 April 1787, Historical Records of Australia, series 1, vol. 1, 1788-1796, Library Committee of the Commonwealth Parliament (1914), 13-14.

clarify British jurisdiction, the writer argued plainly, 'no part of the soil is ours!' (*Sydney Morning Herald*, 25 November 1858).

As Henry Reynolds has most recently put it in *Forgotten War*, legal theory was one thing and the reality of the Australian frontier 'quite another' (72). In practice, governing Aboriginal people within the terms of evolving colonial law, and successfully prosecuting settler violence against them, proved to be two of the most controversial dilemmas faced by colonial governments across the Australian colonies. In some parts of the continent where settlement was slow to develop, the practical difficulties associated with administering districts remote from the seat of government extended well into the twentieth century.

This chapter will consider a case that came before Western Australia's Supreme Court in the late nineteenth century as a means to explore some of the wider social realities that underpinned the uncertain status of Aboriginal people as British subjects, and to examine the frailties of British law in regulating the Australian frontier.[2] This case, in which an Aboriginal man was tried and acquitted for the murder of his white employer, is important for the ways in which it speaks to the unstable character of Australia's still-evolving frontiers on the cusp of the twentieth century, less than a decade before Federation. Most tellingly, however, it opens a deeper glimpse into the inherent gap between the law's stated imperatives to uphold the rights Aboriginal people nominally held as Her Majesty's subjects, and its more pragmatic contribution to building the kind of colonial social order that excluded Aboriginal people from those rights. Considered at the immediate level of its resolution in court, this case appears to be an exceptional one in upholding the law's promise to protect Aboriginal people's legal equality as subjects of the British Crown. Yet examined in the wider context of the circumstances that brought its actors into the court-room, it emerges as a case encapsulating the structural inequalities that the law not only struggled to resolve, but also helped to justify.

The events of the case came to public notice in late April 1895, when prospector James Gibbs and an Aboriginal woman known as Polly arrived at a mining camp near Siberia in inland Western Australia. They had walked from their own isolated camp some miles away to relay the news that Polly's

---

2   The case dealt with here is based on a legal case history entry published as 'Phillips' Brief: The Severest Provocation' (2013) 37 *Criminal Law Journal* 267.

husband Yalya, alias 'Jacky', had fatally speared the man he and Polly worked for, prospector James Anderson. Anderson's body still lay at the camp where they had left it, and Jacky had run away into the bush.

Western Australia at the end of the nineteenth century provides a window on to a particularly complex picture of frontier social relations, because while the colony had a long history of cross-racial interaction, it also had a particularly protracted experience of frontier conflict. From the colony's earliest years, settlers had sought out Aboriginal people's labour, a pattern that remained true late into the nineteenth century as speculators moved northward and inland seeking rewards from pastoralism, pearling and mining. Yet the pattern of settlement northwards and inward was slow and sparse; the very vastness of the colony's territory ensured that European settlement beyond the metropolitan districts remained thin, and that sizable Aboriginal populations continued to remain outside the reach of colonial authority. In these more remote regions, settlers' perception of their own vulnerability perpetuated an aggressive frontier mentality well into the twentieth century.

The region where the lives of Anderson, Jacky and Polly connected in 1895 was the country of the combined Wangai Aboriginal groups in what is now the inland Goldfields district. Jacky and Polly came from this country. Anderson was a Scottish sailor who came to the colony via New Zealand looking for riches from the burgeoning mining sector. The fledgling town of Siberia had sprung up little more than a year earlier with the discovery of gold, drawing in a rapid influx of speculators like Anderson. On the eve of the twentieth century, then, this was a still-evolving frontier, fed by a transient male population and marked by fluctuating degrees of racial separation and cross-racial intimacy.

In the weeks following Anderson's murder, the press pieced together an account of events that at one level formed a uniquely personal saga of jealousy and revenge, and at another represented a familiarly generic colonial narrative of Aboriginal treachery and pioneer vulnerability. According to the press reports, Jacky and Polly had been working for Anderson on a payment of rations without any trouble until Polly started regularly sharing Anderson's tent, whereupon Jacky bided his time until an opportunity arose to murder his employer. There was 'no doubt', speculated one reporter, that 'jealousy prompted the deed'; and there was 'no doubt' that the murderer's next object was 'to kill the woman' Polly, who was now so much 'in terror of her life' that she could not be moved from the camp. The darkness on the night of the murder had provided the opportunity for the murderer's cruel deed, for it had enabled him 'to steal close upon poor Anderson, with the result already known'. Anderson, it seemed, was the unwitting victim of his own generosity: he had 'always treated the natives well, and gave them a hearty meal on the very night of the murder' (*The Inquirer*, 10 May 1895). A fellow miner had 'often warned the dead man against being too kind to the natives', yet he had ignored this warning with fatal results (*The Inquirer*, 17 May 1895). One press report noted that when Gibbs and Polly came into the camp with news of Anderson's spearing, a 'well armed' party of miners 'immediately got ready to go in pursuit', but because of the darkness of the night and the character of the rocky hills they failed to keep up with Jacky's tracks and were forced to turn back (*The Inquirer*, 10 May 1895). With the nearest police station seventy miles away at Coolgardie and the murderer still at large, all the residents of the district remained in 'much uneasiness' (*The Inquirer*, 10 May 1895).

Eventually, however, Jacky was captured by police sent out from the Coolgardie station, and committed for trial on a charge of wilful murder. Before the case could come to trial, there was another flurry of anxiety in the press when Jacky escaped from the local police cell: he had burrowed a path beneath the temporary galvanised iron walls, and had not 'since been heard of' (*The West Australian*, 20 July 1895). Weeks later, he was successfully recaptured by police after a daybreak raid on an Aboriginal camp near Coolgardie (*The West Australian*, 20 August 1895).

When Jacky came to trial for Anderson's murder in the Supreme Court on 7 October 1895, the case for the prosecution initially seemed straightforward. In July, to the local magistrate and a coronial jury, Polly had stated that Jacky speared Anderson because he was 'too much sulky'. With Gibbs's statement that there were 'no other blacks about the camp', and Polly's identification of the spear as Jacky's, his guilt appeared cemented.[3] At the trial Polly and Gibbs appeared as the prosecution's witnesses, but as it unfolded their evidence opened into other directions. Polly told the court that Anderson and Jacky had argued 'because Anderson had taken her'. She 'wanted to go back to Jacky', and Jacky

---

3   Deposition file Cons 3473, item 186, case 2587; Coronial Inquiry Acc 430, 1895/1086, State Records Office of Western Australia.

had asked Anderson for her return, but Anderson refused and 'made a row'. The men fought and Jacky ran away. Anderson then burnt down Jacky's camp, and claimed 'he would track Jacky up and shoot him'.[4] Settler juries often proved reluctant to accept uncorroborated Aboriginal evidence, despite the fact that it had been admissible in Western Australian courts since the early 1840s, but here Polly's testimony was confirmed by the white witness James Gibbs, who also testified that he heard Anderson 'threatening to kill' the accused. No witnesses were called for the defence, but the Crown's witnesses had effectively done the defence's work. Defence counsel George Leake argued in summary that Jacky 'had been suffering from the severest provocation': 'Anderson took away his woman, fired his hut and threatened to kill him'. If 'a white man were in the dock and a black man had been killed,' he urged, the jury would find no other verdict 'than not guilty'. After brief consideration this was in fact the verdict the jury returned.

The enlistment of a provocation defence to acquit an Aboriginal defendant charged with settler murder makes Jacky's case unusual in Australia's colonial legal history.[5] On Australia's frontiers, the argument of provocation commonly served, along with self defence, as a defence enlisted by settlers to justify their violent acts in response to Aboriginal theft of stock and property. As Lisa Ford has put it, in the creation of 'normative exceptions' to the law's imperative to punish murder, 'killing Aboriginal people was ... acceptable when it accorded to settler notions of self-defence, provocation, and retaliation', and these notions became central strands of a process whereby settler lawlessness could be reconfigured as lawful (85). Although strictly speaking provocation has only ever served as a partial defence capable of reducing the capital offence of murder to the lesser one of manslaughter, its assumption, like that of self-defence, also functioned more loosely to allow settlers to escape all judicial punishment for Aboriginal deaths. Legal scholars have argued that inconsistencies in the applications of the

---

4   Supreme Court Criminal Sittings 7 October 1895, reported in *The Western Australian*, 8 October 1895.

5   *R v Kirkham* (1837) 8 C & P 115 is regularly cited as determining 'reasonableness' as a measure for the provocation defence, captured in the observation of Cambridge J that 'though the law condescends to human frailty ... it considers man to be a rational being, and requires that he should exercise a reasonable control over his passions'. For instance, Spain, 97.

provocation defence over time should be understood in the context of deeper structural social relationships (for instance, Coss, Horder, Nourse). In so far as the argument of provocation usually served to mitigate settler violence against Aboriginal people, the law was complicit in perpetuating the structural social inequalities that defined Australia's frontiers.

In this context, Jacky's acquittal is striking, especially when set alongside other cases of violent interracial crime to come before Western Australia's colonial courts. By the end of the century, thirty-four Aboriginal people had been executed for the murder of settlers, while in the history of the colony only one European, an ex-convict transported for violent crime, was ever found guilty and executed for Aboriginal murder (Purdue 61-71). This isn't to say that more cases of Aboriginal murder by settlers weren't prosecuted — indeed, Western Australia tried more settlers for violent crimes against Aboriginal people in the nineteenth century than did its sister colonies — but in all other cases, the expectation of capital punishment entailed in a murder charge was down-graded. Of a total of thirteen settlers charged with Aboriginal murder before 1900, eight were found guilty of the lesser offence of manslaughter, for which they received lesser sentences or fines, and four were acquitted; another twelve settlers prosecuted in cases involving Aboriginal fatalities were charged not with murder but with manslaughter or aggravated assault, for which they also received minimal sentences or fines (Nettelbeck 2013).

Jacky's case is notable in this sense alone, but it resonates in other ways. For a start, his spearing of Anderson opens the possibility of another kind of law at work in the legally unrecognised sphere of Aboriginal punishment of settler crime. Despite the official understanding after the late 1830s that Aboriginal people came within the jurisdiction of British law, colonial judiciaries remained doubtful that they did. An implicit acceptance that Aboriginal people would continue to exercise their own laws in matters relating to themselves was reflected in the widespread tendency of colonial courts to commute sentences in Aboriginal *inter se* cases. As numerous scholars have argued — most recently, Heather Douglas and Mark Finnane in their book *Indigenous Crime and Settler Law* — this continuing tolerance of Aboriginal law in *inter se* matters not only indicated the co-existence of 'two kinds of law' at an unofficial level, but thereby revealed the unconsolidated nature of British sovereignty (88).

This slippage in the extension of British sovereignty over Aboriginal people via the law was only tacitly acceptable to colonial judiciaries in so far as it did not extend to circumstances involving settlers. However, even if Jacky's act of spearing Anderson was motivated by a different or customary understanding of law than the settler jury's, it appears to have been one made comprehensible to them through the logic of provocation and self-defence that typically helped to normalise and excuse settler violence. In effect, then, the very acceptability of provocation as a defence — one that usually supported the legal privilege of settlers — saw the law working in this case as it professed, but often failed, to do in the service of legal equality.

But if the outcome of Jacky's trial reflected a rare symmetry between Aboriginal and settler defendants in this singular sense, in all other respects the circumstances that brought him into the court-room indicate the asymmetries in social relations that the law typically helped to normalise. Although it is impossible to know what compromises and obligations framed the relationship between Jacky, Polly and Anderson, it was broadly true that the law provided little scope to Aboriginal people within colonial economies for redress against the abuses of white employers (Kercher 111). Not only did Aboriginal workers have little leverage within the judicial system, but they were further burdened by an embedded ethic in colonial society that their labour for settlers would serve as a beneficial step towards their own moral improvement. In the paternalist and punitive spirit that defined this relationship, magistrates and courts over the course of decades supported settler masters' assumed rights over the lives of Aboriginal employees, and dealt lightly with employer abuses when these came to their attention (McQueen 79-80).

This leniency applied not only to settler masters generally, but also to those officials formally responsible for Aboriginal people's legal protection. Not long after Jacky's trial, three of Western Australia's Justices of the Peace were tried on separate charges of assault after punishing their Aboriginal station workers by whipping them, chaining them up and depriving them of food (*Western Mail*, 10 February and 3 March 1899). These cases produced some discussion in the press about the incongruities of a system in which Justices of the Peace were able to adjudicate cases involving 'offences similar to their own'; but this publicity did not alter the lightness with which their neighbouring settler magistrates were able to settle the cases with nominal fines. Even when abuses against Aboriginal employees were investigated by the government, as they periodically were through the 1880s, the realities of economic pragmatism appeared to override the theoretical right of Aboriginal employees to the law's protection. This much was stated by a northern-based Resident Magistrate in 1884 when the Governor queried the negligible punishments of cautions or minor fines imposed by the magistrate on employers charged with the assault of Aboriginal employees in the pearling industry. Dealing with such cases more severely, the magistrate responded, would be detrimental to the region's economic development, an argument which apparently provoked no further response from the Governor's office.[6]

If Jacky's relation to Anderson recalls the law's general indifference to the treatment of Aboriginal people involved in colonial economies, Polly's recalls the law's general apathy towards white men's appropriation of Aboriginal women. In a parallel case from the same mining district six years later, Travelling Inspector of Aborigines George Olivey stumbled upon a case that had been neglected by the local Justices and police, and in so doing opened a door on the normalised hierarchies of frontier sexual politics. During the course of his duties in the district, Olivey was told by a local Aboriginal man known as 'General' that some weeks earlier he had been shot by local miner Jack Stewart when he attempted to retrieve his wife Wanda from Stewart's camp. A doctor's inspection of the wound showed that General had been shot while running away. When Olivey asked local police about the case they 'appeared to know nothing about it', so Olivey himself went to Stewart's camp to retrieve Wanda, asked the police to lay a charge against Stewart for 'shooting a native', and insisted that the two local Justices of the Peace investigate the affair.[7]

When the case was heard at the local Police Court, however, the local Justices of the Peace dismissed the case on grounds of insufficient evidence,

---

6 Colonial Secretary to Laurence, 16 May 1884 and Laurence to the Colonial Secretary, 3 July 1884, Acc 388, 2815/84, State Records Office of Western Australia.

7 George Olivey to the Protector of Aborigines, 24 November 1901, Acc 255, 1901/975, State Records of Western Australia.

and the Chair of the Bench went so far as to publicly criticise the Aborigines Department for 'bringing forward such paltry cases'. In this district, Olivey reported, court proceedings were lax, the police could not be complimented on their level of 'energy' and the Chair of the Bench, the local Justice of the Peace who had dismissed the case, had revealed his 'utter ignorance of the law and his duty'.[8] As for Wanda, the only 'protection' Olivey could envisage to prevent Stewart from reclaiming her was to have her assigned as a servant to the local constable's household. Having begun with conflict over her place in the sexual economy of the frontier, which resulted in the legally unpunished shooting of General, this case ended with Wanda made subject to a different kind of economic indenture. As in Wanda's case, there is no way of knowing how the arrangement between Polly and Anderson was negotiated, or with what degrees of consent or coercion, but Polly's vexed position in this sexual economy was visible in her testimony to the court that Anderson told her 'he would kill her' if she returned to Jacky, and that Jacky told her he had speared their boss because he had kept her 'too much'.[9]

Perhaps the most sinister echo of the law's limitations in regulating the frontier is the newspaper's reference to the 'well armed' party of miners that went out in Jacky's pursuit before police were sent from the nearest station seventy miles away. Although not explicit, it is an oblique reminder that some settlers considered limited availability of police as justification for undertaking private reprisals against Aboriginal people, and that such cases were rarely prosecuted. In the late 1920s, one reminiscing Western Australian pioneer wrote quite openly about the nature of this 'rough justice':

> They went out, meeting the blacks at no great distance, and gave them a warm time … The bushman's code of honour is this way: Either stand in with the mob and keep your mouth shut or refuse to stand in and also keep your mouth shut. In either case you will be respected and no more will be required of you in the matter. A man who came part of the way with our party from Queensland threatened to violate this rule. He said he would report on our treatment of blacks when he got back to civilisation. He was

---

8 Ibid.

9 On the sexual exploitation of Aboriginal women on other northern frontiers see for instance Bottoms, 79-95.

told that if he intended to go back on his mates he would have done far better to keep his intention to himself or he might never reach the end of the trip alive.[10]

The year after Anderson was speared, Coolgardie police investigated rumours that an undefined number of Aboriginal people had been 'ruthlessly shot' in that district in reprisal for the spearing of white men. Prospectors told the investigating constable James Glass that some time previously 'a party of miners went out and on returning said they had shot some Blacks'; but, the constable reported, they claimed to 'know nothing of the matter themselves'. Inevitably, in the absence of any firmer evidence, the investigation lapsed.[11] By the time of Jacky's trial in 1895, Aboriginal people had for many decades been officially deemed equal subjects of the British Crown in the eyes of the law. In reality their unequal status, particularly in the ongoing culture of the frontier, was still very much in evidence. If Jacky's case appeared exceptional for the fact that his retaliation against settler provocation earned the law's leniency, at every other level the circumstances surrounding it were emblematic of the law's failures to protect Aboriginal people as Her Majesty's subjects.

The failure of colonial governments over the course of the nineteenth century to ensure the protection of Aboriginal people's rights as subjects of the Crown was extended through the twentieth century in the form of policies of centralised governance which saw Aboriginal people's daily lives brought within the controlling surveillance of Aborigines Departments. Two years after Jacky's trial in Western Australia, the passing of the Aborigines Act of 1897 led to the establishment of an Aborigines Department under the management of Chief Protector Henry Charles Prinsep. In the years to come, the era of the frontier would give way to the era of the reserve, where Aboriginal people would be subjected to new forms of governmental oversight and restraint affecting almost every aspect of life (Haebich 1992).

---

10 'Kimberley Scenes: Rough Justice' by A Pioneer, *Western Mail*, 29 August 1929. 'A Pioneer' was the pen name of Donald Swan and the reminiscences he published in the press were subsequently republished in Cathie Clement and Peter Bridge, eds. *Kimberley Scenes: Sagas of Australia's Last Frontier* (Perth: Hesperian Press, 1991).

11 Report of PC James Glass, 28 August 1896, Acc 430, 1896/2209, State Records Office of Western Australia.

Changing the Victorian Subject

When Queen Victoria died on 22 January 1901, Australia had just three weeks earlier formally transformed from a collection of colonies into a federated nation. As the Victorian age transitioned into the Edwardian age, new legislation was introduced that excluded Aboriginal people from the right to vote, unless they had earlier been listed on colonial electoral rolls.[12] The ongoing uncertain status of Aboriginal people in a federated Australia attracted little attention within a new nation setting its eyes to the future, apart from some commentary in the press about the 'anomalous state of affairs under which the remnant of the aborigines of this great continent now drag on their begrudged existence' (*Sydney Morning Herald*, 28 September 1901). An event that did capture the new nation's attention in 1901 was the visit to Australia of Queen Victoria's grandson and his wife, the Duke and Duchess of Cornwall and York, as part of their broader trans-imperial tour. Western Australia was the last stop of their visit, and it was from there that the Duke dispatched a long letter to the Secretary of State expressing his pleasure in having presided at the inauguration of Australia's first Parliament, his interest in all he had witnessed in the progress of the Australian nation and his hopes for 'the strengthening and welding together of the Empire through the sympathy and interest which have been displayed in our journey' (Wallace 326-8). Nowhere in his letter did the Duke make mention of Aboriginal people, who indeed had had little presence during the royal tour of the Australian states other than to feature in the displays that offered a uniquely local spectacle to the royal visitors.[13]

In Western Australia, Chief Protector of Aborigines Henry Prinsep made arrangements for more than a hundred Aboriginal people from around the state to be brought to Perth for the Duke and Duchess's visit. They were not to be included as active participants, however, but as witnesses to the occasion who would observe the celebrations from a monitored distance. Prinsep arranged for

---

12 For a detailed history of the Aboriginal rights movement see Bain Attwood and Andrew Markus, *The Struggle for Aboriginal Rights* (Sydney: Allen & Unwin, 1999).

13 In Queensland, the Protector of Aborigines Archibald Meston designed an 'Aboriginal arch' to form a decorative human entry-way to Brisbane's George Street, comprised of seventy 'old lords of the soil, resplendent in war paint and armed with shield and spear'. The press reported that the Aboriginal arch created 'a delightful effect' surrounded 'by decorations with characteristic flora and fauna' (*Australian Town and Country Journal*, 1 June 1901; *Clarence and Richmond Examiner*, 15 June 1901).

the Aboriginal group to be established in their own camp at Perth's south-eastern fringe, and he appointed four constables to watch over them and ensure that they would only enter the town when supervised. The occasion of the royal visit served as a 'treat' for them, Prinsep reported, but also as a test and demonstration of their progress in civilised conduct, for 'they behaved in a very exemplary manner; contrary to expectation, not a single complaint was made against them for loitering about the city or becoming troublesome'. They were able to see 'everything that was to be seen … and having witnessed the departure of the Duke and Duchess from the town, were quietly sent back to [their] different districts' (Aborigines Department Report 1902, 9).

Under the auspices of Western Australia's Aborigines Department, much had already changed in the governance of Aboriginal people in the six years since Jacky's trial, justified in the name of protection. However, the marginal presence of Aboriginal people during the royal visit in the year in which Queen Victoria died and Australia embarked on a new age of nationhood still had much in common with the state of uncertainty that had defined their relation to the colonial state through the course of Victoria's long reign. The recommendations of the Select Committee report issued in the year she came to the throne were designed to bring legal regulation to the British settler frontier, and to extend the benefits and responsibilities of British subjecthood to Aboriginal people. Ultimately these goals were undermined by the demands of settlers for land, by the neglect of local colonial governments and by the application of the law in the protection of settler privilege rather than Aboriginal rights. As Julie Evans has put it, 'British subject' as it applied to Aboriginal people was a pliable term, one that appeared to reconcile their status within a framework of protection and liberty at the same time as it worked to facilitate a division of 'privilege and exclusion' (70).

Works Cited

Primary sources

Aborigines Department Report for the Financial Year ending 30 June 1902. Perth: Government Printer, 1902.

Historical Records of Australia, series 1, vol. 1, 1788-1796, Library Committee of the Commonwealth Parliament, 1914.

House of Commons Sessional Papers, Report of the Parliamentary Select Committee on Aboriginal Tribes (British Settlements), 1837, 7 (425).

State Records Office of Western Australia: Aborigines Department files (Acc 255 and Acc 388), Deposition files (Cons 3473) and Police Department files (Acc 430).

Newspapers

Australian Town and Country Journal (1901).

Clarence and Richmond Examiner (1901).

The Australian (1843).

The Inquirer & Commercial News (1895).

The Sydney Morning Herald (1858).

The Western Mail (1899-1929).

The Western Australian (1895).

Secondary sources

Attwood, Bain and Andrew Markus. *The Struggle for Aboriginal Rights: A Documentary History.* Sydney: Allen & Unwin, 1999.

Bottoms, Timothy. *Conspiracy of Silence: Queensland's Frontier Killing Times.* Sydney: Allen & Unwin, 2013.

Clement, Cathie and Peter Bridge. Eds. *Kimberley Scenes: Sagas of Australia's Last Frontier.* Perth: Hesperian Press, 1991.

Coss, Graeme. 'A Brief History of the Doctrine of Provocation in England.' *Sydney Law Review* 13 (1991): 570.

Douglas, Heather and Mark Finnane. *Indigenous Crime and Settler Law: White Sovereignty After Empire.* London: Palgrave Macmillan, 2012.

Evans, Julie. 'The Formulation of Privilege and Exclusion in Settler States: Land, Law, Political Rights and Indigenous Peoples in Nineteenth Century Western Australia and Natal.' *Honour Among Nations? Treaties and Agreements with Indigenous People.* Ed. Marcia Langton, Maureen

Tehan, Lisa Palmer and Kathryn Shain. Melbourne: Melbourne UP, 2004. 69-82.

Ford, Lisa. *Settler Sovereignty: Jurisdiction and Indigenous People in America and Australia 1788-1836.* Cambridge, MA: Harvard UP, 2010.

Haebich, Anna. *For Their Own Good: Aborigines and Government in the South West of Western Australia.* Perth: UWA Press, 1992.

Horder, Jeremy. *Provocation and Responsibility.* Oxford: Clarendon Press, 1992.

Kercher, Bruce. *An Unruly Child: A History of Law in Australia.* Sydney: Allen & Unwin, 1995.McQueen, Rob. 'Master and Servant Legislation in 19th Century Australia.' Law and History in Australia 4 (1987): 78-110.

McQueen, Rob. 'Master and Servant Legislation in 19th Century Australia.' *Law and History in Australia* 4 (1987): 78-110.

Nettelbeck, Amanda. '"Equals of the White Man": Settler Prosecution for Violence against Aboriginal Subjects of the Crown.' *Law and History Review* 31.2 (2013): 355-90.

——. 'Phillips' Brief: The Severest Provocation.' *Criminal Law Journal* 37 (2013): 267.

Nourse, Victoria. 'Modern Law Reform and the Provocation Defense.' *Yale Law Journal* 106 (1997): 1331.

Purdue, Brian. *Legal Executions in Western Australia.* Perth: Foundation Press, 1993.

Reynolds, Henry. *Forgotten War.* Sydney: Newsouth Publishing, 2013.

Spain, Eimear. *The Role of Emotions in Criminal Law Defences.* Cambridge: Cambridge UP, 2011.

Wallace, Sir Donald Mackenzie. *The Web of Empire: A Diary of the Imperial Tour of their Royal Highnesses the Duke and Duchess of Cornwall and York in 1901.* London: Macmillan, 1902.

3

Identifying with the frontier: Federation New Woman, Nation and Empire

Sharon Crozier-De Rosa

Introduction

As the colonial period advanced, negative aspects of the Australian bush were often figured as feminine, represented as harsh, un-nurturing, and barren; as a land hostile to man's desires to conquer or even to just survive. But, by the late nineteenth century, the bush was rarely imagined as a place for women (Schaffer, *Women and the Bush* 52-76). Likewise, the emerging new Australian nation was increasingly symbolised as female — as Britannia's daughter or younger cousin, for example. At the turn of the twentieth century, however, the role of women in the construction of that new nation was rarely acknowledged. Late-nineteenth and early-twentieth-century Australia then provided little place for women in imaginings of either the bush or the nation, despite the paradoxical reality of women's active involvement in both as, for instance, pastoral workers or as voters. More than ever in white Australian history, women were imaginatively consigned to the domestic hearth, to British middle-class notions of domestic ideology.

Changing the Victorian Subject

Catherine Martin's New Woman novel, *An Australian Girl* (1890), published and sold in both Australia and Britain, challenged these gendered omissions. Critically well-received in both the imperial metropole and colonial peripheries, *An Australian Girl* not only feminised the Australian landscape, it also injected the Australian woman into national imaginings. In telling the story of South Australian New Woman, Stella Courtland — by tracing her connection with and love for the untamed, 'uncivilised' land — this novel made visible the woman in the bush. Through descriptions of its Australian-born protagonist's impassioned longing for both national and international recognition of her country's independence from Old World ties, it also confirmed the presence of women in the construction of a national consciousness, one that was pivotally important to the process of federation and nation-building.

This chapter builds on recent works that have used the fact that this 1890s novel was both written by a female author and showcased a female protagonist to write women back into national narratives. It argues that by connecting a female writer and a female character to the Australian landscape, *An Australian Girl* challenged contemporaneous moves towards excluding women from the bush; it challenged the late-nineteenth-century tendency to declare the bush 'no place for a woman'.[1] The chapter also maintains that by allowing her female protagonist to voice such strong and impassioned views about Australia's potential for rejuvenating the human race at a time of much-expressed British anxiety about a decaying civilisation, Martin added another feminine voice to those that were helping to shape the collective consciousness of a newly emerging nation, a voice that favoured the 'Australian' over the 'European' and that championed the New World over the Old. She put a feminine stamp on *fin-de-siècle* understandings of Australia, both of the bush and the newly emerging nation.

It is not only constructions of the bush and the nation as masculinised subjects that Martin challenges and changes, it is also the notion of turn-of-the-century Australia as a stable entity: a closed frontier. In the process of using *An Australian Girl* to insert women back into the national narrative, this chapter diverges from other works in that it also contributes to a different but related and highly critical discussion — the discussion surrounding the definition of Australia as an ongoing frontier society. Martin's evocation of a specific, uniquely

---

1 The title of a short story by Henry Lawson and a much-used term at the time.

Australian national identity draws on an abundance and complexity of shifting or negotiating relations between a number of key categories: 'settler' and indigenous; 'native'-born and migrant; domesticated landscape and uncivilised bush; and Old World and New World. The Australia portrayed in this late-nineteenth-century story of an Australian girl is an ever-evolving site of exchange. What this story casts light on, then, is an ongoing process of renegotiation of what is meant by 'Australian' through landscape, cultures, ethnicities and allegiances or loyalties, an ongoing process of negotiation that helps to defy any notion of Australian society as either stable or static. In this way, not only can *An Australian Girl* be called on as an example of a late-nineteenth-century text that placed women at the centre rather than the margins of discussions about the nature and future of the nation, but it can also be used to contest the notion that the Australian 'frontier' was permanently closed and Australian identity fixed or settled.

The frontier(s) and women

The notion of a colonial frontier has excited much recent debate among not only Australian historians and anthropologists, but also those from other settler colonies, such as North America and South Africa.[2] These discussions have, for the most part, centred on the issue of the rigidity or looseness of definitions of 'frontier' and the consequent usefulness of that term. They have also explored some of the repercussions of applying, for example, a tight or rigid understanding of the term 'frontier', one that could deny the existence of ongoing indigenous resistance to colonial advancements. The closing or ending of frontiers and frontier periods either by nineteenth-century discourse or by later historians, Nathan Wolski in his study of Aboriginal resistance has argued, has been an arbitrary decision, one based largely on limited understandings of the many and diverse forms that indigenous 'resistance' could assume, all too often notions of resistance being reduced to physical violence (216-36). 'Frontier', then, has a contentious history of its own.

Part of this contentiousness relates to the locating of frontiers. As historian Clive Moore points out, far from being a static or motionless 'reality',

---

2 For example, Lynette Russell's 2001 edited collection, *Colonial Frontiers. Indigenous-European Encounters in Settler Societies*, brings together a number of chapters examining, or re-examining, the relevancy and usefulness of the notion of a 'frontier' across a number of geographical and temporal categories.

the 'frontier' in Australia was a 'shifting reality'. Frontiers emerged at different times and in different locations across the Australian colonies, in many ways mimicking the staggered founding of those colonies, from that of New South Wales in 1788 to Western Australia, 'a slow starter until the 1890s' (Moore 35). Indeed, as Mary Ann Jebb and Anna Haebich point out, 'Even into the late 1960s, isolated areas of the north, being the least settled by Europeans, continued to be perceived by many as frontiers and were still referred to as such' (21). Frontiers, then, were often designated the 'outskirts of civilisation', those regions where, as historian Marilyn Lake puts it, the 'truth' of Australian life was more often than not 'exposed' (Lake, 'Frontier Feminism' 12).

The problematical nature of defining frontiers does not stop with pinpointing specific locations. It also extends to the exact nature of a frontier — whether, for example, it should be defined as a geographical site or, as has been generally agreed by those recently examining frontiers, as a 'process' of contested and negotiating intercultural relations. Boundaries and frontiers, as Lynette Russell argues, are produced by cross-cultural encounters (1). They are not only physical places, but also intellectual spaces; spaces 'which are therefore never neutrally positioned, but are assertive, contested and dialogic' (1). Frontiers, Russell contends, are 'interactive, contested and entangled' (13). Here, Jan Critchett concurs: a frontier, she argues, is 'a very local phenomenon' with the disputed area being not an area of neutral ground with the 'enemy' on the other side of that area but rather 'the very land each settler lived upon'. Not only that, but a frontier could be represented by a person, place or activity — by those, for example, who embodied the meeting of cultures, from the 'boy used as guide for exploring parties' to the bedding of white settler man and Aboriginal woman (qtd in Wolski 232). According to Critchett's argument, then, the frontier is better understood as 'cultural difference'. Therefore, the frontier period, Wolski concludes, 'cannot be neatly packaged and cannot be brought to a close, as though we now stand in some post-frontier period'. 'We remain', he argues, 'firmly in the "ongoing colonial present"' (Wolski 233).

It is with the notion of the frontier as an enduring entity, one that cannot be neatly closed or brought to a halt, that I approach Catherine Martin's depictions of late-nineteenth-century South Australia. The novel is set over 50 years after the region has been 'settled', when many there believed that they had firmly established a 'settler' colony, thereby negating any further reliance on the notion of the 'frontier'. But Martin's novel demonstrates an ongoing process of negotiation between numerous categories: white 'settlers' and the colony's Aboriginal inhabitants, a negotiation exemplified by characters such as the missionary, Mr Ferrier, and the mission's ongoing work with the Aboriginal people; 'native'-born Australians and those who continue to migrate to the colonies from the so-called mother country and their respective allegiances or national and cultural loyalties; and male and female understandings of belonging and identity. The frontier, therefore, assumes a geographical dimension in Martin's text in that the domesticated, tamed landscape — exemplified by settlers' gardens, whether planted in ways demonstrating more allegiance to Europe or to Australia — is situated alongside its 'native' or untamed other in the form of the bush. Here nurture meets nature; control meets chaos. But it also assumes a most important, complex and multifarious social dimension in that it draws on a group of binaries: racial, ethnic and cultural.

Whatever the preferred understanding of the Australian 'frontier', one thing most commentators agree on is that such a boundary or intercultural space was overwhelmingly identified as masculine at the end of the nineteenth and beginning of the twentieth centuries. 'Frontier societies', Lake has argued, 'women have long observed, enshrined masculine values and interests'. And in late-nineteenth- and early-twentieth-century Australia, this image of the frontier certainly held 'powerful mythic force' ('Frontier Feminism' 12-20). Even though Catherine Martin (1848-1937) and multiple others, including, for instance, fellow novelists Miles Franklin (1879-1954) and Rosa Praed (1851-1935), situated women on that frontier or frontiers, such placements were resisted in popular imaginings of that space. These denials were intertwined with a corresponding push for a masculinised concept of the emerging nation, one championed by Australia's democratic nationalists. Australia's 'liberal urban bourgeois', composed of urban writers, artists and critics whose interests were notoriously upheld by the Sydney men's paper, *The Bulletin*, constructed this Australian myth of manliness. Reacting against the so-called model of the 'Domestic Man', with its links to British, urban and, increasingly, suburban middle-class, Evangelical Christian respectability, they created the resourceful, independent white Bushman (Moore 43-4). 'Home life', *The Bulletin* argued, emasculated Australian manhood.

It 'trammelled a man's spirit and sapped his energy' (Lake, 'The Politics of Respectability' 266). It was the bush, then, that epitomised the Australian man. It allowed him the freedom to roam the land, unrestrained by woman or child. It provided him with the much-desired opportunity of proving his toughness, independence and self-sufficiency. In short, the frontier offered Australians an ideal of manhood that would serve to represent the newly emerging nation as it took its place on the world stage, separate from, but of course still connected to the British 'mother country'.

In the British mother country, this ideal of the Australian man held its own mythic force, fed as it was by a proliferation of print material emerging from Australia, including the travel writing of Francis Adams, a migrant from England to Australia in the 1880s. Adams, who published *The Australians* in London in 1893, has since been most often credited with spreading the word of the Australian Bushman and his legend to the imperial centre.[3] Writing like Adams's had the effect of rendering popular imperial imaginings of the frontier as exclusively masculine. There this manly myth served not the prerogatives of a newly emerging nation, but rather those of an imperial centre beset by anxieties. Historian John Tosh agrees. In his chapter on 'Manliness, Masculinities and the New Imperialism', he argues that within the imperial metropole, empire 'was seen as a projection of masculinity' (193). 'Empire', he continues, 'was a man's business'. Men fought for and acquired the colonies, and it was their 'energy and ruthlessness' that maintained Britain's imperial holdings (193). And given the harsh physical conditions on the colonial peripheries, 'a masculinity based on physical strength, forbearance, a belligerent belief in progress, and a militaristic style of organisation was seen as an almost necessary component of both settlement and scientific inquiry' (Cameron and Gibson 174). Because of all of this, empire and manliness merged in the popular imagination, aided by 'literary and visual images which consistently emphasised positive male attributes' (Tosh 193). Masculine insecurity resulting from gender confusion or ambiguity in a 'decadently over-civilised' England — a form of gender insecurity brought about by such things as 'the bogey of the hen-pecked, lower middle-class clerk' and the existence of the 'manly' New Woman — increased the desire for empire

---

3   For a discussion of Adams's impact on Australian nationalist discourse, see Schaffer, *Women and the Bush* 52.

on the national domestic front (Deane 213; Jusová 1; Ledger 22). More than ever, empire became a site for the consolidation and extension of British manliness.[4]

The enduring potency of masculinised myths of the bush and the frontier has made the project of reinserting women back into narratives of the frontier something of a major undertaking. Indeed, the very act of having to reinsert women into narratives of the frontier has caused a great deal of incredulity on the part of those historians who have pointed out the very obvious, all too painful, presence of indigenous women, at least, on those frontiers (Jebb and Haebich 27). And this emphasis on the presence and agency of indigenous people is a significant one. For, as Wolski, drawing on the theories of Homhi Bhabha, has argued, the role that the 'native other' plays and has played in the formation of a frontier, in the 'negotiation of the identity of both the colonial self and the native other' — with the 'native other' being far from 'a passive "effect" of the colonial self' — has until recently been ignored.[5] In specific relation to Australia and indigenous women, Ann McGrath's work demonstrates that recognising the role that Aboriginal women have played in the construction of the 'frontier', recovering indigenous women's varied and diverse experiences on the various Australian frontiers, has in fact worked to unsettle the very notion of the frontier, demanding, as Schaffer writes in reference to McGrath's work, 'new paradigms for historical research' ('Handkerchief Diplomacy' 137).[6]

As a result of these historiographical shifts, women and their experiences now form, Jebb and Haebich argue, 'a significant part of frontier history' (20). Such female experiences, they continue, have been diverse and dependent on

---

[4] Whether or not experiences of empire actually had the effect of 'masculinising' the home front, is something that historian of imperialism, Bernard Porter, believes cannot be affirmed with any empirical certainty, and is certainly a consideration that is beyond this scope of this short chapter (Porter 243-4).

[5] Referring here to Homhi Bhabha. *The Location of Culture*. London: Routledge, 1994: 110, qtd in Wolski 220.

[6] Not all histories of women on the 'frontier', however, incorporate the experiences of indigenous women into their analyses. Glenda Riley, writing about the lives of women on the North American frontiers, while drawing attention to an American historiography that had excluded women from frontier narratives, also purposely omitted indigenous women from her account, arguing that the term 'frontierswomen' did not include such women. See Riley 11.

individual 'wealth, ethnicity and race' (Jebb and Haebich 26). This is certainly one of the conclusions reached by scholars like Amanda Nettelbeck, Jane Haggis, Patricia Grimshaw and Julie Evans, who have undertaken studies of individual white women on the colonial frontiers — women such as Christina Smith, Rosa Campbell Praed, Mary Bundock and Katie Langloh Parker (Nettelbeck, 'Seeking to Spread the Truth' 83-90; Haggis 91-9; Grimshaw and Evans 79-95). Such individual examples of women who identified with the Australian frontier, and who not only revealed the degree to which they were complicit with the dispossessing and racist elements of the colonising endeavour but who also demonstrated an appreciation for aspects of indigenous culture and recognition of Aboriginal peoples' humanity, have acted to demonstrate that there were women on the frontiers who, while they contributed to colonial discourses, also unsettled aspects of those discourses.

Particularly, and of interest to this chapter, they unsettled those aspects that supported exclusively masculinised notions of frontier settlement. As Nettelbeck argues, white women like Christina Smith were active agents in ongoing cross-cultural encounters and their criticisms of settler behaviour, such as Smith's condemnation of the extreme violence accompanying Aboriginal dispossession in South Australia, often worked to challenge existing constructions of Australianness. Such critiques acted to disturb constructions of a settler colony and emerging Australian identity which many in the colonies at the end of the nineteenth century liked to view as 'safely secured' (Nettelbeck, 'Seeking to Spread the Truth', 83). The existence of such white women on the Australian frontiers and their rediscovery in recent academic writing has also had the effect of providing alternative narratives to those of colonial violence and dispossession. Jane Haggis has argued that the memorialisation of the life and writing of Christina Smith, particularly her memorialisation in a regional South Australian museum, has produced something of a feminising of stories of colonial conquest, offering current audiences a story of an Australian past that represents a 'softer option than complicity in violent destruction', that is to say, that of 'the good white woman upholding the "true" values of civilised, European society' (Haggis 96).

The 'powerful mythic force' of the masculine frontier, then, as supported by the literary movements of the Federation era, has been dominant, but, importantly, it has also been challenged. As Nettelbeck argues, women did contribute to that body of literature, fictional and non-fictional, that helped to construct such a myth. However, not all these contributions supported the maleness of the adventure myth; some refuted it (Nettelbeck, 'Introduction' viii). Catherine Martin, through *An Australian Girl*, is one such example. This novel, Nettelbeck continues, like other more manly tales of the colonies, celebrates the bush but, importantly, she argues, it does so through 'a feminine consciousness' (Nettelbeck, 'Introduction' viii). Given that this book was sold in both England and Australia, it can be argued that by the time of Federation, readers at all ends of the imperial spectrum were being offered literary images of the Australian frontier which were more than simply masculinised (however they ultimately processed such offerings). Martin changed existing and exported images of the bush by feminising it. Whether she intended it or not, by accommodating the many previously mentioned ever-shifting binaries in her popular text she also painted a picture of Australia as a site of ongoing exchange: a place of multiple frontiers.

Catherine Martin's *An Australian Girl* (1890)

Catherine Martin's *An Australian Girl* contributed to a body of literature at the end of the nineteenth and beginning of the twentieth centuries focusing on the nationalist trope, the Australian Girl. This 'superior Australian type' — whether epitomised by the heroines of Ada Cambridge's *The Three Miss Kings*, Tasma's *The Pipers of Piper's Hill*, Rosa Campbell Praed's *Outlaw and Lawmaker*, Stella Miles Franklin's *My Brilliant Career* or Martin's *An Australian Girl* — emerged at a time when debates about the international New Woman were rife (Magarey, *Passions* 44). Whether a local manifestation of that international icon, as Susan Magarey argues, or a specifically Australian figure who voiced concerns that were unique to settler colonialism, as Tanya Dalziell asserts, the Australian Girl stood for independence, self-determination and 'the possibility of a new gender order' (Magarey, *Passions* 47-8; Dalziell, 'As Unconscious and Gay' 20-1). Certainly, this nationalist trope articulated the rebelliousness of the New Woman in a way that was deemed characteristic of a newly emerging nation.

Set for the most part in regional South Australia, Martin's *An Australian Girl* follows the story of Stella Courtland, a young woman who proudly asserts her Australianness, as well as the benefits of her keen intellect and her thirst for knowledge. In addition to reading and discussing the works of numerous German philosophers, Stella also enjoys exploring the physical side of life, by spending a great deal of time outdoors, riding horses, watching the habits of animals and insects and eating fruit straight from trees and vines (72, 74). Despite a previous secret engagement to an Anglo-German doctor with whom she is intellectually and spiritually attuned, Stella eventually finds herself disappointed in love, in an intellectually and spiritually incompatible marriage to a devoted, thoughtful young Australian friend. After experiencing a nervous breakdown, brought about by the frustration of her ambitions, Stella rediscovers Christianity, resolves to reform her alcoholic husband and then promises to invest the larger portion of her life in using 200 acres of her and her husband's land to help poor incoming European migrants to settle and farm, thereby helping the economic and social development of the newly emerging Australian nation. Considered 'widely read at the time', in both England and Australia, particularly among the 'circles of the Intelligentsia', *An Australian Girl* went into three editions within four years (Allen, 'She Seems to Have Composed Her Own Life' 29).[7] It was also well-received critically, although the reasons for this positive form of reception differed between metropole and periphery, as I will discuss.

According to Lake, 'For white men, the frontier was a fantasy of freedom; for white feminists it was a focus of fear and anxiety, a place beyond their ken, where undomesticated men turned feral threatened, rather than secured civilisation' ('Frontier Feminism' 12-20). Undoubtedly, this was a very 'real' view of the frontier for a multitude of women. However, not all women, nor indeed all feminist women, imagined or represented the frontier as such. Catherine Martin did not. Instead, she imagined the frontier, which stretches outwards from the landscaped environment of her character, Stella Courtland's family property, as a place of beauty, awe, imagination and, for the most part, unrestrained

---

[7] The first edition was published anonymously in London in three volumes; the second was published in London in one volume in 1891; and then the third, in 1894, was published as an Australian edition (Nettelbeck, 'Introduction' xii). Margaret Allen quotes the critic Patchett Martin claiming that the book was widely recognised and that the 'clever novel is now receiving in the higher social and literary circles of London' (Allen, 'She Seems to Have Composed Her Own Life' 29).

movement for women as well as men.⁸ It is a land over which Stella looks 'with glad recognition' (167). The 'squatting life', Martin writes, is open to 'all the most healthful forms of recreation, as opposed to pleasure-seeking'. Here, one can have access to the better parts of 'civilisation', to books and magazines. But here one can also have 'buggies to drive in, horses to ride, visits to be received and paid', and, best of all, 'unpeopled places' in which to 'exercise a fascination, all their own, over the mind'. Here, she continues, are 'tranquil gullies', 'scrubby ranges' with 'radiant' colours, 'swelling hills', treeless plains, and

> [t]he sombre vegetation, the gleam of brilliant desert flowers, the calls and songs of birds, all [of which] have a charm of their own, and rise up in the memory of the Australian exile with an allurement which he never finds in the crowded cities — nay, not even in the scenery of the Old World. (173)

Martin's appreciation for the bush is not to imply a corresponding lack of recognition of its harshness. She well understood the dangers presented by a vast, isolated, rugged terrain at the mercy of a demanding, sometimes capricious climate that could spark up a storm of 'incredible velocity', led by a changing wind that had 'suddenly lost its warmth, and seemed to be gathering strange voices from the wilderness' (234). Indeed, it is in a storm such as this that her protagonist Stella finds herself in peril, falling off her horse and injuring herself, only to be serendipitously discovered and rescued hours later by a passing traveller (who happens to be the Anglo-German doctor with whom she is in love). And Martin also appreciates that it is not simply human beings who are at the whim of the bush and the weather. She comments, for example, on the irony of the presence of tall eucalyptus trees that are at their finest near water, 'yet they have to live through centuries in waterless wastes':

> It is often forced upon the observer of nature in Australia that in the past she has been playing strange pranks; among other trifles, brewing pepper for her children instead of nourishing them. (166)

---

8   I write 'for the most part' because, as is pointed out in the chapter, at one point in the novel Stella does fall off her horse and injure herself. Still, it is not only the bush that has the capacity to injure. 'Civilisation' also holds such power. At another point in the novel, a story is recounted of a man who 'came in from the Bush' to get a very painful toothache attended to, only to die from a complication after the administration of chloroform (168).

Still, on the whole, the bush is portrayed as an overwhelmingly positive force. Balancing its deserved reputation as a scorched and parched landscape, it is also acknowledged as a place of sustenance, producing pears, citrons, mulberries, figs, grapes and grains of such fine variety that, in a letter written to her brother, Stella confesses herself humbled by what 'Nature [*sic*] can do in our land when her lap is shaken out' (76). It is also sustaining in a more metaphorical sense in that it provides nourishment for the soul. It is a land, the narrator explains,

> noble in its vast breadth, its virgin promise of fertility — fit to be the dwelling-place of a race strong, free and generous; careful not only for the things that advance man's material prosperity, but caring infinitely as well for all that touches the human spirit with quick recognition of its immortal kinships. (257)

The Australian land offers itself as an answer to the human race's anxieties; to fears about racial degeneration, immense inequalities and civil unrest. Yet it also offers a more individualised form of fulfilment. Living by the 'great unmeasured woods of her native land' presents itself as absolutely 'delightful' to this Australian New Woman (173). Divorced from the irrelevant or obsolete conventions of the Old World, and as a site for the 'progressive' and 'civilising' forces that advance past the 'primitive stage of savagedom' of the Aboriginal race, the bush is intrinsic to Stella's self-development (166). As Nettelbeck contends, the Australian landscape provides Stella 'with her sense of Australianness, which is equally her sense of self' — it is not simply 'the province of men's exploration and adventure'. Rather, 'it is personalized, even feminized, by Stella's identification with it' ('Introduction' viii, xvi).

The frontier here, then, was a meeting place for domesticated landscape and untamed bush. But it was also an intercultural site. Martin's protagonist, Stella, is not impervious to Australia's pre-European, indigenous past. In many ways, she is sensitive to Aboriginal culture. Her interest in such a culture is exemplified by the fact that she collects not only Aboriginal myths but also artefacts, like an Aboriginal shoe that Ted Ritchie, her friend and eventual husband, brings to her early in the novel (21). However, like many of her contemporaries at the time, Stella seems to ponder a pre-European culture as a noble remnant of a long-gone past and her collecting of indigenous stories and artefacts attests to this. Such a gathering of 'relics' seems to imply an understanding of a race that is either no longer existent or at least doomed to be so (22). In this way, Stella's perceptions of the inevitability of a doomed race, along the lines of Social Darwinism, are in line with those of mainstream white society (Nettelbeck, 'Introduction' xviii). Illustrating this support of mainstream opinion is a story that Martin narrates in which she details the relations between an Aboriginal woman, a white man and the child they bring into the world: a tale that involves a father beating his child, the mother and child running away, and the eventual deaths of both mother and child — deaths that haunt the surviving white father. Here Martin presents a narrative of indigenous tragedy and death in the face of white complicity and survival which lends force to contemporary theories about the inevitable extinction of a primitive race in the face of an apparent white supremacy (94-9).

However, Stella's corresponding description of surviving Aboriginal families — one, for example, 'a father, mother, and two picaninnies' who were 'all barefooted' and encumbered only with 'a tattered Government blanket, a couple of waddies [clubs], and the rakings of a dust-bin, by way of clothing' (63) — belies any understanding or representation of intercultural relations as dead, closed or consigned to the distant past. So does her awareness of the work of missionaries in the area — such as the ongoing endeavours of the ex-missionary, Mr Paul Ferrier, to collect money for missions devoted to Aboriginal conversion to Christianity and the work of the Mandura Mission. Instead, such observations and comments indicate an ongoing negotiation of cultural relations. Stella claims that in his eagerness to convert, Mr Ferrier has been blind to the myths and to the culture of the very people whose souls he is hoping to convert (73). Revealed in this ironic observation is the 'reality' of a continuous effort to affect change in relations between white missionaries and indigenous people, to transform Aboriginal cultures and practices: a continuing process of modification that points to the existence of an ongoing, not a dead, frontier. The mention of the 'tattered Government blanket' does much to recall a continuing legacy of dispossession and white governance. And the very story of a white man unable to escape at least the emotional repercussions of a past encounter with an indigenous woman, an encounter that produced a child, helps to defy any notion of the irrelevancy of frontier interactions. Therefore, whatever late-nineteenth-century white Australians, like the character of Stella, wanted to believe about the inevitability of a doomed black culture, the very real presence of indigenous people, the continuous work of white missionaries and ongoing evidence of inter-racial mixing in this text, act to verify the existence of an intercultural meeting place, a frontier of interaction and reciprocal effect.

Catherine Martin's portrayal of intercultural negotiations did not only apply to settler-indigenous interaction; it was also pertinent to relations between incoming migrants, long-term and short-term, and non-indigenous but so-called native-born Australians. It is here, in passages detailing the many differences between settler Australians and the ongoing flow of migrants, that Stella reveals a level of passionate empathy with a newly emerging Australian nation that equals her zealous attachment to the untamed Australian landscape. The Australian-born Stella identifies with being a 'natural' or a 'native' Australian — 'natural' and 'native' here being highly contentious terms given the dispossession of the native inhabitants of the land by migrants and their descendants like the fictional Stella and Ted, and like the very 'real' Catherine Martin herself. However, Martin applies such categories in the quest to distinguish between those people born in Australia and those continuing to enter the country from the Old World, especially those in search of fleeting experiences like holidays, business opportunities, or exotic tales of the adventurous colonies for consumers 'back home'.

A sense of affinity with a relatively new notion of Australianness and allegiance to a 'native'-born idea of Australia as opposed to any conception of the soon-to-be nation as being dependent solely on British or European culture is as intrinsic to Stella's whole sense of being as her connection with the bush. 'Who', this Australian New Woman asks, 'could be born in such a place and not love it for its beauty and fertility?' (71) True love and loyalty for a social, political, cultural and regional entity does not require a shared history as old as that of the Old World, she adamantly maintains. Those born in Australia can 'love it as their native land' in the same way that those born in Germany, for example, do (70). And here, Aboriginal history is typically omitted from such nationalist debates. Australians, then, were as capable of 'true patriotism' as their European counterparts (70).

Moreover, and contrary to the opinions of some in the imperial metropole, Martin argues that Australians were also as capable of managing their own nation as they were of loving and pledging loyalty to it, however 'new' it may be.

Certainly, the two main Australian-born characters of *An Australian Girl*, Stella and Ted, believe in the right to national self-determination. They both deplore the idea of the country that they were born in as existing only in relation to the 'motherland', rather than as a national land in its own right. Indeed, Ted is quite unambiguous, as when he writes a letter to Stella, informing her of his jealousy when he meets independent Americans and his sense of indignity when he hears the English refer to Australia as 'our colony'. In the letter he exclaims, 'We must have a country of our own, governed by ourselves, and not have the name of being ruled by fellows sent out of the heart of London', a sentiment with which the Australian New Woman, Stella, agrees (371). What is ironic, given Miles Franklin's critique of Martin as a mere Anglo-Australian writer (Allen, 'Catherine Martin' 184), is that Martin's protagonist is quite similar in sentiment to Franklin's uniquely Australian New Woman protagonist, Sybylla Melvin, who at the end of *My Brilliant Career* declares herself to be 'a daughter of the Southern Cross, a child of the mighty bush'. Like Franklin's Sybylla, Martin's Stella also represents what Susan Magarey terms 'a local manifestation of an international icon'. She represents a New Woman who 'stands for independence and self-determination', essential ingredients of a newly emerging Australian nation. She is a feminine figure who identifies wholly with frontier landscape and society, and with the newly emerging nation, whether she is incorporated into the national, masculinised myth or not (Magarey, 'History' 108).

Still, as strong as Stella's and Ted's support of national self-determination and riling against Old World imperialism is, they are not precluded from incorporating many elements of the varying cultures of that Old World into their conceptions of a new Australian nation, a factor that makes Stella's vision for a future Australia as internationalist as nationalist. Stella condemns the slavish following of Old World customs which she witnesses in her immediate environment — customs such as planting English-style gardens and hanging heavy imported European curtains, both entirely unsuited to Australian conditions. And yet much of her understanding of civilisation, manners and progress is based on European ways of thinking, making her quite internationalist in outlook. She believes, for example, that the new Australian nation should be built according to the political and geographical imperatives of this 'new' land, but that its governing ideals should also be based on a set of universally-based cultural artefacts: on the works of German philosophers, texts of the classical eras, European literature and the Bible. And this merging of Old World ideas and New World realities is in line with much historical writing on not only the construction of the Australian nation and identity, but also those of other former settler colonies. As David Lambert and Alan Lester argue of colonial lives across the British Empire, by the end of the nineteenth century most of the descendants of early settlers had 'constructed new national identities — for example as Australians, South Africans, Canadians or New Zealanders — that were distanced both metaphorically and literally from Britain itself' (1). Imperial culture in the peripheries of the Empire then, far from being stable, was contested and therefore in a continual state of flux, of reformulation. Relations between imperialism, Britishness and a newly emerging Australian nationalism were, therefore, also not unproblematic, as Martin's text demonstrates.

This notion of antipathy or at least complication between understandings of Britishness and Australianness is one that has received considerable attention lately. Historians like Neville Meaney and Russell McGregor have argued that Britishness was intrinsic to early notions of Australianness (Meaney 79). McGregor, for example, contends that to build an Australian nation required 'a repertoire of myth and symbol' (McGregor 493). Given that an overwhelming proportion of the population were of British origin, it follows, he argues, that the only repertoire available to those living in the colonies at that time was also of British origin.[9] This assertion is complicated by an appreciation of the varying ethnicities that are included or excluded from the term 'British' — did those of Irish origins in late-nineteenth-century Australia, for example, identify with an understanding of the new nation's origins as being wholly or even overwhelmingly 'British'? The assertion is further obscured by Catherine Martin's approach to the ethnic make-up of her heroine — Stella 'is rooted in two nationalities', Australian and 'Keltic', each being, to one character's mind, as 'eerie' as the other for all their 'superstitions' (377). This ethnic make-up is more than unproblematically 'British'. Moreover, whether readers would agree that

---

9 Aboriginal myths were present. However, late-nineteenth-century perceptions of an 'inglorious' Aboriginal past, 'deplorable' present and inevitable extinction, McGregor explains, did not recommend Aboriginal 'history' as one on which to base a white settler society and nation (McGregor 502).

'British' simplifies the ethnicity issue or not, what is obvious from a reading of *An Australian Girl* is the tension existing between an imperial attitude towards Australia — the British notion of Australia as 'our colonies' — and a nationalist one. This tension is evidenced by the narrator's repeated espousals of values like egalitarianism and autonomy which, she says, are much more suited to the newly emerging Australian nation than those unwanted vestiges of colonialism, such as an inherited class system and loyalty to a notion of aristocratic entitlement. These assertions are of course made in the face of the very obvious gain that the colonial process, with its ideas of hierarchy and entitlement, has brought to the white 'settlers'.

However, for all of Martin's campaigning on behalf of the Australian-born nationalist, she does not ignore the invaluable contribution made by the most diligent of the newly arrived migrants to the welfare of the country, as revealed when Stella reproaches Ted: 'You're like a good many more Australians. You'll never do as much for your native land as your fathers did for their adopted one' (15). Stella's internationalist vision for Australia was that it would be a land that would harness not only the hard work and skill of its long-term inhabitants but also the energies of the best of the newly arriving immigrants. Australia would take from migrants, in that it would use their gratitude, enthusiasm and toil all for the good of the nation, but it would also give to them, in the form of offering prospects for self-improvement and material advancement. Moreover, by offering opportunities for the bettering of deserving migrants from the Old World, not only did Australia benefit directly from this reciprocal relationship, but it also offered itself up as a site of rejuvenation, much needed in an Old World that was anxious about its racial stock.

This idea of the New World as a site for the rejuvenation of humankind is not a new one. As Cecily Devereux has argued, within white settler colonies there existed the notion that 'virgin soil' and a healthy climate brought forth 'a new and stronger race' (Devereux 179). But what is interesting about Catherine Martin's approach to this issue is her inversion of the British metropole's reasoning that the frontier was a place suited to the extension of British manliness. Exploration of this notion in *An Australian Girl* elicits a feeling of nationalist indignity because such an imperial view of Australia threatens the very future of the approaching nation, primarily through attacking its manhood. For, in many ways in this novel, the crowded cities of the Old World are associated with physical weakness, even degeneration and decay (433) — a sense of weakness and decay which can all too easily be imported to Australia. Men raised in this old, decaying climate and transported to Australia, or those men raised in homes in Australia where parents still slavishly follow the obsolete customs of the Old World, for example, are likely, in the end, Stella thinks, to go 'completely under, in the rough, wild manner of the veriest waifs' (57).

Stella agrees that this white settler colony is a prime environment to host the rejuvenation of the race, but the frontier as a site for the moral and physical renovation of the race could only be guaranteed if weak or degenerate elements did not infiltrate this 'virgin' soil. Stella's ideas about how to appropriately build the nation, then, make her complicit with an exercise of nation-building and national-identity-shaping which excluded undesirable elements, including non-white elements.[10] Notably, Stella's concerns about the possible degeneration of Australian manhood should it come into too close a contact with Old World manhood is akin to anxieties in the imperial metropole about a domestic manhood that was seen as increasingly over-feminised and at risk of losing its virility.

Some concluding thoughts

What remains to be asked here, then, is how could a novel that celebrates the Australian frontier as a place of freedom for colonial women — and that was substantially read and critically well-received in Australia as well as in England — not have more of a hand in reshaping the national and the imperial imaginings of the colonial frontiers as a place also for women? The answer to this might lie with the differing imperial and colonial receptions of the novel according to differing social and political imperatives at either end of the Empire.

English reviews of *An Australian Girl*, Christopher Lee explains, were, on the whole, positive, with one major exception — negative appraisals of deviations from the Romance form. Romance fiction, some critics complained, was intended as a feminine form of light entertainment. Catherine Martin's inclusion of long

---

10   This national ideal that excluded undesirable elements — particularly non-white elements — was epitomised, for example, by the White Australia Policy. See Grimshaw et al., *Creating a Nation*, who discuss in detail the varied roles that women assumed in the creation of this new nation.

and complicated passages on intellectual and philosophical subjects on the part of her New Woman character deviated from those light intentions, thereby contravening gendered expectations of the genre (Lee 68). Although imperial critics held the book up as a '"truly" Australian novel', by concentrating their reviews on how Martin committed the sin of deviating from the feminine form, they favoured the 'Girl' over the 'Australian' in *An Australian Girl* (Nettelbeck, 'Introduction' xi).

Australian critics, on the other hand, although they too were disposed to disagree with the deviation from light feminine entertainment, tended to concentrate their appraisals of the novel on its Australian content, thereby, as Lee argues, favouring the 'Australian' in the title over the 'Girl' in it. In line with nationalist imperatives at the time, namely the push for a recognised Australian nation, colonial critics celebrated the book 'as the representation of a colonial ideal which should be encouraged' (Lee 73). But as Lee points out, in 'seeking to celebrate the "Australian" in *An Australian Girl*', colonial or Australian reviews 'perhaps inadvertently' celebrated 'the feminine aspects of the novel' (Lee 75).

For example, the reviewer for *The Sydney Mail* held Stella up as 'a new or original type of Australian heroine', as a colonial female who was in 'no way inferior in either education, intelligence, manner, culture or appearance to her English counterpart' (qtd in Lee 76). Celebrating the nationalist sentiments in *An Australian Girl*, in line with political imperatives at the time, meant that it was often too difficult to extricate the 'female' sentiments and sensibilities of the novel, and so each aspect was, to a degree, celebrated alongside the other (Lee 75). The uniquely Australian New Woman, like the much-celebrated 'Australian Girl', worked her way to a small degree into the newly emerging national consciousness, into frontier and nation alike. One only has to look to *The Bulletin*'s lauding of Franklin's *My Brilliant Career* in 1901, a praise for a portrayal of an Australian landscape if not a womanhood that sat alongside the journal's celebration of a very masculine radical nationalism, for demonstration of this (Dalziell, 'Colonial Displacements' 39).

However, it was not in the imperial metropole's interests to celebrate a feminine portrait of either frontier or emerging nation. Such a celebration did not fit with imperial imperatives of the time. Although imperial critics held up the novel as a 'truly' Australian book, they simultaneously overlooked the text's insistence on the frontier as a site for femininity. Why? Probably because it was much more of an imperative for the metropole to retain the image of the frontier as a site of masculinity. By maintaining this notion in the public imagination, it protected the popular idea that the empire was a place for the consolidation and extension of British manliness — a balm for metropolitan anxiety about an increasingly feminised domestic manhood.

Works Cited

Adams, Francis. *The Australians: A Social Sketch.* London: T. Fisher Unwin, 1893.

Allen, Margaret. 'Catherine Martin, Writer: her Life and Ideas.' *Australian Literary Studies* 13.2: 184-97.

——. '"She Seems to Have Composed Her Own Life": Thinking about Catherine Martin.' *Australian Feminist Studies* 19.43 (2004): 29-42.

Cameron, Jenny and Katherine Gibson. 'Land and Place.' *Australian Feminism: A Companion.* Ed. Barbara Caine. Melbourne: Oxford UP, 1998. 173-7.

Dalziell, Tanya. 'As unconscious and gay as a trout in a stream?: Turning the trope of the Australian Girl.' *Feminist Review* 74 (2003): 17-34.

——. 'Colonial displacements: Another look at Miles Franklin's *My Brilliant Career.*' *Ariel* 35.3-4 (2006): 39-56.

Deane, Bradley. 'Imperial barbarians: Primitive masculinity in lost world fiction.' *Victorian Literature and Culture* 38 (2008): 205-25.

Devereux, Cecily. 'New Woman, New World: Maternal feminism and the new imperialism in the white settler colonies.' *Women's Studies International Forum* 22.2 (1999): 175-84.

Franklin, Miles. *My Brilliant Career.* 1901. New York: Penguin, 2007.

Grimshaw, Patricia and Julie Evans. 'Colonial Women on Intercultural Frontiers: Rosa Campbell Praed, Mary Bundock and Katie Langloh Parker.' *Australian Historical Studies* 27.106 (1996): 79-95.

Grimshaw, Patricia, Marilyn Lake, Ann McGrath and Marian Quartly. *Creating a Nation, 1788-1990.* Ringwood, Victoria: McPhee Gribble Publishers, 1994.

Haggis, Jane. 'The Social Memory of a Colonial Frontier.' *Australian Feminist Studies* 16.34 (2001): 91-9.

Jusová, Iveta. *The New Woman and the Empire.* Columbus: The Ohio State UP, 2005.

Jebb, Mary Ann and Anna Haebich. 'Across the Great Divide: Gender Relations on Australian Frontiers.' *Gender Relations in Australia. Domination and Negotiation.* Ed. Kay Saunders and Raymond Evans. Marrickville: Harcourt Brace Jovanovich, 1992. 20-41.

Lake, Marilyn. 'Frontier Feminism and the Marauding White Man.' *Journal of Australian Studies* 20.49 (1996): 12-20.

———. 'The Politics of Respectability: Identifying the Masculinist Context.' *Pastiche 1: Reflections on Nineteenth Century Australia.* Ed. Penny Russell and Richard White. Sydney: Allen & Unwin, 1994. 263-71.

Lee, Christopher. 'Women, Romance, and the Nation: The Reception of Catherine Martin's An Australian Girl.' *Australian Feminist Studies* 8:17 (1993): 67-80.

Lambert, David and Alan Lester. 'Introduction: Imperial spaces, imperial subjects.' *Colonial Lives Across the British Empire: Imperial careering in the long nineteenth century.* Ed. David Lambert and Alan Lester. Cambridge: Cambridge UP, 2006. 1-31.

Ledger, Sally. 'The New Woman and the Crisis of Victorianism.' *Cultural Politics at the Fin de Siècle.* Ed. Sally Ledger and Scott McCracken. Cambridge: Cambridge UP, 1995. 22-44.

Magarey, Susan. 'History, Cultural Studies, and Another Look at First-Wave Feminism in Australia.' *Australian Historical Studies* 27.106 (1996): 96-110.

———. *Passions of the First Wave Feminists.* Sydney: UNSW Press, 2001.

McGrath, Ann. 'The White Man's Looking Glass: Aboriginal-Colonial gender relations at Port Jackson.' *Australian Historical Studies* 24.95 (1990): 189-206.

McGregor, Russell. 'The Necessity of Britishness: Ethno-cultural Roots of Australian Nationalism.' *Nations and Nationalism* 12.3 (2006): 493-511.

Martin, Catherine. *An Australian Girl.* 1890. Oxford: Oxford UP, 1999.

Meaney, Neville. 'Britishness and Australian Identity. The Problem of nationalism in Australian History and Historiography.' *Australian Historical Studies* 116 (2001): 76-90.

Moore, Clive. 'Colonial Manhood and Masculinities.' *Journal of Australian Studies* 22.56 (1998): 35-50.

Nettelbeck, Amanda. 'Introduction.' *An Australian Girl.* Catherine Martin. Oxford: Oxford UP, 1999. vii-xxxi.

——. '"Seeking to Spread the Truth": Christina Smith and the South Australian Frontier.' *Australian Feminist Studies* 16.34 (2001): 83-90.

Porter, Bernard. *The Absent-Minded Imperialists: Empire, society, and culture in Britain.* Oxford: Oxford UP, 2004.

Riley, Glenda. *The Female Frontier.* Lawrence, Kansas: University of Kansas Press, 1988.

Russell, Lynette. 'Introduction.' *Colonial Frontiers: Indigenous-European Encounters in Settler Societies.* Ed. Lynette Russell. Manchester and New York: Manchester UP, 2001. 1-16.

Schaffer, Kay. 'Handkerchief Diplomacy: E.J. Eyre and sexual politics on the South Australian frontier.' *Colonial Frontiers: Indigenous-European Encounters in Settler Societies.* Ed. Lynette Russell. Manchester and New York: Manchester UP, 2001. 134-50.

——. *Women and the Bush: Forces of Desire in the Australian Cultural Tradition.* Cambridge: Cambridge UP, 1988.

Tosh, John. *Manliness and Masculinities in Nineteenth-Century Britain: Essays on gender, family and empire.* London: Longman, 2005.

Wolski, Nathan. 'All's Not Quiet on the Western Front — Rethinking resistance and frontiers in Aboriginal historiography.' *Colonial Frontier: Indigenous-European Encounters in Settler Societies.* Ed. Lynette Russell. Manchester and New York: Manchester UP, 2001. 216-36.

4

A 'Tigress' in the Paradise of Dissent: *Kooroona* critiques the foundational colonial story

Margaret Allen

Kooroona: a Tale of South Australia, a novel published in Britain in 1871 under the pseudonym of Iota[1], poses a challenge to the social imaginary of colonial South Australia as the 'Paradise of Dissent'. It contests the key features of the foundational story of the South Australian colony and casts a new and critical light upon the dissenters, who had hitherto been accorded an important role in that foundational narrative. Much of the novel's critique of colonial South Australia focuses upon the white settlers' cruel treatment of the Indigenous peoples. In exploring *Kooroona*'s challenge to the colonial foundational story, this chapter examines the circumstances of the novel's creation and the involvement of its author in struggles during the 1860s to improve the life chances of Aboriginal people who were faced by the onslaught of a violent settler community that was dominated by Methodist and other dissenters.

Unlike other Australian colonies, the colony of South Australia was founded in 1836 by free settlers, rather than convicts, and the 'voluntary principle'

---

1   This Iota should not be confused with the Irish-Australian novelist, Kathleen Mannington Caffyn, who used the pseudonym Iota from the 1890s.

of religious affiliation was enshrined. Subsequently the notion of the South Australian colony as a 'Paradise of Dissent' was elaborated in representations of the colony by a number of South Australian writers, such as Matilda Evans and C.H. Spence, and public figures from before settlement; it was also later analysed in Douglas Pike in *Paradise of Dissent: South Australia, 1829-57* (see Pike). This notion represented South Australia as a place where dissenters — Methodists, Baptists and other Protestant non-conformists — could enjoy freedom and opportunity away from the social power and condescending attitudes of the powerful Anglican establishment which characterised early nineteenth-century Britain. In Britain, despite the repeal of some legislation that had privileged members of the Established Anglican Church in the 1820s and 1830s, 'Dissenters were still subject to many civil disadvantages and humiliations' (Hilliard and Hunt 195). In the South Australian colony, however, equality between Christian denominations was a crucial foundational principle, along with the 'voluntary principle'. Indeed, from 1850 the colony was 'the first colony in the British Empire to dissolve the last remaining vestiges of the traditional connection between church and state' (202).

Dissenters, many of whom were from the lower- and middling-classes, flocked to the young colony. Whilst the Anglican Church was always large in nineteenth-century South Australia, it did not flourish in the voluntary environment without state aid. However, the non-conformists did well and indeed Methodism was 'the most potent religious movement' in the colony in the nineteenth century (204). The influx of Cornish miners immigrating to work in the rich copper mines of Kapunda, Moonta and Burra added significantly to the numbers of Methodist adherents (205).

Without a state church and a privileged class of gentry and aristocrats, colonists from the middling and even lower ranks of British society prospered and some became leaders in business, politics and society (Richards 123). The liberal ideas that guided the colony's founders and the experience of the dissenters, who created their chapels with voluntary support from their congregations without the overweening power of an established church and upper-classes, encouraged the growth of democratic ideals. In 1856 manhood suffrage and the secret ballot made the colony one of the most democratic in the world. Such developments, and the pride of successful dissenters in the prosperity and social authority they had crafted in the young colony, fostered the foundational story of worthy settlers, unable to prosper in hierarchical and unjust British society, but coming into their own in religious, political, social and financial terms in this 'Paradise of Dissent' (see Curthoys).

Another foundational myth of the South Australian settlers was the belief that their colony 'was different in its treatment of Indigenous people' (Foster, Hosking and Nettelbeck 2). The founding documents of the colony argued that rather than 'an invasion of the rights of the Aborigines', the colony was to be settled by 'industrious and virtuous settlers' who 'would protect them from the pirates, squatters and runaway convicts who infested the coast' (Foster, Hosking and Nettelbeck 2). However, as Foster, Hosking and Nettelbeck note, the reality on the ground was that Aboriginal people were subject to violence and dispossession in South Australia just as frequently as they were in the other colonies across the continent. And, just as in the other Australian colonies, 'Violence by settlers against Aboriginal people often went unreported' (7). The comfortable belief that South Australia was different remained unchallenged until quite recently (see Rowley; Reynolds).

The 14 novels of the South Australian writer, Matilda Jane Evans (1827-1886), furnish exemplars of these foundational narratives. Published under the pseudonym Maud Jean Franc, Evans's novels are set in colonial South Australia and explore themes of interest, even of anxiety, to settler culture. Thus they discuss emigration and settlement and in particular whether it is possible to establish a worthy society and raise decent families in the new rude and crude colony. Settlers were concerned that the rising generation might be corrupted by the colonial environment. Emigration and settlement meant leaving a known and settled society for one in which one's fellow colonists came from all parts of Britain, and even from other countries. Settlement meant mixing with people from diverse and even unknown social backgrounds. All colonists sought to make good but the notion of a society founded upon acquisition and greed was troubling. Inherent to settlement was the dispossession and devastation of the Indigenous peoples which posed deep moral questions about the whole colonial venture. As will be discussed below, colonial novelists dealt with these issues in a variety of ways. However, usually questions about Indigenous ownership of land were strongly repressed.

Evans's novels articulate the foundational myths of South Australia through their plot denouements, which involve the central characters becoming worthy settlers by adapting themselves to their new colonial environment. The novels represent the colony as a worthy place where those who have been thrust out of their homes in England due to social injustice or perhaps some legal fraud can find their reward and redemption (Curthoys; Allen 'Homely Stories'). For the Baptist Evans, Methodists, Baptists and other dissenters are central to South Australian life. Evans was a settler and hers are novels of settlement. In *No Longer a Child*, published in 1882, she writes of seeking to inspire pride, even a colonial 'nationalist spirit' among her local readers:

> The fact is, we South Australians are not half proud enough of our country, with its rapidly growing buildings, its wealth of minerals, developed or undeveloped, its thousand-and-one improvements, and its immense capabilities. We do not make as much capital of its wealth as we should. We allow ourselves to be too easily crushed by the idle comparisons of the 'newly arrived' ... Sometimes we need to stir up the languid blood of our youth, something to inspire them with a love for the land of their birth. (71-2)

Kooroona: Mrs Mary Meredith

Kooroona stands as a challenge to settler tales such as these. In *Kooroona*, that which is seen as central to the foundational narratives of South Australia's history, to the powerful story that has been rendered a 'truth', is cast under a harsh light and strongly criticised. *Kooroona* has scarcely been discussed in the small field of literary scholarship focusing upon colonial South Australia. One of the few critics to examine the novel, Paul de Pasquale, describes it as a 'High Church novel' that is 'determinedly anti-South Australian in every way and, in particular, deplores in the most revolting manner the prevalence of dissenters in the colony' (157-8). He notes that the author, Iota, was a Mrs Meredith, described in a colonial newspaper of 1882 as 'a lady formerly well known here as taking a deep interest in religious matters and the welfare of the aborigines, and who left the colony some two or three years ago for England' (qtd in de Pascquale, 157).[2] The further exploration of her life in colonial South Australia in this chapter

---

2   Here de Pasquale quotes from the *Areas Express*, 7 October 1882, 2.

deepens the analysis of the novel as a critique of the colony and its foundational narratives.

The author was in fact Mrs Mary A. Meredith (c. 1818-1897), whose husband, John, was the first surgeon to the Moonta Mines on Yorke Peninsula. The novel draws upon her experience of life in South Australia between about 1858-1869, and especially on Yorke Peninsula during the period 1863-1868. Mary and John Meredith came to the colony in 1858 with John's brother, E.W. Meredith, and his family (*South Australian Register*, 11 November 1858, 2).[3] It seems that their first years in the colony were spent in Burra and then the Mitcham district, before they proceeded to Moonta on the Yorke Peninsula. The couple were charitable and public-spirited Anglicans. Mary Meredith was active in fundraising for the Anglican Church in both Mitcham and Moonta and laid the foundation stone for All Saints in Moonta (*South Australian Register*, 9 August 1862, 1 and 24 September 1864, 1).

As this chapter will discuss, she agitated for the establishment of a mission for Aboriginal people on Yorke Peninsula. Her husband supported her in that work, and he also served as a Justice of the Peace and was involved in a number of other campaigns: he raised funds for Lancashire workers during the American Civil War in 1862 (*South Australian Register*, 9 October 1862, 1); he was the president of the Moonta Institute (*South Australian Register*, 24 May 1864, 1); he was a Trustee of All Saints Church in Moonta (*South Australian Register*, 31 July 1865, 2); and he sought to organise a clean water supply for Moonta (*South Australian Register*, 30 September 1864, 3). As the surgeon of the Miners' and Tradesmens' Club in Burra (*South Australian Register*, 29 June 1860, 3), and later in a similar position in Moonta, another copper mining township, he seems often to have been associated with schemes to assist working men.

Kooroona is set against the background of South Australia in the 1860s, and it features pastoral ventures and, in particular, mining ventures. In the novel we read of sharp characters salting mines, floating mining companies such as the aptly named 'Bunkumgorum Mining Venture' (127) and then selling out at the appropriate moment, so that inevitably the 'new chum' loses his money.

---

3 Edward William Meredith was in business as a wine and spirit merchant and was a Church Warden at St Matthew's Kensington. He left the colony in 1879, and died in 1886 at Wharton Court, Herefordshire (*South Australian Register*, 23 January 1886, 7).

The novel discusses contemporary controversies such as the state of the South Australian legal system, the abolition of the Grand Jury system and particularly the sacking of Justice Boothby (257). The narrator trenchantly criticises the treatment of the Indigenous inhabitants by the South Australian people, the government and, in particular, the dissenters.

Like so many colonial novels, *Kooroona* tells the story of a family cast out of Britain by some injustice or misfortune, which comes to the colony with the hope of recuperating its fortunes there. The Vernon family, headed by the gentle widow Mrs Vernon, includes her children Harry, Isabelle and Edith. Having lost the family fortune, her late husband has had to sell their ancestral manor, the Hermitage. Fortuitously, it is bought by a wealthy old friend, Sir John Carleton, who undertakes to sell it back to the young Harry Vernon, when he has made his fortune in Australia. This sets up a potential scenario that will enable the family to return to their ancestral home. As the plot turns, however, their return to England is facilitated by the romance and subsequent marriage between young Isabelle Vernon and Arthur Percy, a 'true' Englishman and 'an aristocrat in the true sense of the word' (166) who befriends the Vernon family in the colony (404-11). He is, in fact, the heir of Sir John Carleton and thus the family is able to return to the Hermitage and their rightful place in English society.

This conventional plot device notwithstanding, *Kooroona* challenges the foundational myths of colonial South Australia in a variety of ways, most notably through its depiction of religion, of the relationship between money and the colonial social order, and of the treatment of the Indigenous people. A comparison of *Kooroona* with the novels of Matilda Evans brings *Kooroona*'s challenges to the foundational story of colonial South Australia into sharp focus. *Kooroona*, for example, articulates some decided opinions about religion. It is written from a High Anglican position[4], and not only is it highly critical

---

4 It is interesting to note that Mary Meredith published in 1883 a work entitled *Theotokos, the example for women* (London: Kegan Paul and Co., 1882). The work sought to 'contribute something towards directing profitably the thoughts of members of the Church of England to the position which God has assigned to the Blessed Virgin Mary in the economy of grace' (*South Australian Register*, 11 July 1883, 5). The British Library catalogue also lists a book by M.A. Meredith, which may also be by Mary Meredith, entitled *Thoughts of the months: their beauties and lessons* (Bath, 1852). This book was revised by Archdeacon George Denison, a High Church clergyman.

of the dissenters, who were a very important element in colonial society, but it also portrays the Established Church as being in a degraded state in the South Australian colony. As the character Arthur Percy declares:

> The clergy of South Australia, speaking of them as a body, are not churchmen … as I understand the meaning of the word … There are some honourable exceptions, but the majority consists of men who ought to join the dissenters, and who would join them, or, at any rate, give up their office in the Church, if they were true honest men. (282)

But it is the Dissenters, rather than this debased Anglican clergy, who are depicted as unseemly, alien and the source of disorder within the colony. When the aristocratic Arthur Percy decides to visit a Primitive Methodist Chapel, he observes an 'Elocutionary Treat' telling the story of Joseph and his brothers. The narrator states that Arthur had known of dissenters in England, but that as far as he knew

> [h]e had never spoken to a dissenter until he landed in Australia. There he found schism in the ascendant, the protestant element widely diffused, very pretentious, very aspiring. He could not walk out in Adelaide, on Sunday, without being in danger of being run over by some man in black clothes and a white choker, on his way to a conventicle of some kind, where he was going to teach others what he did not know himself. (159-60)

Percival is shocked to find dissenters everywhere, even in positions of some status and authority. His own notion of worship is, we are told, restrained and dignified: 'Besides being thoroughly English in everything, he was though he made little profession or outward shew of his belief, an intelligent member of the Church' (160). Arthur goes to the chapel, reluctantly, to know 'to what lengths these professing bibliolators would travesty the sacred volume' (160). Initially amused by 'the absurd burlesque', he becomes disgusted by 'the irreverent scene [and] the wretched buffoonery' and leaves — 'It was his first and last visit to a dissenting meeting-house' (162). His restrained and unemotional masculinity and religiosity are depicted as being appropriate for a true English gentleman, and stand in strong contrast to what is seen as the noisy, ignorant and emotional colonial dissenter version. The narrative voice exclaims: 'Poor Arthur! He was certainly out of his element in Australia' (160).

The Cornish, who were an important ethnic group in the copper mining districts of South Australia, are represented as almost savage and Other, and their Methodism is represented as a show of unseemly and trivial business. Captain Treloar, a Cornish mining captain, is denigrated as being 'a constant attendant at class-meetings, tea-fights, love-feasts, and revivals' (126). Meredith represents the Church of England as the true church, if somewhat under siege from the rising tide of distasteful dissent (see Hilliard and Hunt 203).

The contrast with the positive depiction of Dissenters in the novels of Matilda Evans is striking. Indeed, most of Evans's central characters are chapelgoers. For example, Marian, the heroine of Evans's first novel, *Marian, or the Light of Someone's Home*, is a non-conformist. Marian defends Methodists when an upper-class character denigrates them as 'Ranters', describing them as 'simple, earnest people' (147). When she attends the Wesleyan chapel, she approves the minister's style, praising it as gentlemanly, in refutation of the association with Anglicanism and high social class that comes through so strongly in *Kooroona*. The preacher, we are told, was not fiery: 'He did not thunder out his message to his audience … but he carried their hearts with him by his deep rich voice, his persuasive tones, his affectionate exhortations' (169).

Yet there are a few churchgoing characters who are treated in a sympathetic fashion in Evans's fiction. Thus in *Golden Gifts* the Wallace siblings, thrust out of England by a downturn in their family's fortunes, show their worth in adapting to a simpler and humbler life running a smallholding in the Adelaide Hills. But the Established Church is generally represented as being rather 'aristocratic' and unsuited to the colony, and good colonists are generally chapelgoers, whose religion is represented as being more honest and sincere. For example, in Evans's novel *Into the Light*, Bessie Bruce has a nominal adherence to Anglicanism. However, it is the Fosters, a humble but worthy couple, who, through reading the Bible and the psalms, bring her to Christ. Bessie becomes a chapelgoer while the locals desert the Anglican Church and the clergyman returns to England. This is something of a trope in Evans's novels: upper-class characters, often Anglicans, are likely to show their unworthiness by returning to England. Thus in *Into the Light*, Nina Templeton trifles with Bessie's brother Sid, then throws him over to marry into a wealthy, aristocratic family and returns to Scotland to live on her husband's estate. Evans repeatedly has the dissenters stay in the colony to build a good society for their descendants.

By way of contrast, at the end of *Kooroona*, as noted above, the Anglican Vernon family returns to England resuming their place in the social order, since, as one character declares, 'everything in South Australia is repugnant, invalid and illegal' (257). They are happy to leave behind a colony where life is grubby: merely 'a scramble after money, place and power' (280). Like many colonial texts, *Kooroona* displays an anxiety about what is seen as the colonial obsession with money — the besetting colonial sin. In Evans's novels, however, the masculinity of the self-made colonial man, the man who has pulled himself up by his bootstraps, is to be admired. The character of Bennet Ralston in *The Master of Ralston*, for example, perfectly embodies the colonial ideal of the man who seizes his chances. Ralston seeks to make his fortune within the capitalist economy by whatever means are available to him. The fact that he is always looking out for opportunities to make money is commended by the narrative voice:

> He had no particular system, excepting the very common one, patent to all — that of taking the chances that fell in his way and making the most of them. And there could be no doubt at all that it was this last clause — the 'making the most of them' — that was the real secret of his success — He never suffered any favourable season to go by unimproved; he took up the opportunities for bargains as they came to him; he always had his eyes open, his senses alert, and his muscles in full play. That was all the account he could have given of his prosperity. (9, emphasis in original)

In *Kooroona*, however, only inherited wealth is depicted as being worthy, and the colony is represented as base because of the ubiquitous concern of its inhabitants with self-advancement. As one character notes, 'In the first place every man, with a few rare exceptions, comes to Australia to improve his position in life by acquiring money; that is the object, and, as a rule, he is indifferent as to the means by which he attains his object' (317). Another comments that 'Expediency is the motto in everything' (385).

According to *Kooroona*, such a place is unlikely to prove suitable for the bringing up of children. Mrs Graham, a most respectable woman who has lived in the colony for some years, expresses the view that '[t]he boys here are no sooner out of the nursery than they begin to smoke, and express their opinion on every subject, using slang phrases, [and] speak of their fathers as "the governor'" (43). Mrs Vernon evinces a similar concern, and is very glad that, with the help of the Grahams, she can take her young family to live on the station, Kooroona, where 'we are likely to live in the Bush, far away from these fast young people' (43). Whilst Evans also explores these concerns, in her texts the colony is ultimately shown to be a good place to settle to bring up a family; thus it is possible to be colonial *and* worthy. In Meredith's work the social order of the colony is almost irrevocably corrupted and polluted.

Meredith extols the virtues of a hierarchical social order and of social deference. For instance, Graham, who has lived in the colony for a number of years, is highly scornful about the local parliamentarians who are represented as not valuing the traditional wisdom of England. In a classic statement of Burkean conservative ideology, Graham declares that

> the united and progressive wisdom of centuries, must surely be sounder and deeper than the raw and undigested theories of men who have lived behind a counter and until the wealth they have acquired in their various occupations, enables them to leave the shop for the House of Assembly. (56)

This valuing of old social hierarchies contrasts with foundational narratives which applaud the fact that the decent and lowly can make their way and be rewarded with comfort and even honour in the colonial environment. The colony offers an egalitarianism for white settlers: it is their Eden. In such foundational narratives, Britain's social hierarchies, valued in *Kooroona*, are represented as promoting social injustice.

But what is really striking in *Kooroona* is Meredith's representation of the Indigenous peoples. This contrasts markedly with Evans's work, in which there is virtually no discussion of the Indigenous peoples — neither of their dispossession nor of the harsh relationships between Indigenous and non-Indigenous people in South Australia. Such an omission is, I argue, strategic and crucial to the creation of foundational narratives and the legitimation of settlement. I have noted elsewhere that Evans's works represent

> a colony in which 'white' European settlement is assumed and not contested. In depicting a colonial landscape void of Aboriginal people, these texts are implicated in the ideological work of settling the Europeans into the

South Australian colony ... By continually representing South Australia as *terra nullius*, a smiling agricultural landscape where those who have been cast out of Britain by economic troubles or by its harsh class system, may rightfully come into their own, these texts advance the colonial venture. (Allen, 'Homely stories' 114-5)

Indeed, there is only one passage in Evans's 14 novels in which Aboriginal people are discussed. It seems likely that Evans included this passage in her 1867 novel, *Golden Gifts*, after a reviewer of an earlier novel commented, 'She should put a blacky or two in her next work, and describe them as they really are' (*South Australian Register*, 17 September 1866, 2). In *Golden Gifts*, Evans represents Aboriginal people as intruders in the colonial social order, as ugly, alien, marginal and as thieves and greedy beggars, likely to place great economic demands on the settlers. One character questions the humanity of the Aboriginal people, referring to the contemporary debate about the unity of human species (see Gardner): 'And then to think that these beings are really of one blood with us! Does it not seem strange? They have souls; and yet how near they seem to approach the lowest order of animals' (61). Another briefly wonders 'whether there is really any effort done to do them good?' but the responsibility 'for doing good' is seen as belonging to some unspecified others (61). This topic is not pursued and this brief encounter ends with the settlers withdrawing into their home to enjoy a comfortable normative domesticity whereas the 'weird' Aboriginal people gather around a campfire for a 'corroberry' (62): the Aboriginal people are Other and are contained as a marginalised spectacle in the text.

The contrast with *Kooroona* is marked. Meredith generally writes from a humanitarian position (see Reynolds) and at times positions Aboriginal people as Australian and as the hosts and owners of the land. Early in the novel the narrator comments, 'as a rule the white man need not fear to meet with the native Australian in his own wilds. He will give him a seat by his wood fire, and the shelter of his wurley [bough shelter], and he will be his guide through the forest, unless the white man has previously injured him of one of his tribe' (106). The white man need fear the 'native Australian' only if he has harmed him: 'If he have done that, he must pay the penalty; for the black man will have his revenge as well as the white man, unless fear or some other motive restrain him' (106). Here, faith in Christianity rather than skin colour is the determinant of morality: 'Revenge is a virtue among the savages. It always was and always will be, for the mere fact that it is natural to fallen man. The colour of the skin makes no difference. It is only Christians in *deed* who return good for evil' (106, emphasis in original).

A telling incident occurs in *Kooroona* when the Vernon family is first travelling to the station and gets lost in the bush. They come across a party of Aboriginal people, including the couple, Wahreep and Koonid, who help them by bringing water to them. The children of this group have a friendly exchange with Mrs Vernon and her daughters: 'Not a word did the little natives understand, though they seemed to know instinctively that kindness was intended, returned the smiles that greeted them with interest, and laughed heartily as they received a gentle pat on the cheek or shoulder' (116-7). The passage is somewhat patronising, but the narrator refutes contemporary notions about Aboriginal intelligence, stating, 'These poor Australians, whose capacities for learning are so much underrated, are wonderfully quick of comprehension, and remember accurately everything once seen or heard' (117).

However, Meredith's representation of Indigenous people can be ambivalent, and is at times framed within discourses of scientific racism, with references such as those to 'thick hideous lips' (114). Other familiar tropes of colonial discourses appear, such as infantilising the Indigenous people and likening them to animals. The small girls, Caudeto and Muhnard, are described as follows: 'Those two little animals are like kittens' (185).

Inherent in the colonial gaze is the study of peoples and their customs and their classification in racial hierarchies. Thus, the reader is assured that 'Revolting as are many of their habits and customs, Mrs. Vernon and her family felt a deep interest in them' (190-1). The narrator describes the customs and beliefs of the Indigenous peoples. She notes they had 'no permanent habitations; they wander from place to place' (188). At their destination, they set up wurleys and cook on open fires. She recounts the notion of Indigenous people being outside of history: 'They have no written language … they take no notice of time. No memento remains of past generations; not a trace exists of those who century after century have been born, lived, and died on this vast island' (188). In relation to their beliefs, 'They believe in the existence of good and of a Bad spirit' (188-9). Their 'customs and legends' derive from ancient times (189). She writes of deities and heroes: Wyungare, Nurundere and Neppele (189). It is not known if she gained this information from discussion with Indigenous peoples, but as Nurundere is well-known as relating to the Njarrnindjeri peoples of Lower River Murray, it is likely that some of it came from her reading.

Meredith describes Wanganneen [*sic*], a 'northern savage', in terms of the 'noble savage'. A 'man, born and reared on the wilds of Australia', he 'was one of nature's gentlemen … the untaught Australian had God's own patent of nobility' (219).[5] It is interesting to note that Indigenous characters in this work have names — apparently Indigenous names; thus the reader meets Wahreep, Koonid, Menulta, Caudeto, Muhnard and Wanganneen. This is in contrast to Evans's work in which Indigenous people are merely a homogenous, nameless group of natives, and also to Catherine Helen Spence's novel *Clara Morison* in which we briefly meet 'Black Mary' (Spence 130, 165). In *Kooroona*, Indigenous ownership of the land is acknowledged and Mrs Vernon is aware that she is 'a stranger in a black man's land' (118).

Whereas Evans wrote about Aboriginal people briefly in order to represent them as weird and savage, they are key to Meredith's motivation for writing *Kooroona*. In *Kooroona*, the Aboriginal people are shown as suffering under the bad treatment of the settlers and the colonial government, whose actions were driving them into rebellion rather than 'trying to raise them in the scale of humanity by drawing forth and encouraging the good that is in them' (218). An awareness of the injustices visited upon the Indigenous population is articulated via the consciousness of Mrs Vernon, who knows that 'the so-called Christian Government of South Australia ignored, as far as possible, the existence of the native inhabitants, regarding them and treating them as a degraded race, doomed to die out before the white man' (118).

The message within *Kooroona* is that the misguided treatment of the Aboriginal people is linked to the settlers' abandonment of true religion: Anglicanism. The narrator advises us that Mrs Vernon considers

---

5   Meredith misspells the Wanganeen family name. This is now an important Indigenous family in South Australia. In the late 1860s, Meredith may have known or known of James Wanganeen, who was then at the Anglican-run Poonindie mission. Lydon and Braithwaite sketch the Anglican humanitarian network with which Meredith must have been associated. See also Kartinyeri, *Wanganeen*.

> [t]hat those who have not learnt to govern themselves are unfit to govern others, and she was not surprised, therefore, that those who had separated themselves from the Church — the teacher appointed by God; those who had cast aside all restraint, who acknowledged no rule in religion or politics, who, self-wise, made their own creed, and tried to make laws to suit their own ideas of right and justice — should commence their reign of misrule by disobeying their Queen, and get into a labyrinth of discord and confusion. (218-19)

Once Mrs Vernon meets Wahreep, Koonid and their relatives *en route* to Kooroona, she knows that they have 'given to her in her need the best they had' (118), and she feels that it is her duty to do something for them although she does not know what. Although here there is a sense of reciprocity, Mrs Vernon is also positioned as a superior person, as one who can help the Aboriginal people.

In the novel, Mrs Vernon and her family have to battle the prejudice of the settlers, who will not give Aboriginal people work. When the Northern tribes come down, the mounted troopers, fearing trouble, come onto the Vernon property, Kooroona, to protect the Vernon family. Harry Vernon sees the police as the cause of much racial strife:

> I wish the fellows would keep at a distance: they have been making free use of their revolvers lately. I don't suppose it will ever be known how many they have killed. Wahreep has heard somehow that the blacks are infuriated with them, and are determined to have their revenge. Old Duncan has been told by a shepherd, that in the last skirmish, as soon as the natives rushed forward and threw their boomerangs, the revolvers were fired, and many fell. They were carried off into the scrub, whether dead or alive he did not know. If they find the police here we shall never be secure again. (202)

Although the trooper assures Harry that he need not fear the Northern Aborigines, for 'a few shots will soon frighten them' (202), Harry sends the troopers packing. With regard to the Aboriginal people, Harry declares:

> Be kind to them and trust them, and they will repay it in the only way they can — by honesty and gratitude. To rob them of their land, and of the very means of existence and then shoot them like wild dogs for carrying off a few sheep, is a disgrace to humanity'. (203)

The Vernons treat the Aboriginal people somewhat like faithful retainers. De Pasquale writes of their 'oily condescension' (159), which emphasises the almost feudal relationship the Vernons establish with them. For instance, when the Aboriginal people have a corroboree, the Vernons supply them with provisions: 'Harry did not go empty handed. A cart followed him. Sheep, roasted whole, an abundant supply of plain substantial cake, which Isabelle and Edith had been helping Mrs. Brown to make, with tea and sugar' (221).

Meredith draws contemporary politics into her novel. Harry and his sister Isabelle have a long discussion on the position of the Aboriginal people around Lake Hope, and on the expanding northern frontier of white settlement. Harry reads out a letter in the press critical of the settlers' and government's behaviour (212-14). This letter is taken almost word for word from a letter, entitled 'Christians and Aborigines in the North', written by another Anglican, John Bristow Hughes, to the *South Australian Register* in February 1866 (Hughes 3). Harry's comment sheets home the government's failures to the dissenters:

> What especially disgusts me … is that the men who manage the affairs of the colony and expend public money, are all methodist preachers of some kind … you constantly see their names in the papers as speakers at meetings and tea-fights, where they profess to feel the deepest interest in every conceivable good deed that man ever has done or can do under the sun; their love for everybody is unbounded. (215)

According to Harry, after these men have slept off the flow of hot tea and 'heart rending oratory' at 'a methodist tea-fight', they 'get up the next morning to assist in some little arrangement for robbing the natives of a further portion of their territory' (215).

When a white man is found murdered on Kooroona station, Mrs Vernon's vow to assist the Aboriginal people is really called upon. The local magistrate charges Wahreep and he is taken hundreds of miles to Adelaide, along with his wife Koonid and other Aboriginal witnesses. They are 'hand-cuffed and chained together' (243) and then locked up for three months pending the trial. Harry Vernon hopes that an Aboriginal man who can clear Wahreep will come forward, but he cannot be found. Harry goes to Adelaide to visit the prisoner and witnesses, and discovers some of the difficulties for Aboriginal people mixed up with the law. Whilst staying at the York Hotel he has a long discussion with Jones, another guest, who shares his jaundiced view of the colony. They discuss the way the courts deal with Aboriginal defendants, as well as the 1860 Select

Committee of the Legislative Council, which had dealt with 'the utility of trying native prisoners in the Supreme Court' (249-58). Jones advises him to avoid colonial lawyers and to 'leave your black friend in the hands of the judge' (256).

When Wahreep's trial begins he appears almost powerless: 'There he stood, one of a degraded race, alone, despised, to be judged by men who had taken possession of his land, and who knew no more of his language than he did of their laws' (301). However, both Harry Vernon and his genteel sister, Edith, take the witness stand and speak for Wahreep at the trial. But curiously, in a work that maintains the common humanity of settler and indigene, it is some scientific evidence about 'race' which enables Wahreep's acquittal. Harry arranges for a German medical practitioner to appear as an expert witness. His testimony sees Wahreep acquitted and released. He testifies that the hair on Wahreep's spear belongs to an Aboriginal person, stating:

> I have examined the hair by the aid of a powerful microscope, and have clearly detected the difference that distinguished the hair of different races of men. The hair could not have grown upon the head of a European, and is different from the hair of a white man, as is that of the negro or of the red Indian. (306-7)

While Wahreep and Koonid are able to return to their country at Kooroona station, the Vernon family does not go back there. Their eyes are set firmly upon England. In a neat twist of the plot, Arthur Percy, whom they have befriended, is revealed as the nephew and heir of Sir John Carleton. He falls in love and becomes engaged to Isabelle Vernon and the family is able to resume their ancestral seat, the Hermitage. Edith expresses the family's regrets:

> There is one thing we shall regret whenever we leave Australia, and that is, not having been able to do more for the aborigines, We have thought about it and talked the matter over [and basically no good will come] until Government recognises its responsibility, and that Harry says will never be … [but] if the colonists were different, they would be able to make the Government do more for the natives. (418-19)

While Evans's novels can be seen as novels of settlement, which affirm foundational narratives, *Kooroona* is a novel of sojourn. The colony is a place where one might recoup one's fortune, but not a suitable place to raise one's children. In this novel, the colony is found to be polluted and immoral but the morality of recouping one's fortune on Indigenous land is not questioned.

The autobiographical elements of this novel seem evident since Mary Meredith did take up the situation of the Indigenous people on Yorke Peninsula in 1866. She began a letter to the *South Australian Register*, signed over her own name, in January 1866, with the following words:

> It is difficult to understand how any one who has had opportunities of observing the social and moral degradation of the native inhabitants of this country can really believe that he is not failing in a positive duty when, while enriching himself with the produce of the land, or with mineral wealth, he leaves the original possessor untaught and uncared for. (Meredith, 'A Native Mission' 2)

She asserted that the local Aboriginal people trusted her family, 'because we have been kind to them; they believe us, because what we tell them we will do we do' (2). She referred to the authoritative Aboriginal leader, King Tom, 'a fine old man — full six feet in height; he is intelligent and speaks English very tolerably' (2).[6] She reported that the Aboriginal people would support the establishment of a school for their children whom they had agreed to leave there. Indeed, King Tom's child had 'been at our house many times, on one occasion for part of a week'.[7] Clearly she had been discussing this matter with Aboriginal people for at least a year, but presented her ladylike reticence as holding her back from going public as 'a natural disinclination to take any but a private part in the matter' (2). She commented that it is 'painful to reflect that for more than a year they have been looking for their teacher, while I have been waiting and hoping that others would do that which now it seems I should have tried to commence myself' (2).

Her appeal gained some support from the leader writer in the *South Australia Register*, but clearly there were concerns about a woman making such a public, critical statement of the social order. The following day the leader read:

> We honour her [Mrs. Meredith] for her courage as well as her kindness in doing violence to her gentle nature by coming forth publicly on behalf of the poor natives. There are some women who are very enthusiastic for savages at a distance while they neglect those at their very doors … But Mrs. Meredith is not a Mrs. Jellaby, mad about her pet natives at Bhorrioboola Gha, while she neglects those who have immediate and pressing claims

---

6 King Tom 'was widely recognized as a Narungga leader' (Krichauff 130, 139-168).

7 It is interesting to note that in the novel Edith Vernon teaches the children, Caudeto and Muhnard, to read in the family home (184-5).

upon her sympathies and assistance. She boldly and yet modestly states the case of the aborigines who have come under her notice, and speaks in the name of humanity and of religion that they should be better cared for than they are now. (*South Australian Register*, 11 January 1866, 2)

Mary Meredith was one of the concerned Christians in the district who formed a Missionary Association and invited two Moravian missionaries to come from Adelaide in February 1866 to discuss the needs of the local Aboriginal people (Edwards 4; Wilson 4-5; Krichauff 139). Pastor Kuehn stayed and 'commenced a school with twenty children attending, conducted services, provided medical care and distributed rations provided by the government for the fifty Aborigines at Kadina' (Edwards 4). However, Meredith became increasingly frustrated by the failure of the government to provide further assistance. In a letter to the Protector of Aborigines in June 1866 she claimed that for five months they had had a missionary to teach the natives and described herself as 'the originator of the movement' for a mission on Yorke Peninsula (GRG 52/1/1866/59). She reported that they had been waiting five months for the government to grant land for a mission house.

The Merediths were strongly associated with the campaign for the mission and Mary Meredith wrote more letters to the press on the matter (*South Australian Register*, 21 May and 20 July 1866 and 12 September 1867). She was very critical of the colonial government and in some of these letters she quoted the replies she had received from government officials. The Yorke Peninsula Aboriginal Mission, later known as Port Pearce, was founded in 1868 and Mary Meredith and her husband were on the committee.

However, the Merediths were soon engaged in controversy with other members of the mission committee. John Meredith was moved to defend his wife against a member of the mission committee at Wallaroo, who was telling what he saw as an 'amusing anecdote' about Mary Meredith putting the natives through a 'catechistic drill' in order to gain a meal. John Meredith wrote: 'I shall take this opportunity of expressing my regret, that anyone connected with the mission should, even if he believed it, circulate a low story, calculated to bring ridicule upon one who takes such a warm interest in the success of the mission' (J. Meredith 1). It is possible that this incident led to their quitting the colony at short notice and may account for some of the rancorous tone of the novel.

Only a fortnight after John Meredith's letter in support of his wife, the sale by public auction of the Meredith house on Ryan Street, Moonta, was notified, for they were leaving the colony (*Wallaroo Times*, 28 October 1868, 1). They appear not to have had any children living and died within two months of each other in 1897 in Cheltenham, England (*South Australian Register*, 17 August 1897, 3 and 30 October 1897, 4).

Reception of *Kooroona*

It is not known how widely *Kooroona* was read and discussed in South Australia in the 1870s, although it is known to have been sold in Adelaide bookshops. Clearly some of the characters in the novel were closely modelled upon people Meredith knew in South Australia and some of the discussion of the text centred upon that. A reviewer in the *Observer* found that 'the least pardonable fault of the work' was that

> some of the caricatures are avowedly intended for personal sketches. We do not pretend to recognise the individuals thus lampooned, but it is easy to see that the portraits, if professedly from life, are unfairly taken. Every human foible is exaggerated and emphasized, while better qualities of worthy and useful colonists are carefully kept out of view. (Anonymous 15)

In relation to the novel's discussion of Indigenous issues, the reviewer merely noted, 'A vivid picture is drawn of the farcical proceedings before a Court, the laws and often the language of which are equally unknown to the prisoner and the witnesses' (15); and that 'The book abounds with denunciations of the conduct of the white men towards the natives' (15) without any further discussion of the contentious issues raised. The novel was too troubling to the settlers and its challenge was firmly repressed. Certainly this reviewer felt the need to respond in terms of a foundational narrative: 'That we have amongst us persons who have risen from the ranks — wealthy men whose fathers were poor — is a fact which we proclaim with pride rather than confess with shame' (15).

Evidently this novel aroused some controversy in Adelaide. Indeed, two readers felt moved to furnish their own reviews of the work to the *South Australian Register* in 1872. The newspaper published extracts from both reviews. One declared that, while some claimed that characters were easily identified, there was 'no spite in the book' ('Kooroona' 24 May). For those who found the work too critical of South Australia, this reviewer commented, 'Let them know that their society is not perfect, nor all-wise, nor all-benevolent — let them think that sickness is known in South Australia as well as elsewhere, and needs at time the wholesome and bitter draught of the kindly physician'. The other attacked the author, clearly knowing her identity, referring to her as 'Mrs. M.', and showing the dangers of presenting 'alternative readings that contested aspects of the dominant colonial discourse' (Grimshaw and Evans 81). This reviewer was vicious:

> The countenance of Mrs. M. had treachery written upon it. A bold, thick, unladylike nose; near, furtive eyes; a hanging mouth, and dowdy dress, were quite sufficient to send their owner to Coventry. There was nothing to attract men, everything to repulse women, and with no social ties to make her human, Mrs. M. became a sad tigress. ('Kooroona' 17 May)

The comment on social ties seems to refer to the fact that she had no children.

In conclusion, this anti-foundational narrative contests the main features of the South Australian foundational narrative. It allows for a critical view of relationships between the settlers and Indigenous peoples: a view that foundational narratives cannot allow. Foundational settler narratives, such as those by Matilda Evans, ignore Indigenous peoples and their prior ownership of the land that the settlers have taken. They fail to acknowledge settler violence against Indigenous peoples. To do so would be incompatible with the foundational narrative, which represents the settlers as worthy and the colony as their promised land.

Although knowledge of *Kooroona* disappeared from literary memory in South Australia, a trace remained and surfaced years later. Another South Australian writer, Catherine Martin (1847-1937), used the name Kooroona for a young woman of Aboriginal descent in her novel, *The Silent Sea* (1892), published under the pseudonym of Mrs Alick MacLeod. Possibly Catherine Martin learnt of this book from her husband Fred, who had lived in Moonta from 1873-77 (Allen, 'Fred Martin' 100). *The Silent Sea* makes some criticism of the settler project, with some of its action taking place in the outback area of South Australia, described as 'regions red with black men's blood and stained with white men's crimes' (vol. 2, 49-50). Kooroona, the daughter of a Mr White and Jeanie, a woman of Aboriginal descent, has to flee with her mother to avoid being separated by the heartless White. Jeanie has a difficult life '[w]ith her timid eyes and shy, kindly ways, cut off from her own people, avoided by others, her health ruined, meek and submissive always to this tyrant, who talked of her more heartlessly than he would of one of his sheep or cattle' (vol. 1, 133-4). By the 1890s, when the settlers had taken over a considerable portion of the Indigenous lands of South Australia, it was possible to challenge the settler myth, albeit in this muted manner.

Works Cited

Allen, Margaret. 'Fred Martin.' *The Hatbox Letters*. Ed. Martin family committee. Adelaide: privately published, 1999: 99-104.

——. 'Homely stories and the ideological work of "Terra Nullius".' *Journal of Australian Studies* 79 (2003): 105-15 and 234-6.

Curthoys, Ann. 'Expulsion, Exodus and Exile in White Australian Historical Mythology.' *Imaginary Homelands*. Special Issue of *Journal of Australian Studies* 61 (1999): 1-19.

De Pasquale, Paul. *A Critical History of South Australian Literature 1836-1930*. Warradale, SA: Pioneer Books, 1978.

Edwards, Bill. 'The Moravian Mission at Lake Kopperamanna.' Unpublished paper, c. 2005.

Franc, Maud Jeanne [Matilda Jane Evans]. *Marian, or the Light of Someone's Home*. 1859. London: Sampson Low, Marston & Company, c. 1925.

——. *Golden Gifts*. 1867. London: Sampson Low, Marston & Company, c. 1911.

——. *No Longer a Child*. 1878. London: Sampson Low, Marston, Searle, & Rivington, 1882.

——. *The Master of Ralston*. 1885. London: Sampson Low, Marston & Company, n.d. [c. 1907].

Foster, Robert, Rick Hosking and Amanda Nettelbeck. *Fatal Collisions: The South Australian frontier and the violence of memory*. Kent Town: Wakefield Press, 2001.

Gardner, Helen. 'The "Faculty of Faith": Evangelical missionaries, social anthropologists, and the claim for human unity in the 19th century.'

Foreign Bodies: Oceania and the Science of Race 1750-1940. Ed. Bronwen Douglas and Chris Ballard, Canberra: ANU E-Press, 2008. http://press.anu.edu.au//foreign_bodies/html/frames.php, accessed 6 September 2011.

GRG 52/1/1866/59 qtd in Doreen Kartinyeri, *Narungga Nation*. Point Pearce, SA: D. Kartinyeri, 2002, 15.

Grimshaw, Patricia and Julie Evans, 'Colonial Women on Intercultural Frontiers: Rosa Campbell Praed, Mary Bundock and Katie Langloh Parker.' *Australian Historical Studies* 106 (1996): 79-95.

Hilliard, David and Arnold D. Hunt. 'Religion.' *The Flinders History of South Australia: Social history*. Ed. Eric Richards. Netley, SA: Wakefield Press, 1986. 194-234.

Hughes, Jno. [*sic*] B. 'Christians and Aborigines in the North.' Letter to the Editor *South Australian Register* 20 February 1866: 3.

Iota [Mary A. Meredith]. *Kooroona: A Tale of South Australia*. Oxford and London: A.R. Mowbray and Simpkin, Marshall and Co., 1871.

Kartinyeri, Doreen. *The Wanganeen family genealogy*. Adelaide: D. Kartinyeri, 1989.

'Kooroona.' *South Australian Register*, 17 May 1872: 5.

——. *South Australian Register*, 24 May 1872: 5.

Krichauff, Skye for the Narungga Aboriginal Progress Association *Nharrungga wargunni bugi-buggillu: A journey through Narungga history*. Kent Town, SA: Wakefield Press, 2011.

Lydon, Jane and Sari Braithwaite. '"Cheque Shirts and Plaid Trowsers": Photographing Poonindie Mission, South Australia.' *Journal of the Anthropological Society of South Australia* 37 (December 2013): 1-30.

MacLeod, Mrs Alick [C. Martin]. *The Silent Sea*. London: Bentley, 1892. 2 vols.

Meredith, Mary A. 'A Native Mission on Yorke's Peninsula.' *South Australian Register*, 10 January 1866: 2.

Meredith, John, 'The Native Mission.' *Wallaroo Times*, 17 October 1868: 3-4.

'Original Reviews: *Kooroona*.' *Adelaide Observer*, 24 June 1871: 15.

Osborn, Pamela. *Letters from Mitcham: St Michael's Anglican Church: 150 years of parish life 1852-2002*. Mitcham, SA: Anglican Parish of Mitcham, 2002.

Pike, Douglas. *Paradise of Dissent: South Australia, 1829-57*. Melbourne: Melbourne UP, 1957.

Richards, Eric. 'The peopling of South Australia.' *The Flinders History of South Australia*. Ed. Eric Richards. Netley, SA: Wakefield Press, 1986: 115-42.

Reynolds, Henry. *This Whispering in Our Hearts*. Sydney: Allen & Unwin, 1998.

Rowley, Charles. *The Destruction of Aboriginal Society*. Canberra: ANU Press, 1970.

South Australian Register. Various dates.

Spence, Catherine Helen. *Clara Morison*. 1854. Intro. Susan Eade. Adelaide: Rigby, 1971.

Spry, Y. *All Saints Moonta, Centenary 1874-1974*. Moonta, SA: 1984.

Wilson, William. 'The Aborigines.' *Wallaroo Times*, 3 February 1866: 4-5.

5

The making of Barbara Baynton

Rosemary Moore

Barbara Baynton's oeuvre, though small, has always been a challenge. It has been viewed as somehow at odds with the work of her male contemporaries, while ostensibly covering much of the same ground in terms of setting and genre. Her work remains challenging, and this is not just in terms of her position in the national canon. Two characteristics of her writing serve to alienate the reader: her use of fractured narratives and her failure, deliberate or otherwise, to provide an authorial position with which to assist the reader's interpretation. Furthermore, as Hergenhan suggests, her writing — short stories and a novel — involves 'a symbolic elusiveness, almost a concealment, possibly to evade censorship' (211), probably to protect the discovery of truths that her protagonists themselves seek but fear to acknowledge.

There is a consensus amongst readers about one feature of Baynton's work. She is a dissident writer, but what does she dissent from? The notion that her writing fails to support the national ethos espoused by her male compatriots is not in doubt. Similarly, the view, first stated by feminist readers, that the target of her criticism is the sexism of a male-dominated society is not in dispute. Yet, these views do not account sufficiently for 'the pervading vision of moral chaos and cruelty' which her work delineates (Krimmer and Lawson xxiii). Hegenhan suggests that 'her quarrel is with the universe, its disorder rather than with a specific national ethos or with gender relations, though she is deeply critical of these'. It is a response to 'injustice' which is 'ultimately part of a cosmic ethos' (Hegenhan 8). However, though Baynton is aware of social injustice, this seems too abstract for the intensity and specificity of her themes.

Whilst 'meaninglessness and malice' characterise her 'vision of the bush' (Krimmer and Lawson xxvi), it is necessary to consider further the reasons behind 'her attack on man's animality' (xxix) and the reasons for the way that her use of symbolism often appears to obscure meaning. I will draw on Freud's theory of hysteria to account for these elements in Baynton's work. This reading will fall outside of what has too often been a restrictive frame in Baynton criticism: that of Australian nationalism. By drawing on hysterical symptoms, Baynton draws attention to the unspoken. These symptoms establish a relationship between symbols and actions in daily life, thus permitting the expression of that which cannot be openly said. Hysteria allows for the symbolic expression of psychical conflict as somatic symptoms of various kinds — emotional crises accompanied by theatricality, hysterical paralyses, lumps in the throat.[1] The symptoms draw attention to an impasse, to a barrier to speaking out and actually giving a name to what causes the horror pervading her work: Baynton's anger at the consequences for women, children and the family at large of the licentiousness of men who are prepared to rape women, and who commit adultery and incest as if by right, albeit under the influence of alcohol. The nationalist frame has tended to pit Baynton against the radical nationalist writers of her time, but it need not do so. Leigh Dale points out that Baynton is, in fact, a

> chronicler of her culture's most brutal truths. In the latter role, she cannot be set apart from any Australian or bush tradition, as so many critics have claimed; on the contrary, *on this basis*, she must be central to it. (380, emphasis in original)

While not wishing to use Baynton's biography as a definitive mode of reading her fiction, I believe it is nevertheless relevant to refer to some of the

---

1 The definition of two forms of hysteria given by Laplanche and Pontalis are appropriate to Baynton's epoch and usage: '*Conversion hysteria** [*sic*], in which the psychical conflict is expressed symbolically in somatic symptoms of the most varied kinds: they may be paroxystic (e.g. emotional crises accompanied by theatricality) or more long-lasting (anaesthesias, hysterical paralyses, 'lumps in the throat', etc.); and *anxiety hysteria** [*sic*], where the anxiety is attached in more or less stable fashion to a specific external object (phobias)' (194).

factors in her life which appear to be linked to her practice of narrative elusiveness. The complicated subjectivities produced by displacement and dislocation are typical, rather than unusual, in the colonial world. Such complications are evident in Baynton's own life, and in her explanations of it, as well as in her fictional narratives. I will first outline a brief biographical account, in order to illuminate the reading of *Human Toll* which will follow. I will then consider how similar themes play out in some of the stories from *Bush Studies*.

Baynton was aware that society and religion held women responsible for sin and believed them to be the source of male lust. And she must have had a reason for obscuring the identity of her father, which remains a mystery today. She was born Barbara Jane Lawrence in Scone, New South Wales, on 4 June 1857. Her mother, Elizabeth Lawrence, arrived from Ireland with her husband, John Lawrence, on the *Royal Consort* in 1840 (Krimmer and Lawson x). She was brought up in poor circumstances, but went on to marry three times and to advance her social status each time, unlike her sisters, who married 'gangers and gardeners' (Hackforth-Jones 84). To meet the strictures of respectability *de rigueur* at the time she reshaped her past. Yet it remained the inspiration for her work, it defined her themes, and it led to the creation of her unique narrative style.

According to her own account she was born Barbara Kilpatrick. As her grandson, H.B. Gullett, states, her mother, Penelope Ewart, who was then married to her cousin, Robert Ewart, came out to Australia in 1858. In Bombay she met and fell in love with Captain Kilpatrick, formerly of the Bengal Light Cavalry, after which she left her husband and entered into a de facto relationship with her lover (21). Baynton's great-granddaughter, Penne Hackforth-Jones, aware of variant accounts, surmises that Elizabeth Ewart arrived in 1840 married to a farm labourer, John Lawrence, and that she left him for Robert Fitzpatrick, a carpenter who had arrived in Australia some months before her and who, for propriety's sake, later took on John Lawrence's name in order to live with Elizabeth (6). But this is speculation: whoever Robert Kilpatrick may or may not have been, he was not in the Bengal Light Infantry (established to deal with the Indian Rebellion of 1857-58) or in the cavalry regiments of the armoured corps of the Indian Army, which did not bear the title of Bengal Lancer until 1896. It seems that Baynton's imaginative bent was such that the truth was to her a variable quantity depending on 'what she chose to believe it ought to be at any given moment' (Gullett 21).

The discovery of Baynton's marriage certificates begins to suggest why she may have needed to disguise her parentage as her social status increased and she was able to put the past behind her. Her parents' names were not cited on the certificate of her first marriage to Alexander Frater, but her father's name was cited as John Lawrence on her marriage certificate to Dr Baynton and as Robert Lawrence Kilpatrick on her marriage certificate to Lord Headley (Krimmer and Lawson x). As Krimmer and Lawson observe, it seems curious that Baynton should have invented a de facto relationship for her parents that rendered her siblings illegitimate (xi). However, the date of birth she claimed, 4 June 1862 — five years later than her actual date of birth — coincided with the date on which John Lawrence died and her mother married Robert John Lawrence (Hackforth-Jones 6). Thus she confirmed her own legitimacy. Given that, in Freud's view, the uncertainty of fatherhood can lead to the exaltation of a father's identity, she may have invented a father 'of higher social standing' in accordance with Freud's theory of 'Family Romances' (239), and the fact that she claimed to have been born Barbara Kilpatrick may also have been a protective disguise.

In light of this biography it is significant that her novel, *Human Toll*, looks at the impact of illegitimacy, incest and male licentiousness upon the growth of a young child, Ursula, who, like Baynton's illegitimate brother, James, bears her mother's maiden name, Ewart. It is a complex narrative that draws attention to its themes through mirroring symbolic events with realistic ones. Despite the presence of lascivious men, there is an underlying association between female sexuality, sin and death, partly because Baynton grew up with a mother who 'never lost her sense of guilt and regarded her harsh life as a sort of judgement for her behaviour' (Webby 24), as her 'Mother's God was a vengeful God' (Hackforth-Jones 12).

The narrative begins with the death of the man believed to be Ursula's father, but the facts surrounding her birth remain unclear. She is surrounded by potential father figures: her immediate guardian, Boshy, their neighbour, Cameron Cameron, his son-in-law, Hugh Palmer, and her aunt's second husband, Mr Civil. Both Boshy and Hugh take false names, presumably to disguise their identity as English convicts. The question the child puts to Boshy, "'W'y am I?'" (Baynton, *Human Toll* 129), is fundamental to the work as a whole.

Boshy has 'memories connected with the child that he, like Mary, has "pondered in his heart"' (143). He does not know whether her father and mother were married or not and fears for Ursula's future security if they were not. All he knows for certain is that "'he pick 'er up in some towen, w'en 'e went down wi' some sheep, a' w'en they come 'ere I arst no questions, so they tell me no lies, for she'd an eye in 'er 'ead that 'ud coax a duck — a nole duck — off ov the water'" (132). Fearing Cameron's plan to take Ursula away to be "'schooled'" in a nearby town (138), Boshy poses a moral question. Who has the greater right to the child, the man who has "'weaned 'er from 'er mother a'most'" (141) and who loves her as his own or the man who has "'a-snavelled'" (138) her father's papers (apparently with his marriage lines) and thus assumes legal possession of her?

Claiming he has her father's permission, Cameron takes Ursula away to become the ward of his sister, Mrs Irvine. There her destiny is shaped by the events that occur on her first Sunday, from which she learns her place as a female. And, from a complicated series of juxtaposed episodes, the child is led to believe that she has bad blood, is sinful, and that God is out to get her. When in a violent storm she flees from God's wrath and chooses to hide in a brick oven, she dramatises her fear of having been a bun in the oven, born illegitimately. After the death of her protectors, Boshy and her aunt, Mr Civil becomes her de facto father. In this capacity his new interest in her culminates in a visit to her bedroom one night with the intention of possessing her treasure. She flees and is taken in by the Steins, formerly shanty-grog providers, to share a room with their daughter, Mina. Mina becomes her rival for Andrew Cameron and her double, taking over the role of the girl with bad blood.

Mina taunts Ursula with her uncertain parentage by asking to whom she is related. "'W'at are you? An ole Boshy, an' old Civil, an' Andrer even, if ther truth was known?'" (240). However, although Mina doesn't know it, she is herself the fruit of an incestuous relationship between her father and his sister, Barbara, as his wife divulges. Mr Stein's ignorance of the fact results from his having been too drunk at the time to know what he was doing. For this eventuality there is a biblical precedent in the story of Lot's daughters who, after their mother's death, get their father drunk in order to have sex with him and thus preserve his seed.

Andrew awakes after a drunken spree during which he and Mina have had sex to find that he has been forcibly married to Mina, who is then evicted from her parental home and sent with Ursula to a property part-owned by himself and Hugh. However, since Andrew has sworn not to live with Mina, she is free to carry on an adulterous affair with Hugh, now a widower. When 13 months later she has an illegitimate baby, like the bad mother in the story of Solomon's famous judgment, she kills it by partially smothering it in sleep, thus prolonging its death. Ursula becomes the true mother who thinks only of the baby's welfare. However, she is forced to flee with it into the bush as Mina intends to kill them both. Bushed and suffering from exposure to intolerable conditions Ursula becomes mentally unhinged, unable to tell if the baby is alive or dead, but determined to claim it as her own, fathered by Hugh.

Biblical references serve to give plausibility to the novel's illicit sexual encounters and to give meaning to the life it recounts. When Ursula is bushed she resembles Miriam destined to die in a waterless desert. But she hopes to be saved by her true love, Andrew, who like Jacob has been falsely married to Mina-Leah. The conclusion brings to a climax Ursula's practice of reading the landscape in relation to the Bible. For example, after the death of Ursula's aunt she revisits the 'old haunts that had tempted and terrified her childhood', the place she designated 'Mount Murillo … where Satan had led Christ, to tempt Him with the kingdoms of the earth'; the place where 'Christ, lonely, had wept'. Nearby is the place where her aunt lies buried, her 'childhood's Garden of Gethsemane' (213). Ursula's fantasies when bushed do not diminish the power of Baynton's description of her spiritual trial and its outcome — the expiation of sin and redemption.

When she encounters the devil as a goanna he does not tempt her, and when the sword of vengeance hangs above her head it does not fall on her. The bush-Christ is a figure of forgiveness who enables her to feel forgiven and to forgive herself, so that when she believes her saviours have come to rescue her she identifies herself with Mina's body in words she can barely articulate, pointing to '"[t]his poor woman"' who is also '"I — I — … I"' (299). Now that the baby and mother are dead, Ursula can re-enter the world without bearing the burden of being the child born in sin. Thus the inheritance of bad blood is finally overcome, and the wages of sin is death no more.

Her initial carer, Boshy, is biologically male, but anatomy does not determine his sexual position as he oscillates between male and female symbolic positions. He behaves like a hysteric who, in Lacan's view, poses a question about gender identity: 'What is the woman-hysteric saying? Her question is this — *What is it to be a woman?* (*The Psychoses* 175, emphasis in original). He wears Ursula's father's boots and a carpenter's cap, and he also makes coffins. However, he has a mother's love for the child of his heart; he instructs her through parables; and he uses storytelling as a means of disguising the truth. His discovery of Baldy's hoard marks a traumatic moment that seems to refer to some original event which is inaccessible to consciousness, but which is symbolised in part through a series of representations carrying a traumatic impact for him. His discovery constitutes a secret so momentous that it must be repressed and buried with the dead. He will never speak of it openly because it involves the theft of a treasure, a symbolic representation of the rape and dishonouring of a woman. Baynton establishes links between various strands of meaning connected with the discovery of the gold coins, and these form a nodal point of meaning which binds associated ideas together, such as secrecy, inheritance, treasure, theft, rape and reputation. In addition, in both symbolic and realistic registers, incidents recur which indicate the characteristic of hysteria to offer 'ever new versions of reworked memory traces addressing without ever touching the initial traumatic event' (Bronfen 42).

Before Mrs Civil dies she tries to impart a secret to Ursula associated with her birthplace, but is prevented from doing so by her husband. When Ursula receives papers associated with her inheritance, they are stolen from her. But she also has a biological inheritance from her mother, whom she resembles. This becomes the cause of dread for Boshy. Grave-robbing, theft and digging for treasure are associated with rape and the unearthing of a secret that will damage a woman's reputation. Ursula evades Mr Civil's assault when he comes with a pick and shovel to take her treasure. Jim exposes Fanny to the local shopkeepers' jokes because he has sex with her outside of marriage, and when he robs a grave of flowers to put on Mrs Civil's grave it is a reminder that grave-robbing is a form of violation and that Mrs Civil was done to death by a husband who forced his will upon her. Boshy's last words to Ursula are a warning: '"Remember w'at comes over the divil's back goes under 'is belly; an' a narrer getherin' often gits a wide scatterin'" (Baynton, *Human Toll* 229). The context of these proverbs suggests that the burden of sin is sex, and ill-gotten gains may be inappropriately spent if semen is too widely scattered.

The drunkenness of men appears to have been a social right, although it led Baynton's first husband, Alexander Frater, into adultery. He was a drunkard and a womaniser who seduced the wives of their neighbours, and whose children were raised in the families into which they were born (Hackforth-Jones 48). Furthermore, he seduced Baynton's nineteen-year-old niece, Sarah Glover, who later told her children that she had tried "'to stop him — I said no, no … but he wouldn't listen'" (qtd in Hackforth-Jones 47). Male brutality is condoned by the society Baynton depicts and there is little sympathy within her stories for women who are abused, isolated and lack social support. But in spite of being silenced, her women find in hysterical conversion and the language of the bodily symptom the means to make their feelings known.

Baynton's writing can be described as hysterical due to its obsession with sexual misconduct, deceit and betrayal, and she characterises Boshy as a hysteric whose silence results from overwhelming feelings of anger and outrage. When he fears that Ursula will repeat her mother's life by being subjected to the sexual predation of men, he behaves like the stereotypical hysterical old woman. When he sees that she has matured into a woman 'his mouth opens helplessly' and 'for a time his tongue click[s] inarticulately against his dry palate' (Baynton, *Human Toll* 194). He can barely articulate the words "'yur gut yur mother's eyes'" (194) because he remembers that as a young woman her mother had the kind of eye "'thet 'ud coax a duck — a nole duck — off ov the water'" (132). When Ursula is in fear of Mr Civil's attentions she becomes aware of 'the inequality of her struggle to alter the thing that is' (225) and, as Boshy says, the look in her eyes is just the same as if "'yer mother's eyes [were] a-lookin' et me ther same'" (225). Boshy's death is finally brought on by his inability to protect Ursula. His breath fades 'in a thwarted throttle' only to rise again 'successively in a seething gurgle that forced his mouth apart' (23), after which his heart stops.

Boshy illustrates Freud's view that hysterics are unable to give an ordered account of their lives because they omit, distort and rearrange information due to repression. He is incoherent because he narrates in fragments, leaves out vital information, and prevents an auditor from making sense of what he says. His mental anguish is also expressed in somatic symptoms through paralysis, a dry palate, choking, loss of breath, purpling of the face, aimless hands and words that refuse to come or cannot be said. He thus conforms to the type of hysteric defined by blocked speech and communication: 'the *globus hystericus*, or sense of choking, the *tussis nervosa*, or chronic nervous cough; *aphasia*, or the inability to use words, and *aphonia*, or loss of voice' (Showalter, *Hystories* 87).

Exhausted by the effort of writing *Human Toll* — of 'dredging up more of her past, scraping through her memories of childhood, and casting up old hatreds and grievances' — Baynton was hospitalised. She was 'unable to work at all' on the manuscript. She sent it to Duckworth 'as it was', and proofreading was later confined to 'half an hour a week' (Hackforth-Jones 93-4). When she received her copy of the novel she wrote the word 'Desormais' ['henceforth'] on the title page (Hackforth-Jones 95), signifying her intention to move on and leave the past behind her.

When *Human Toll* was first published in 1907, it received mixed reviews. As the reviewer from *The Times* noted, it was difficult to know what to make of the story, since it employed 'a narrative style that is ... often unintelligible', requiring 'hard and repeated study' in order to discover who the characters were 'and sometimes what they [were] doing and why' (Hackforth-Jones 96). At the same time, reviewers were struck by the power of the story, the truthfulness of its depiction of life and the originality of its vision. In Australia it has been consistently regarded as a flawed work that fails to follow accepted narrative forms. Yet reading it through the lens of hysteria makes sense of the oddities of its composition, reveals why its material required oblique representation and offers a perspective from which to look back at Baynton's better-known short stories.

Bush Studies (1902) covers the same terrain and shares many stylistic features with *Human Toll*. The collection was well-received at the time of its publication in England, made possible by the enthusiastic support of Edward Garnett, writer and literary editor, who also supported such writers as Joseph Conrad, D.H. Lawrence and Henry Lawson. It is probable that Baynton failed to find a publisher in Australia because Australian society was dominated by parochial attitudes and the ethos of respectability (Hackforth-Jones 75). Indeed, interest in her work lapsed partly because it was too dark and unpatriotic, especially in contrast with the bush tales of her male contemporaries — whose tales promoted nationalistic pride as well as mateship between men who felt an affinity for the bush. And the malevolence of her representation of the bush has been held to account for the brutality of her male characters, though — as John Kinsella claims in relation to 'The Chosen Vessel' — 'it is not the bush per se that is inimical to the woman here, but the transgressing male' (45). However, if the generic male figure in her work is founded on the behaviour of her first husband, it is possible that an antecedent figure prefigures him, the unknown and unnameable man within the family who could have been her biological father. Though the men in *Bush Studies* use every means available to them to humiliate and dehumanise women, the women are not merely silenced by male aggression. They experience a barrier to speech so complete that recourse to hysteria is the only way in which they can express the kind of emotional and psychological pain they feel, which seems to arise from a deep and more obscure source of outrage.

It is an aspect of Baynton's originality that she could draw on the popularisation of the discourse of hysteria to represent feminist protest. Because she could not state the plain truth, the paradigmatic narrative of consciousness characteristic of the novel of development was unsuited to her use. Similarly, she could not employ the presence of an implied author to substantiate a reading position. It is therefore left to the reader to make sense of fragmented narratives primarily concerned with the psychic effects of acts of violence, rape, murder and incest: acts that can be narrated only by means of somatic symptoms and the psychological mechanisms of displacement, substitution, doubling and symbolism.

The short story 'A Dreamer' represents a pregnant daughter's return to her maternal home in a dreamlike sequence. To reach the house she must ford a creek at night. Her pregnancy marks her own transition to motherhood, and her emotions alternate between moments of feeling comforted by memories of a mother's care and moments of distress when she is threatened by a hostile power. She is sustained by the expectation of a reunion, aware that the mother-daughter bond is the most profound human attachment, one that 'dwarfed every tie that had parted them' (Baynton, 'A Dreamer' 7).

Though her memories are stirred by the landscape, she, being near-sighted, finds everything at night unfamiliar. The daughter thus suffers 'all the horror of the unknown that this infirmity could bring' (6). At the same time the fearful passage she must make in crossing the creek in flood is symbolic of the time when her own waters will break and she will give birth. As a daughter of Eve she is doomed to bear her child in pain. Thus crossing the creek is fraught with difficulty and the threat of death. As she feels the child stir 'for the first time' near her heart, 'the instincts of motherhood' awaken in her (5), yet at the same time the force of the wind's anger, through which God speaks, takes her breath away. Sex and death are already linked in her mind through the memory of a drunken rider on a runaway horse who was crushed against 'the Bendy Tree' (6) she has just passed.

When she finally fords the creek she is overcome by giddiness, loss of breath and an inability to speak. The wind makes a funnel of her mouth and throat and she is literally choked. She can only hope that 'the sweat of her body' may redeem 'the sin of her soul' (8). The enactment of her battle with the elements resembles 'the hysterical seizure', *grande hystérie* or 'spasm of hyper-femininity, mimicking ... both childbirth and female orgasm' deemed to dramatise female sexual experience (Showalter, *Hysteria* 287 n6). The analogy between the throat as a funnel for the production of speech and the uterus as a conduit for the production of new life is a reminder that speaking out for a woman is a taboo based on the construction of gender.

The daughter calls, '"Mother!"' (Baynton, 'A Dreamer' 8), thereby reaching out to an idealised figure who promises completion and plenitude in contrast to a wrathful God who speaks only of death through the wind. Though she must pray to Him for safekeeping, when 'a giant tree's fallen body' prevents the 'furious water' from carrying her to her death (9) it signifies her mother's care. But when she reaches home she is led silently by a stranger to view her mother's corpse, whilst another woman, virtually her double, nurses a baby. There are no words that can convey the horror of that moment, and all is silence. Bronfen argues that because hysteria 'commemorates the traumatic enjoyment of the abundant presence of the maternal body', it also refers to the fact that 'the subject's desire [is] doomed to endlessly seek an impossible satisfaction' (42).

Motherhood may be 'the hope for humanity' (Krimmer and Lawson xxiii) but Baynton's wives and mothers are treated with contempt. The childless wife, Mary, in 'Squeaker's Mate' is part of an unequal, abusive, one-sided relationship.

She is stunned by a fallen tree and later by Squeaker's behaviour when, with money gained from selling her sheep, he returns from town with a pregnant young woman, having decided that a broken-backed wife is of no further use and that a second mate must do her work. However, the girl is town-bred, fearful and ignorant of bush ways. Fearing 'what people might say and do if [Mary] died' (Baynton, 'Squeaker's Mate' 19), the second mate tries to pass herself off as Mary's carer but fails to allow for her jealousy, which is fuelled by anger at Squeaker's suspected adultery. Mary does not know the identity of the father of the second mate's child. Being unlearned 'in these matters' she fails to discover 'by calculation' that 'the paternity was not Squeaker's' (20).

However, Mary is among those hysterics who tend to 'move into a psychic state in which their own body function, psychological functions and character traits are experienced as an apparent *other*, a quasi-altered, self-representation' (Stavros Mentzos qtd in Bronfen 40, emphasis in original). Her anger and outrage are expressed through physical symptoms. Her broken back speaks of a life of toil. Like the 'thick worm-eaten branch' of the tree that felled her, a 'worm' has been 'busy in the heart' (Baynton, 'Squeaker's Mate' 11). She habitually views objects as if they were a part of her self — even her tools are friends — but animals are brethren who speak to her and for her. The voices of the bush which break the silence of the night tell of her pain: 'the whine' of the dingo near where she was felled, 'the quivering wail' of 'the fearing curlew' (16) and the 'cries for help' of her pet sheep destined for 'the town butchers' (17).

Hysteria is related to the question of the subject's position, and the fundamental question, *'What is it to be a woman?* (Lacan, *The Psychoses* 178, emphasis in original), informs Baynton's use of role reversal, which challenges the way gender characteristics are constructed and applied. In addition, she questions the right of man to be the Master. Squeaker boils the billy and fixes the food: Mary requires a pipe. He evades hard work: her reputation is built on hard graft. He is passive and moody: she is active and energetic. He complains about work: she gets on with the job. He is '"a nole woman"', a term designed 'to eliminate all virtue' (Baynton, 'Squeaker's Mate' 15): she is 'the best long-haired mate that ever stepped in petticoats' (11). He complains like the proverbial woman: Mary is 'straight and square' (14), the epitome of uprightness, honesty and integrity, as men are supposed to be. Squeaker is garrulous and has the privilege of direct speech. However, since Mary 'kept silent always' (20), her thoughts are conveyed in the third person, through body language, and through her dog and other doubles. As Kahane has noted, 'in an era that constructed sexuality as a predominant gauge of psychosocial identity' the question of sexual difference was 'increasingly prominent' and 'symptomatically articulated' in the way the narrative voice was handled in some nineteenth-century texts (xi).

Though to others Mary seems curiously supportive of Squeaker and passive to her fate, her symptoms — paralysis and aphonia — are a form of protest, and she implicitly questions Squeaker's entitlement to be her 'lawful protector' (Baynton, 'Squeaker's Mate' 14). The hysteric characteristically 'pursues a paternal figure who might represent symbolic consistency, who could fulfil her phantasy of a love that would abolish all flaws' (Bronfen 42), but who turns out here to be a liar and a deceiver. Her dog is everything the man should be: faithful, loyal and dependable, her defender at all times and a source of unconditional love.

Mary's virtue undermines Squeaker's authority and exposes the flaws in their marriage. However, in attempting to steal that which is vital to her life, the young woman arouses the older woman's anger and outrage. Thus in attacking the adulteress with the ferocity of 'a wounded, robbed tigress' (Baynton, 'Squeaker's Mate' 25), Mary makes her feelings plain, hastens her own death and leaves her dog to attack Squeaker in person. As Squeaker is left alone complaining, trying to cast blame on the other woman while excusing himself, Mary's implicit criticism of him hits home.

Even if paternal authority appears to be upheld, it is constantly undermined. 'The Chosen Vessel' figures another silent and denigrated wife who seeks to expose her husband's abuse and betrayal of her. The story implies that the shearer husband is responsible for the death of his wife, though it is the swagman as his double who finally kills her. Both men dehumanise her by treating her as an inferior species on a par with animals. The husband humiliates her by verbal abuse and insult, and discounts her fear of isolation as ridiculous: '"Needn't flatter yerself, nobody 'ud want ter run away with yew"' (Baynton, 'The Chosen Vessel' 82).

The freedom to move around provides the husband with sexual opportunity and conquest, like the swagman when he comes like a thief in the night to steal another man's property. The swagman's gleaming teeth and lascivious eyes, and the short-bladed knife, proclaim his sexual dominance and his intentions as he treads a well-known path from 'the dismal, drunken little township' (82) along a well-worn 'track' 'in front of the house' that 'had once been a wine shanty' (81).

When the wife places her mother's brooch outside the hut for the swagman to take, the jewel is a symbol of her treasure, which will hopefully prevent his attack on her body. But the hut is likewise a symbol of her bodily integrity, and both woman and hut have a crack — a point of vulnerability to attack, a place where the swagman can get in. At the moment when she is sure he has found the entrance, knowing her barricade is no defence, she runs out into the night in the hope that a passing horseman will save her. Because the horseman fails to stop, she finds herself in the swagman's 'outstretched arms that caught her as she fell' (85). Unable to accept his terms, silence and acquiescence, she is finally forced as his hand grips her throat to cry out the single word, '"Murder"' (85), which is taken up by the curlews that fly above the horseman's head 'wailing "Murder! Murder!"' for all to hear (85).

When the boundary rider sees the crows circling above her corpse he believes he is looking at a dead ewe with a lamb at her side, since her body is discarded in an open field like that of a dead animal. However, once he discovers the truth he exclaims '"Jesus Christ!"' (85) and goes off to tell the world how the child would have died in the night 'but for the hand that still clutched its little gown', allowing it to suck on its ravaged mother's 'warm breasts' and sleep 'till the morn' (85).

The reviled wife proves to be an exemplary mother: a dualism that exemplifies male attitudes to women. Society trained women to be weak, passive and dependent, but women were required, especially in the conditions of the bush, to be strong, assertive and self-sacrificing. Smith-Rosenberg has argued that the prevalence of hysteria at the end of the nineteenth century stemmed from sex-role conflicts then emerging:

> The discontinuity between the roles of courted young woman and pain-bearing, self-sacrificing wife and mother, the realities of an unhappy marriage, the loneliness and chagrin of spinsterhood, may all have made the petulant infantilism and narcissistic self-assertion of the hysteric a necessary social alternative to women who felt unfairly deprived of their

promised social role and who had few strengths with which to adapt to a more trying one. (Qtd in Showalter, *Hysteria* 303)

The dead mother remains caught in the contradiction that sexual ideology imposes, between revered mother and abhorred whore — a woman whose psychic pain is converted into hysterical symptoms that provide evidence for understanding hysteria as a 'dis-ease of women in patriarchal culture' (Kahane qtd in Showalter, *Hysteria* 331).

However, the language of hysteria is as mutable as are the theories that serve to explain it, and Freud's understanding of 'the bisexual nature of hysterical symptoms' (Freud 165) lie behind Lacan's reworking of hysteria. Freud notes that the analyst must 'be prepared for a symptom's having a bisexual meaning', as the patient who acts like a man and a woman 'avails himself during the analysis of the one sexual meaning, of the convenient possibility of constantly switching his associations as though on to an adjoining track, into the field of the contrary meaning' (166). The horseman, Peter Hennessey, is viewed as the dead woman's double. His story mirrors her ordeal in life, caught between the conflicting symbolisations of sinner and saint. When he sees her robed in white 'with a babe clasped to her bosom', Peter thinks he has had a vision from God, has seen the Virgin Mary and, like Saul on the road to Damascus, has become His chosen vessel. Thus he would have confirmed his faith in Mary as the model for women and would have been exonerated from the sin of disobedience to his mother. However, when he reaches the priest, expecting confirmation of his transformation, his question, '"My Lord and my God ... And hast Thou chosen me?"' is met with the priest's horrified denial: '"Great God! ... and you did not stop to save her! Do you not know? Have you not heard?"' (Baynton, 'The Chosen Vessel' 87). Peter's mistaken interpretation arises in the context in which the redemption of women, as the daughters of Eve, lay in following Mary. Thus, since Peter remains tainted by sin, his story reflects the contrary case to the dead mother's story.

It is in the coda of 'The Chosen Vessel' that 'a man' (88), an amalgam of husband and swagman, is finally accused of murder. He is described 'many miles down the creek' throwing 'an old cap into a water-hole', which his dog fetches and places on 'the opposite side to where [he] stood' (88). The dog evades the man's attempt 'to wash the blood of the sheep from his mouth and throat ...

for the sight of blood made the man tremble. But the dog was also guilty' (88). Since the man is a dingo in sheep's clothing he is no different from the dog, and both have spilled the blood of an innocent lamb. But without his hat the dog has exposed 'the man', so that he is seen for what and who he is.

The abuse of an innocent woman caught between inconsistent gender roles is also the subject of the short story 'Billy Skywonkie'. She is an unnamed "alf chow' (Baynton, 'Billy Skywonkie' 58) who answers an advertisement for a housekeeper at Gooriabba Station only to discover that she is unwanted because she is not 'a young "piece"' prepared to service the men at the station (48). As an aging 'Sally Ah Too' (51) she is humiliated, abused and inappropriately accused of sexual impropriety. Her availability is assumed. As Billy, the rouseabout who transports her to the station implies, there will always be someone prepared to have sex with her: '"some one would soon buck up to 'er if their boss wusn't on"' (56).

Sex is used as a tool of aggression, and the newcomer is viewed and judged as a sex-object. Even the drovers on the train from Sydney expose her to 'obscene jokes', 'snatches of lewd songs' and foul language (47). On arriving at the siding Billy nearly drives away because the newcomer fails to match expectations and he realises that '"there'll be a 'ell of a row somew'ere"' when it is discovered (48). But his first aim is to meet '"Mickey ther 'Konk' t' leave 'im 'ave furst squint at yer"' (50). Both Mickey and Billy look sideways at the woman as if they don't trust themselves to view her face-on. But, though Mickey judges her to be beneath consideration, the observed woman claims the power of observation and sees him as a 'little hairy horror', 'grotesquely monkeyish' and possessed of a nose so big that it 'blotted the landscape and dwarfed all perspective' (50). She is divided between fascination and repugnance, half-inclined to pat him on the nose like a horse, yet overcome by disgust.

David-Ménard argues that hysteria is an epistemology of disgust because the hysteric feels a pleasure which cannot come into existence since it is regarded as improper: that disgust produces excess and this prevents it from forcing its way through to action (David-Ménard vii). For, as Freud wrote to Fleiss, the hysteric's defence against sensations of 'improper pleasure' is to repress a memory that 'stinks': 'In the same manner as we turn away [*abwenden*] our sense organ (the head and nose) in disgust [*Ekel*], the preconscious and the sense of consciousness turn away from the memory. This is *repression*' (Freud qtd in David-Ménard vii, emphasis in original). The unnamed woman's sense of disgust is fuelled by a brain 'over-fed' with ghastly images, and together with an 'under-fed liver' she falls prey to a 'ghastly' 'bilious sickness' (Baynton, 'Billy Skywonkie' 48). 'Little matters became distorted and the greater shrivelled' (55) and consequently she loses her sense of mental balance.

Billy's aim is to get 'shanty-grog' (52) and flirt with Mag, but the delay this causes is such that his wife, 'Lizer, suspects him of an 'offence' that constitutes a 'terrible injustice to a respectable married woman', '"aslavin' an' graftin' an' sweatin' from mornin' ter night, for a slungin', idlin', lazy blaggard"' (57). 'Lizer blames the wrong woman, yet the newcomer feels in 'an indefinable way' that 'both of them are guilty' (57) as Billy is willing and she accepts 'Lizer's designation.

The heat is such that the terrified woman in the buggy is silenced because her mouth and throat are too dry for speech. She is given nothing but a sip of tepid, mosquito-infested water, green with algae, to 'moisten her mouth and throat' (54). But her speech is also blocked in reaction to the horrors she witnesses, which upset her mental and physical balance. She is forced to see herself in horrific images, especially when she is solicited by 'the old hag' (54), Mag's mother: a 'creature' so dishonoured in age that her appearance inspires horror in an onlooker. Like the snake in the story of Genesis, she is forced to crawl in the dust as she begs for a coin to get a 'dose' (54). Her disgraced age is expressed physically in her reduction to intolerable thirst and voracious need: 'Entrenched behind the absorbed skin-terraces' of a 'cavernous mouth', her 'stump of purple tongue' makes unsuccessful 'efforts at speech' as she shakes 'a warning claw' at the giver of the coin, then flops back 'whining in the dust, her hands ostentatiously open and wiping her eyes' before being forced to surrender the coin to her daughter (54).

In Lacan's reading of Freud's specimen dream, the back of a woman's throat offers 'a terrifying anxiety-provoking image':

> the revelation of this something which properly speaking is unnameable, the back of this throat, the complex, unlocatable form, which also makes it into the primitive object *par excellence*, the abyss of the feminine organ

from which all life emerges, this gulf of the mouth, in which everything is swallowed up, and no less the image of death in which everything comes to its end. (Lacan, *The Ego* 64)

Lacan draws attention to a gap in symbolic reality so that when faced with 'the revelation ... of the ultimate real', 'the object of anxiety *par excellence*', 'all words cease and all categories fail' (64, emphasis in original). There is a point beyond symbolisation, which interpretation cannot bridge. At the same time, the paternal authority that the symbolic supports is endlessly questioned by Baynton's silenced women. While the men behave like beasts in this story, a woman is branded with bestiality, treated as a worthless slut and viewed on a par with the snake that tempted Eve. Billy tells her from the first that 'he knew what she was' (Baynton, 'Billy Skywonkie' 56), and when she arrives the Chinese cook confirms her place at Gooriabba Station by announcing his availability.

The horror she inspires in her onlookers reaches a climax when she is finally introduced to the Boss in a state 'too giddy to stand' without the support of a table and obliged to face the full force of his rage as he rebukes her for having had the '"infernal cheek ... to come"' (58). Outraged by her appearance, he asks, '"How old?"' and without waiting for a reply expresses his disgust by striding out and leaving 'his last thrust' to have 'the effect of a galvanic battery on her dying body' (58).

She must be got off the Station at once, but before she can get away Billy has to slaughter some sheep and, as he draws the knife across the first sheep's neck, the woman's consciousness of her plight is mirrored back to her in the sheep's awareness of its doom, visible in 'the glitter of the knife ... reflected in its eye' (60). The woman's bodily awareness speaks for her as she faces the crippling conflict between her self-image and the image imposed upon her owing to her gender. The disparity between her actual being and the distorted representation of her femininity is therefore the cause of her mental anguish.

Freud thought that hysterical symptoms, like dreams, produced an 'unplumbable' spot: 'its point of contact with the unknown', which he called 'the navel' (qtd in Bronfen 77). This point of resistance to penetration returns us to the fact of 'the impenetrability of trauma' which, being 'constructed like knots' (Bronfen 33), is built on a plethora of associations and memories which make the discovery of its origin an ever-receding possibility. It is impossible to unravel the threads in Baynton's fiction connected with her life, but the impact of her work is not confined to her own personal circumstances.

She preserved for posterity a language and a way of life otherwise lost to history. And, drawing on the concept of hysteria, she developed a unique, complex and original narrative style that enabled her to write about unmentionable aspects of family life: the abuse of women, rape and incest. It is clear that she did not espouse the form of nationalism promoted by her literary contemporaries, for whom the bushman was the hero of legend, the exemplar of Australian identity and the model of mateship. However, although the myth continues in some sense to influence the concept of Australian identity today, Baynton's representation of life as it was experienced in her youth enlarges our understanding of Australia's colonial history and confronts questions that remain critical today. Though she exposed the roots of misogyny in a bush setting that allowed men unparalleled freedom, she did not hate the bush itself. On the contrary, the bush served her creative imagination, allowed for the emergence of the unconscious and provided a mental landscape in which she could develop a language of trauma and spirituality. Her stories were indeed the means by which she remade her life and established a lasting literary reputation.

Works Cited

Baynton, Barbara. 'The Chosen Vessel.' 1896. *Barbara Baynton: Bush Studies, other stories, Human Toll, verse, essays and letters.* Ed. and intro. Sally Krimmer and Alan Lawson. St. Lucia, Qld: Queensland UP, 1980. 81-8.

——. 'A Dreamer.' 1902. *Barbara Baynton: Bush Studies, other stories, Human Toll, verse, essays and letters.* Ed. and intro. Sally Krimmer and Alan Lawson. St. Lucia, Qld: Queensland UP, 1980. 4-10.

——. 'Squeaker's Mate.' 1902. *Barbara Baynton: Bush Studies, other stories, Human Toll, verse, essays and letters.* Ed. and intro. Sally Krimmer and Alan Lawson. St. Lucia, Qld: Queensland UP, 1980. 11-26.

——. 'Billy Skywonkie.' 1902. *Barbara Baynton: Bush Studies, other stories, Human Toll, verse, essays and letters.* Ed. and intro. Sally Krimmer and Alan Lawson. St. Lucia, Qld: Queensland UP, 1980. 46-60.

———. *Human Toll*. 1907. In *Barbara Baynton: Bush Studies, other stories, Human Toll, verse, essays and letters*. Ed. and intro. Sally Krimmer and Alan Lawson. St. Lucia, Qld: Queensland UP, 1980. 115-300.

Bronfen, Elisabeth. *The Knotted Subject: Hysteria and its Discontents*. Princeton: Princeton UP, 1998.

Dale, Leigh. 'Rereading Barbara Baynton's Bush Studies.' *Texas Studies in Literature & Language*. 53.4 (2011): 369-86.

David-Ménard, Monique. *Hysteria From Freud to Lacan: Body Language in Psychoanalysis*. Trans. Catherine Porter. Foreword Ned Lukacher. Ithaca: Cornell UP. 1989.

Freud, Sigmund. 'Hysterical Phantasies and their Relation to Bisexuality' and 'Family Romances.' *The Standard Edition of the Complete Psychological Works of Sigmund Freud*. Trans. and ed. James Strachey, Vol 9. London: Hogarth Press, 1959. 159-66, 237-41.

Gullett, H.B. 'Memoir of Barbara Baynton.' Elizabeth Webby. *Bush Studies: Classic Australian Short Stories*. North Ryde, NSW: Collins/A and R, 1989. 17-41.

Hackforth-Jones, Penne. *Barbara Baynton: Between Two Worlds. A Biography*. Ringwood, Victoria: Penguin Books Australia, 1989.

Hergenhan, Laurie. '"Shafts into our fundamental animalism": Barbara Baynton's use of naturalism in *Bush Studies*'. *Australian Literary Studies* 17.3 (1996): 211-22.

Kahane, Claire. *Passions of the Voice: Hysteria, Narrative, and the Figure of the Speaking Woman, 1850-1915*. Baltimore: Johns Hopkins UP, 1995.

Kinsella, John. *Contrary Rhetoric: Lectures on Landscape and Language*. Ed. Glen Phillips and Andrew Taylor. Fremantle: Fremantle Arts Centre Press, 2008.

Krimmer, Sally and Alan Lawson. 'Introduction'. *Barbara Baynton: Bush Studies, other stories, Human Toll, verse, essays and letters*. Ed. and intro. Sally Krimmer and Alan Lawson. St. Lucia, Qld: Queensland UP, 1980. ix-xxxi.

Lacan, Jacques. *The Seminar of Jacques Lacan Book II: The Ego in Freud's Theory and in the Technique of Psychoanalysis 1954-1956*. Ed. Jacques-

Alain Miller. Trans. Sylvana Tomaselli. With notes by John Forrester. Cambridge: Cambridge UP, 1988.

———. *The Seminar of Jacques Lacan, Book III: The Pyschoses 1955-1956.* Ed. Jacques-Alain Miller. Trans. Russell Grigg. London: Routledge, 1993.

Laplanche, J. and J.B. Pontalis. *The Language of Psycho-Analysis.* London: The Hogarth Press and the Institute of Psycho-Analysis, 1985.

Showalter, Elaine. 'Hysteria, Feminism and Gender.' *Hysteria Beyond Freud.* Ed. Sander Gilman, Helen King, Roy Porter, G.S. Rousseau and Elaine Showalter. Berkeley: University of California Press, 1993. 286-344.

———. *Hystories: Hysterical Epidemics and Modern Culture.* Chatham, Kent: Picador, 1997.

Smith-Rosenberg, Carroll. *Disorderly Conduct: Visions of Gender in Victorian America.* Oxford: Oxford UP, 1985.

6

A literary fortune

Megan Brown

Mary Fortune wrote for the popular literary miscellany the *Australian Journal*, which began publication in Melbourne in 1865. It was a cheeky copy of the English publication the *London Journal* and Fortune was its most enduring writer. She wrote urban ethnography, romance, autobiography, Gothic serial fiction, poetry, an occasional recipe and detective fiction. Not only did she contribute (almost without interruption) for over 40 years but her work encompassed a range of genres and explored the burgeoning modern metropolis of Melbourne, the turbulence of the goldfields and the 'bush'.

Fortune's work provides an unparalleled literary and historical perspective on a changing colonial landscape because of her longevity as a contributor. Her ability to adapt and change her writing style was extraordinary. It is best illustrated by her contributions published between 1865 and 1885, which coincided with the most tumultuous period of the *Australian Journal*. Not only did she often change the subject within her stories to soften the impact of her incisive critiques of colonial society, but reading her work also changes our perspective on the subject of colonial women. Fortune's very candid reflections on the day-to-day problems faced by immigrant women in the colonies changes the subject and the perspective from the more common male version to the female one and provides an alternative version of colonial experience.

Changing the Victorian Subject

In the latter years, her writing tended to be predominantly detective fiction but it continued to appear in the *Journal* until her death in about 1908. A number of her stories were reprinted irregularly until the *Journal* ceased to exist in the 1960s. However, the extent of Fortune's contribution to the *Australian Journal* has only become apparent since Lucy Sussex's detective work revealed that works by Waif Wander, W. W. and M.H.F were all written by Fortune.[1] Fortune is therefore perhaps unique in Australian literary history. Is there any other writer, male or female, who managed to maintain a publishing presence in the cutthroat world of the periodical press as a paid writer in one periodical over such a long period of time in Australia?

While Sussex has concentrated on uncovering Mary Fortune's biographical history and the transgressive nature of her work, the sheer quantity and variety warrants further exploration.[2] In particular, this chapter will focus on her attempts to change the construction of colonial womanhood by examining her serial memoir entitled 'Twenty-Six Years Ago; or the Diggings from '55'. It consisted of six instalments and ran from September 1882 to May 1883.[3] It highlights women's experience of living in the goldfields. While Fortune's subject choice is uncommon, the experiences she describes are not. Fortune provides a representative voice for a significant number of women in the colonies whose stories have been lost. Their reinstatement cannot help but change the way we think about the colonial Victorian subject and the way women experienced the transition from immigrant to colonist.

Despite the major adjustments that living in the goldfield required of women, Fortune embraced the Australian bush and colonial life. She saw

---

1 In a recent article published in *Australian Literary Studies* I argue that there is enough evidence to suggest that Fortune also wrote the 'Ladies' Page' in the *Australian Journal* for 9 months under the pseudonym of Sylphid (see Brown, 'Mary Fortune').

2 Lucy Sussex's work has been essential to my research on Mary Fortune. Rather than use specific quotes I have synthesised the biographical information that appears a little later in this chapter from the academic research she has conducted. Consequently, I have included an extensive list of Sussex's work in the Works Cited at the end of this chapter. (See in particular *Women Writers*, 126-41).

3 The first instalment was published in September 1882 but the second instalment did not appear until January 1883. The non-appearance forced the editor to publish a note commenting that the writer had not provided the instalment on time.

the change of attitude and behaviour needed to become a successful colonist as a positive rather than a negative. The bush, so often described by colonial women in particular as threatening and frightening, is a place of comfort and solace for Fortune.[4] Many of her stories articulate a need for a new standard or code of behaviour for women. Her writing makes it clear that 'old country' prejudices and the standard by which respectability was judged had to change to suit the environment. More importantly, she celebrates the change towards a more egalitarian society. The bush and by extension the goldfields provide pleasure and a sense of community that transcend class. In 'Fourteen Days on the Roads' Fortune details the delights of camping out in the bush, and in the vignette entitled 'Melbourne Cemetery' she explains she would rather be buried in a lonely bush grave than in Melbourne Cemetery. She philosophises on burial places, noting that despite the loneliness of bush graves there are compensations:

> A lonely place is a primitive burial-ground 'up in the bush.' There are few engraven names there, and not many flowers, save the wild beauties that are at home under the sheltering trees; but there are rustling branches und [*sic*] sweet sighing evening breezes there, and instead of the loud careless laugh, there is the gurgling *reveillé* [*sic*] of the merry magpie, although his notes will not awake the sleepers below. (M.H.F. 181)

Melbourne's hustle and bustle cannot compare to the peaceful scenes of the Australian bush.

It is in 'Twenty-Six Years Ago; or the Diggings from '55' that this philosophy is most clearly articulated (see Waif Wander [W. W.]). The memoir starts in an enthusiastic and confident tone and Fortune positions herself as an authority on colonial life and a hardy adventurous pioneer. She constructs her life as historically significant and her writing as culturally important. She even links all three of her pseudonyms. In the February 1883 instalment Fortune includes an anecdote about writing for the *Mount Alexander Mail* as M.H.F. (*33*). This appeared in the column directly below the attribution:

By W A I F W A N D E R (W. W.)

Unfortunately, while the series starts in a vibrant and confident manner, the break in the delivery of instalments suggests that Fortune experienced some kind of

---

[4] Fortune's writing usually celebrated the bush; however, she did exploit the Gothic or sinister aspects from time to time in her crime stories.

crisis, and the last three episodes see her paradoxically taking a diminishing role in her own memoir. She increasingly focuses on the crimes that she witnessed while retreating to become an observer. Perhaps she was paying the price for her audacious attempt at writing women into colonial history and for her own less than perfect Victorian respectability.

As well as managing to uncover the mystery of Fortune's *noms de plume*, Lucy Sussex also pieced together the extraordinary story of a life that was as changeable and sensational as the stories Fortune wrote. Mary Helena Wilson was born in Ireland in 1833. Her mother died when she was quite young and she emigrated to Canada with her father. In 1851 she married a Quebec surveyor named Joseph Fortune. They had one son named Joseph. Her father moved to Australia to search for gold and she and her son Joseph followed him in 1855. They were reunited in the Victorian goldfields where her father ran a 'canvas' general store. Once in Australia, it appears that change and misfortune accelerated for Mary. According to Sussex's research, Fortune gave birth to an illegitimate child (who became a petty career criminal), her oldest son died and she had a short-lived but bigamous marriage. Her life seems to have remained peripatetic and financial security elusive. She ended up an alcoholic and with failing eyesight. The details of her death and her place of burial remain a mystery.

Given her history, it is hardly surprising that, despite her relatively high writing profile in the *Australian Journal*, she did not allow her anonymity to be penetrated. Her claim of genteel poverty would have been hard to justify and her intimate acquaintance with the position of the fallen woman may have ended her writing career. The paradox is that Fortune's misfortunes in life bring an authenticity to her writing that makes it much more interesting. For the contemporary reader, the discovery of Fortune's powerfully articulated female critique challenges preconceptions about the discourses of gender circulating in colonial Victoria.

The period during which Fortune's work was being published is also of note. It is a period that has been seen traditionally, and particularly in the case of Australia, as male-dominated. European history has told the story of men. As men were the holders of political office and leaders of commercial enterprise, their lives were more likely to be officially documented. In the Australian colony the nature of the settlement and unequal gender numbers meant that this tendency was exacerbated. However, women were not absent from the pages of one of the most popular contemporary periodicals of period, the *Australian Journal*. They were vociferous. Fortune's work and the *Australian Journal* reveal the surprising complexity of those voices in the period from 1865 through to the more renowned 1890s. Fortune's writing examines colonial life from the point of view of a white middle-class woman in the urban centres, rural settings and the goldfields.[5] Her writing makes reference to documented historical events and provides anecdotal evidence of a broad range of women's experiences, which historical accounts do not always include. It outlines a formula for success in the colony which requires a willingness to adapt and change.

Fortune's writing, it must be pointed out, focused on the European settlers in the colony. She was almost silent about the indigenous inhabitants and on the rare occasions when indigenous communities or characters were included in the narrative she portrayed them as non-threatening in most situations and even at times preferable to Europeans. For the purposes of this chapter, therefore, all references to women can be understood to mean 'white' colonial women.

Nevertheless, the importance of her description of women's presence in the goldfields and her attempt to change the perspective on the way colonial womanhood can be viewed cannot be understated. For Fortune the construction of colonial womanhood is dependant on the ability to change and adapt. As she looks back nostalgically at her 'stirring, hardy and eventful life on the early goldfields' ('Twenty-Six Years Ago', September 1882, 33), she writes proudly about the obstacles that she, and the colony, have faced and overcome.

Fortune describes the sensual assault felt by the newly arrived colonists. Even in the city it was confronting but the transition from the city to the goldfields took on a nightmarish quality. The unfamiliar landscape and the primitive methods of conveyance challenge the female travellers in more than superficial

---

5   Fortune's short stories about the trials of being an unprotected woman in urban Melbourne are also worthy of examination. They were published in the *Australian Journal* between November 1868 and February 1871 and provide a candid and critical insight into colonial life by exploring the difficulties of finding respectable lodgings and employment.

ways. Waif Wander (W. W.)[6] dubs the driver of the carriage, for example, 'Jehu'. Jehu was the king of Israel, renowned for his crazy chariot driving. He is both a saviour and a destroyer, a metaphor for the ambivalence about the journey experienced by his passengers:

> The crashing of the breaking branches under our wheels, as our cool Jehu drove his four-in-hand through the tangled mazes of the Black Forest, and the dangerous vicinity of the white gum trees, from whose tall trunks hung long strips of dead bark they were shedding as the snake sheds his skin. (September 1882, 36)

Fortune evokes a phantasmagoric sense of the journey and an almost cinematic vision. So confronting is the experience that it passes like a 'blank' except for seeming like 'one scene of plunging horses and broken traces on a bush track, where our Jehu seemed to thread the mazes of dead and living timber like a phantom driver with a team of phantom horses under his spirit power' (September 1882, 36). The speed and nightmarish quality of the passing images reflect the passengers' fear of the future — they are uncertain whether the dead timber by the roadside symbolises the life they have left behind or the life they will find at the end of their journey, if they can survive it.

The end of the phantasmal journey does not end the nightmare for the 'new chums'. The roadside inn is rough and they cannot read the cultural signs. The colonial world is beyond their experience and the colonial inhabitants, while nominally European, have been transformed by colonial living. At the inn the women are put together in a 'large barn-like room' with female new arrivals and children as well as others who were waiting or about to depart. The descriptions of Waif Wander (W. W.) are poignant, as they explore the painful early stages of the development of a new identity and relationships. The women wear 'mostly a bewildered, half-lost expression in their anxious faces' (September 1882, 36). It is very difficult because, as the narrator says:

> a woman, especially with little ones in charge, can scarcely be expected to feel safe or comfortable in a strange land, and among a class of people she

---

6 Fortune usually wrote as either Waif Wander or W. W., so that in theory the reader did not know they were the same writer. However, in 'Twenty-Six Years Ago; or the Diggings from '55', she used both names, calling herself 'Waif Wander (W. W.)', making it clear that they were one and the same person (see Waif Wander [W. W.]).

has been told were as rough and knobby as the stones from among which they were rooting out their gold. (September 1882, 36)

Fortune's narrator uses the distress of one woman as a representative illustration of the collective sentiment. The lady bends her head and bursts into tears: "'What ever came over me at all to come to such an outlandish place!" she sobbed. "I didn't know when I was well off, or I'd have stopped among my own people'" (September 1882, 36). Those witnessing the emotions are sympathetic and Waif Wander (W. W.) confirms that 'many of us have come to the same conclusion many a hundred times since our voluntary expatriation' (September 1882, 36). The immensity of the decision is outlined for readers in a personal reflective statement as she pinpoints the uncertainty and the numerous questions such a dramatic life change can pose for the actor in the drama:

> I began to realise that I was on the borders of a new life. All the perils of the sea were over, and it lay an impassable barrier between me and the old happy Canadian life. What fate was to be for me and mine in this land of gold over which the shadows of night were slowly dropping? Could the question have then been answered, would I have stopped and retraced my steps? Alas! it is impossible to say, for human nature is a strange thing, and the unknown and untried has always attractions for the sanguine and the youug [*sic*]. (September 1882, 36)

The self-reflective nature of this passage is an important example of Fortune's transformation from immigrant to colonial advocate. There can be no doubt that she acknowledges the trauma of the transformative process and the loss that was associated with it, in what is both a personal expression of grief and an expression of a collective experience. The outward exploration of the new world is combined with the inward examination of the experience, an important process for both the reader and the narrator. As Fortune points out, colonial transformation meant that women needed to be judged by a new standard and this was confronting for the newly arrived immigrant. It was how an immigrant dealt with that confrontation that affirmed her worth in Fortune's eyes and that meant the colonial Victorian subject had to embrace change.

Part of the process of transformation meant meeting the challenge of the colony in more practical ways. The fashionable mode of dress created significant problems. Not only were the dresses and petticoats unsuited to the environment and weather, they were at times dangerous. In a particularly graphic description of the dangers Waif Wander tells readers: 'I saw a scene so strangely illustrative of what might happen [to] a lady in those days that I must tell you of it' (February 1883, 338). She describes the woman as being a passenger travelling on an empty dray to Taradale. She was seated on the old tarpaulin in the bottom of the dray, but the tarpaulin gradually slipped and became caught in the wheel. Every turn of the wheel dragged the tarpaulin further round the barrel of the wheel until the woman's petticoats were caught and she 'was dragged down to the rail and jammed there. Nothing saved her but her dress being turned over her head, for, see, she had slipped out of the petticoats and left them behind' (February 1883, 338). She hurried into the hotel to escape further scrutiny 'with only the black satin skirt and mantilla hanging loosely about her'. Waif Wander, however, highlights the sensitivity the diggers displayed by returning the 'petticoats, in a sadly mangled condition', but 'brought in to her carefully bundled up under a digger's arm' (February 1883, 338).

Once in the goldfields the assault on feminine sensibilities did not abate. It is important to understand the way in which the goldfields formed and reformed.[7] Once a strike was discovered, the itinerant gold seekers would gather at that place staking claims. Tents were pitched close together and canvas service industries would spring up rapidly in their midst, for if one could be the first proprietor on the scene the potential income was enormous. It was edgy living, and this unstable and quasi-urban environment provided an ideal site for Fortune's observations and explorations of the ambiguous moral ground that surrounded gold discovery. Community was important because, as Fortune pointed out, '[a]lmost everybody took an interest in their neighbours in those days, as upon them depended the comfort and quiet of one's lives' (May 1883, 509). If there was trouble, people responded immediately: '[a]s if a blow upon a hive had alarmed the busy tenants at his shout, every man and woman emerged from tent and dwelling, running' (May 1883, 509).

As a form of cultural observation, Fortune's writing is important. She is able to provide a long-term view of what David Goodman describes as

---

7 Fortune's accounts of the goldfields give a good overview of these processes. The information she provides supports historical research (see Serle) and more recent historical accounts (see Goodman; also McCalman, Cook, and Reeves).

'mythical events in Australian history — uproarious [and] larger than life' (34). Goodman suggests that the history of gold has been 'tamed in historians' prose into a comforting story of gold as a maker of cities and nations' (34). Both the personal and the diverse ranges of experience encountered during the gold rush have been buried in the documentary and statistical explication of the period; Goodman suggests that it is important to 'recover a sense of the gold rushes as dangerous, edgy events with unpredictable outcomes' (34). The danger that Goodman finds lacking in historical descriptions is available to the reader in Fortune's accounts. Her descriptions are vivid as she paints a picture of the 'babel' of noise and nationality as well as the uncertain status of the fellow diggers (February 1883, 340).

Fortune's reference to the *Ladies' Companion* in the early 1850s suggests that she may have been aware of Ellen Clacy's recollections of her time in the Australian goldfields, and was aware that stories of the goldfields sold magazines.[8] Clacy's *A Lady's Visit to the Gold Diggings of Australia in 1852-53: written on the spot* was a runaway success. While Fortune may have been engaged by the *Ladies' Companion* because of Clacy's success, the general desire of the English reading public to learn about the 'Fields of Gold' might have provided sufficient impetus for them to engage her. English periodicals and book publications were awash with goldfield narratives, mostly male descriptions of their success or failure. The chaos, disorder and potential for danger which Clacy describes (93) is reiterated by Fortune: 'It was a terrible scene to me, and if I had any ideas of a Pandemonium, they must have been realised there' (September 1882, 37). Fortune hears the noise of the 'prosperous rush' before she sees it: she says there were German bands

> crashing out familiar dance music, dogs were barking, men were shouting, and now and then a sonorous bell rang, while, in the interludes or temporary lulls, hundreds of firearms were being let off — crack, crack, crack — in every direction. (September 1882, 36)

---

8   In an interesting parallel, recent biographical research has uncovered a number of disjunctions between Clacy's idealised version of her respectability and the reality of her circumstances. It has been suggested that the trip to Australia may have been undertaken to cover up a pregnancy outside of marriage (Anderson 240). While their strategies for shielding potentially scandalous information from the reading public differed, they both achieved publication success.

The indiscriminate gunfire was the nightly custom as each digger checked that his gun was in working order, a warning to 'let all whom it might concern know that the owner was in a position to defend the gold he had worked so hard to obtain' (September 1882, 36-7).

Despite the noise and the danger, both women found aspects of the diggings to admire. Clacy suggests that despite the appearance of chaos, and notwithstanding her reference to murder being a commonplace, the diggers were on the whole quite trustworthy:

> Perhaps nothing will speak better for the general order that prevails at the diggings, than the small amount of physical force maintained there by Government to keep some of the thousands of persons of all ages, classes, characters, religions and countries in good humour with the laws and with one another. The military force numbers 130, officers and men; the police about 300. (97)

Fortune's anecdotes also include tales of faithfulness, loyalty and a community spirit despite the temporary nature of the settlements. In fact, despite all of the privations, chaos and danger, Waif Wander shows no sympathy for the women who complained of their lot on the diggings. In a conversation she has with a woman despairing of her fall from gentility to the essential elements of living in a tent, she clearly demonstrates her joy at the independent nature of life in the goldfields:

> 'You astonish me!' I cried, and, indeed, truthfully. 'You are as young as I am and, I hope, healthy; you have your husband and the dearest little girl, *how* can you feel anything unpleasant in your surroundings? As for myself, I do think I never was happier in my life!' (April 1883, 447, emphasis in original)

The early episodes of this autobiographical excursion do indeed celebrate this life removed from domesticity. In this new life Waif Wander was relieved of some domestic chores: 'I was never allowed to interfere with the cooking in any shape or form' (April 1883, 447). She also relished the experiences of '"campings [*sic*] out"', particularly the 'cool and pleasant' evenings, the 'dewy' nights and the 'strange delight' she drew from turning her back on the material comforts of urban life (February 1883, 339). Life without conveniences is compensated for, by the opportunity

> [t]o lounge on rugs under the canopy of pale heaven, broken only by the spreading branches of rustling trees; to see the gleaming of creek or dark water-hole in its denser shadows of bush and bank; to hear the bullock bells "tinkle tinkling," as the grateful beasts cropped the grass for acres around our temporary shelters; and listen to the sighing or rustle of leaves above us was a pleasant thing, and every puff of sweet night air brings the remembrance to me still. (February 1883, 339)

Fortune celebrates the shared experience of this transitory urban community. It is a paradoxical life. The diggers live removed from the trappings of material possessions but the reason they live this way is the quest for money. They are removed from the rigid structures of Victorian society but the goldfields became a makeshift nomadic society with its own rules, a kind of bush morality. These rules are presented as being more inclusive and allowing for greater personal freedom than urban Victorian society, but life was not without its dangers. In this life, so often presented as one that was too harsh and dangerous for women, Waif Wander finds a kind of peace. The opportunity to live outside the social boundaries, to be free of domesticity, to be part of a family structure that makes no unreasonable demands on her and to be so close to the natural world gives her a sense of freedom that she hints is unique to this time and place.

Fortune's work, like Clacy's, was part of a greater trend that colonial enterprise set in motion. Colonies needed women and women wrote of their experiences in them. While Mary Louise Pratt points out that exploration was often the domain of the male, colonising gave women an opportunity to participate in the same transformative process (qtd in Smith and Watson 90). Fortune's autobiographical vignettes formed part of an explosion of life writing, which Smith and Watson describe as the 'democratisation of the institution of life narratives' (97). Like other intrepid female travellers or colonisers, such as Susannah Moodie, Isabella Bird and Harriet Martineau, Fortune's foray into the writing of life narrative was an act of female agency.

For Mary Fortune the goldfields were a life-changing experience, offering a chance to live beyond the domestic and class structures, and an opportunity to start afresh. In the noise and confusion of the goldfields, where hopes were realised and destroyed, the 'dreamers' were all changed:

> The noise was shocking, and toward evening deafening. Hammering, chopping, bellringing, band-playing, shouting, laughing, fighting, and singing were all represented horridly in the babel of a new rush, and one heard and saw as in a dream in which the dreamer's identity is lost. (February 1883, 340)

One digger tells Fortune that at times he doesn't know himself: that when he gets a glimpse of his reflection in a creek he 'sometimes think[s] it must belong to some other man' (February 1883, 339). She describes this destabilising experience in terms of dreams: 'to fall asleep and dream dreams that change as quickly as the forms in an unsteady kaleidoscope, and to awaken with a bewildered feeling that you are not yourself but have changed places with some other identity' (January 1883, 280).

As Penny Russell has shown, class distinction in Melbourne was partially manufactured and required a certain amount of fluidity to accommodate a transient population and burgeoning wealth. For Fortune the more democratic and egalitarian nature of the goldfield population is appealing. However, she points out that she, too, had trouble making sense of it when she first arrived. She asked her 'uncle' 'unbelievingly ... "*where* are all the *gentlemen* we had supposed to have become diggers?"' (January 1882, 281, emphasis in original). Even though he points out that appearances are 'truly deceitful' she has trouble coming to terms with the idea that '"those great brown men, with beards all over their chests, and such rough, ill-fitting shirts and common pants"' are 'gentlemen'; and she remarks that '"surely not even such a change would entirely hide the gentleman?"' (January 1882, 281).

Fortune's priority of creating a new hierarchy of colonial respectability is revealed. She suggests that while appearances may deceive, education never does. She uses her 'uncle's' voice to articulate what has, 26 years later, become her view. The scruffiest-looking individuals will distinguish themselves by their superior intelligence:

> [Y]ou soon recognise the educated man when he speaks. There are amid that very crowd many a man who has taken his degree and abandoned a good profession, at least *pro tem.*, in the pursuit of sudden wealth. Just observe that party of four who are coming toward us, most probably to sell their gold to me; the one at the right who has the pick over his shoulder is a Glasgow M.D.; the next to him [*sic*] a barrister who has left his briefs in

London. The tall one is a Philadelphia Yankee, who came out with capital to speculate in stage-coaching or railways, or something, but who threw up the idea for digging. (January 1882, 281)

In some senses the topsy-turvy nature of the goldfields opened up new opportunities for women and Waif Wander reveals to the reader how she exploited those opportunities even before her writing was published in the *Australian Journal.* She describes her dealings with the *Mount Alexander Mail* when she lived in the goldfields. Ostensibly the anecdote is a description of striking up tentpoles to move to a new location in the goldfields, but in reality it is an opportunity to describe her trip to Castlemaine at the behest of the editor of the *Mount Alexander Mail.* While Waif Wander uses the common female strategy of self-deprecation to downplay the importance of her dealings with the newspaper, the inclusion of the details of the visit to their office in the memoir suggests the opposite. Its prominent position at the beginning of the instalment and its central location on the page reinforces this. She makes sure the reader knows what she has had published but devalues and apologises for the political subject matter:

> Coming almost directly from America, and being young you know, perhaps it was natural that, in a new land and among scenes in which law was of but little account, I should bloom in the Poet's Corner as a thorough Democrat. At all events, some pieces of mine were printed in the sheet I have alluded to, of which Mr. Saint (Charles, I think) was the editor or proprietor, or both. Some of the rhymes I have alluded to I have since reprinted, but with changes that redeemed them from the Republican taint. (Februrary 1883, 338)

Having established that even in the early days of the colony she was being published, she explains that she, or rather 'he', has been invited to call at the newspaper's office:

> The lines I write of were printed with my own initials attached, and just before I left the 'Flat' a line was addressed to me in the answer to correspondents' corner of the *Mount Alexander Mail.* The line was a request that 'M.H.F.' would call at this office at his earliest convenience. I was very much tickled at the personal pronoun, and curious too, so I took the opportunity of passing through Castlemaine to call at the office in question. (February 1883, 338)

This story reveals that the writer's initials are M.H.F. and suggests that she can write in a way that is not identifiably female. However, she prudently plays down her talents, deflecting any accusations of an unfeminine grab for publicity. While Fortune assumes an air of amusement by informing the reader that her writing had impressed the editor so much he wanted to offer 'him' a job there is also a discernible element of pride:

> I was interviewed by a man who stared in open-eyed wonder at me and my youngster, whom I led by the hand.
> 'Are *you* "M.H.F"?' he questioned with evident disbelief.
> 'Yes.'
> 'I can hardly credit it. You had better see Mr Saint; but as for the request that M.H.F. would call, we want a reporter and sub-editor, and thought he might suit.' (February 1883, 338)

This anecdote reveals personal information about Fortune's arrival directly from America: that she wrote and published poetry with republican and democratic sentiments. While she suggests that her political agenda was just the frivolity of youth, it confirms for the reader that the underlying egalitarian message is intentional. This anecdote also confirms the authority of Fortune as a writer — even in those early days her writing was not only worthy of praise, but it also prompted a job offer. While Fortune strategically deflects criticism of female ambition by making light of the episode, the fact that she relates it to the reading public draws attention to her potential and her success. Writing defined her time in the goldfields, writing defined her time in the city and writing defined her sense of personal value. It also suggests that a 'new land' where the 'law was of little account' created an egalitarian environment where one could construct a new writing identity.

In the January instalment (1883), Fortune's narrator detailed the first murder she had encountered in the colonies. While she is still in awe of the new surroundings and people, she starts to watch her neighbours, displaying her exceptional skills of observation and an eye for detail. At this stage in the memoir she still manages to balance the tawdry and distasteful with the amusing and bizarre. An anecdote about a canine-perpetrated theft counters the nasty scenes of domestic violence that lead to death. She intensifies the sensational nature of such murders by lingering on the details with morbid curiosity:

> It was dreadful to know that, hidden only by the still calico, that awfully rigid form was lying within, and I found myself wondering if the red painted spots were still visible on the cheeks of the dead, or if the long curls were dabbled in the stream that cruel knife had drawn from her breast. (January 1883, 284)

The speculation about the appearance of the corpse was not perhaps very 'ladylike' so she makes sure she dissociates herself from any direct contact with the grisly details. In this autobiographical mode, when the narrator is supposed to be a 'real' person, she makes it clear that her detailed information is second-hand: 'But the particulars of what they saw I must, of course, relate from hearsay' (January 1882, 284).

It is during this episode that her role as a *voyeuse* is cemented. She watches in the daytime, the night-time and from multiple viewing positions. She reads people's expressions, their body language and even the magic lantern effect of their tents because the 'effect of the bounding shadows on the unlined calico walls of the dancing-rooms was ludicrous' (January 1883, 283).[9]

Mary Fortune's prominence in the *Australian Journal* meant that her work formed an important part of the discussion that appeared in that journal and typified the uncertain and contradictory nature of colonial attempts at defining gender. Colonial women were expected to conform to English codes of dress and behaviour in an environment where such codes were often physically impractical. Colonial publications, while acknowledging English ideals, started to develop a new code of conduct for women. They became intent on changing the Victorian female subject to suit colonial life. The discussions in colonial publications suggest that the readers and the writers were aware of the debates taking place in the English press but they increasingly admired the virtues of hard work, resourcefulness and practicality. Kathryn Gleadle describes the process as forging a 'new concept of gentility which could incorporate the need for hard, physical work as pioneers' and create colonial 'discourses of womanhood' that could encompass 'bravery and adaptability' (56).

These were the virtues that Fortune's writing makes clear she admired. Her work provides a unique feminine insight into two important aspects of

---

9   When writing crime fiction as either W. W. or even as Waif Wander, Fortune has no hesitation in recounting the details as if from direct observation.

Australian history: the gold rush and the rise of the modern city. Reading her work changes our perspective on these events and, even more markedly, our perspective on colonial women and their role in creating a new cultural identity.

Works Cited

Australian Journal: A Weekly Record of Amusing and Instructive Literature, Science and the Arts. [Melbourne] 1865-1962.

Anderson, Margaret. 'Mrs Charles Clacy, Lola Montez and Poll the Grogseller: Glimpses of Women on the Early Victorian Goldfields.' *Gold: Forgotten Histories and Lost Objects of Australia.* Ed. Iain McCalman, Alexander Cook and Andrew Reeves. Cambridge: Cambridge UP, 2001. 225-49.

Brown, Megan. 'Mary Fortune as Sylphid: "blond, and silk, and tulle".' *Australian Literary Studies* 27.3-4 (October-November 2012): 92-106.

Clacy, Ellen. *A Lady's Visit to the Gold Diggings of Australia in 1852-53: written on the spot.* London: Hurst and Blackett, 1853.

Gleadle, Kathryn. *British Women in the Nineteenth Century.* Houndsmill: Palgrave, 2001.

Goodman, David. *Gold Seeking: Victoria and California in the 1850s.* St Leonards: Allen & Unwin, 1994.

McCalman, Iain, Alexander Cook, and Andrew Reeves. Eds. *Gold: Forgotten Histories and Lost Objects of Australia.* Cambridge, Melbourne: Cambridge UP, 2001.

Russell, Penelope. *A Wish of Distinction: Colonial Gentility and Femininity.* Carlton: Melbourne UP, 1994.

Serle, Geoffrey. *The Rush to Be Rich: A History of the Colony of Victoria, 1883-1889.* Carlton: Melbourne UP, 1974.

Smith, Sidonie, and Julia Watson. *Reading Autobiography: A Guide for Interpreting Life Narratives.* Minneapolis: University of Minnesota Press, 2001.

Sussex, Lucy. 'A Woman of Mystery.' *Crime Factory: The Australian Crime Fiction Magazine* Edition 002, n.d.

——. 'A Woman of Mystery.' http://lsussex.customer.netspace.net.au/index.html, accessed 25 July 2007.

——. 'Cherchez La Femme: Finding Mrs Fortune: Detail of the Search for Mary Fortune's Identity.' *Hecate* 14.2 (1988): 56-65.

——. 'Introduction.' *Mary Helena Fortune ('Waif Wander' / 'W. W.') c. 1833-1910: A Bibliography.* Lucy Sussex and Elizabeth Gibson. St Lucia, Qld: University of Queensland, Department of English, 1998. 1-11.

——. 'Introduction.' *The Detective's Album: Stories of Crime and Mystery from Colonial Australia.* Mary Fortune. Shelburne: Battered Silicon Dispatch Box, 2003. 3-17.

——. 'Introduction.' *The Fortunes of Mary Fortune.* Mary Fortune. Ringwood: Penguin, 1989. xii-xxiii.

——. 'Introduction.' *Three Murder Mysteries by Mary Fortune.* Canberra: Mulini, 2009. 1-5.

——. 'Mary Fortune: The Only Truly Bohemian Lady Writer Who Has Ever Earned a Living by Her Pen.' *Overland* Winter 183 (2006): 54-60.

——. 'Shrouded in Mystery: Waif Wander (Mary Fortune).' *A Bright and Fiery Troop: Australian Women Writers of the Nineteenth Century.* Ed. Debra Adelaide. Ringwood: Penguin, 1988. 117-32.

——. 'The Fortunes of Mary: "Authenticity, Notoriety and the Crime-Writing Life."' *Women's Writing* 14.4 (2006): 449-59.

——. 'Whodunit? Literary Forensics and the Crime Writing of James Skipp Borlase and Mary Fortune.' *Bibliographical Society of Australia and New Zealand Bulletin* 21.2 (1997): 73-106.

——. 'Whodunit? A Postscript.' *Bibliographical Society of Australia and New Zealand Bulletin* 22.2 (1998): 111-13.

——. *Women Writers and Detectives in Nineteenth-Century Crime Fiction: The Mothers of the Mystery Genre.* London: Palgrave Macmillan, 2010.

Sussex, Lucy. Ed. *The Fortunes of Mary Fortune.* Ringwood: Penguin, 1989.

Sussex, Lucy and Elizabeth Gibson. *Mary Helena Fortune ('Waif Wander' / 'W. W.') c. 1833-1910: A Bibliography.* St Lucia, Qld: University of Queensland, Department of English, 1998.

Stories by Mary Fortune Listed by Pseudonym

M.H.F. 'Melbourne Cemetery.' *Australian Journal* Nov. 1869: 180-1.

Waif Wander. 'Fourteen Days on the Roads.' *Australian Journal* (28 November 1868): 217-21.

Waif Wander (W. W.). 'Twenty-Six Years Ago; or, The Diggings from '55.' *Australian Journal* (September 1882): 33-7.

——. 'Twenty-Six Years Ago; or, The Diggings from '55.' *Australian Journal* (January 1883): 280-5.

——. 'Twenty-Six Years Ago; or, The Diggings from '55.' *Australian Journal* (February 1883): 338-43.

——. 'Twenty-Six Years Ago; or, The Diggings from '55.' *Australian Journal* (March 1883): 370-84.

——. 'Twenty-Six Years Ago; or, The Diggings from '55.' *Australian Journal* (April 1883): 445-8.

——. 'Twenty-Six Years Ago; or, The Diggings from '55.' *Australian Journal* (May 1883): 508-10.

7

Olive Schreiner's *From Man to Man* and 'the copy within'

Dorothy Driver

Olive Schreiner's various writings, both fictional and non-fictional, made an extraordinary contribution to late nineteenth- and early twentieth-century feminism, and continue to be of interest today. She is best known for her first published novel, *The Story of an African Farm* (1883), which was received with great acclaim, and *Woman and Labour* (1911), which became known as the Bible of the Women's Movement. *The Story of an African Farm* had advanced views on, among other things, the shaping of women, which — in a jibe at finishing schools and girls' education in general — Schreiner had identified as a process of 'finishing' women: 'our end has been quite completed' (185, 189). Although, in most instances, later critics have been disappointed by the novel's closure, seeing the deaths of the two main characters, Lyndall and Waldo, as a kind of moral failure and even as a failure in Schreiner's composition, it is *The Story of an African Farm* that has kept Schreiner's reputation as a novelist in place.

However, *From Man to Man* is, to my mind, the more interesting text: more mature, more ambitious, and more intent upon struggling through the social problems and contradictions of the time, and — if it is also exemplary of those 'large loose baggy monsters' identified by Henry James (84) — it is nevertheless characterised by magnificent, impassioned writing, evocative descriptions of its various settings and an acute portrayal of a range of (particularly) women's subjectivities. Moreover, the novel shows Schreiner as a precursor of what would later be called intersectionality studies[1] — in this particular case, the intersections between race and gender[2] — and also of the notion of the subject-in-process, which Julia Kristeva would later theorise. Kristeva's work itself — originally published in French in 1977 — developed in part out of *The Second Sex* by Simone de Beauvoir (1949), whose claim that women are made and not born Schreiner also anticipated: 'We all enter the world little plastic beings ... and the world ... shapes us by the ends it sets before us' (*The Story of an African Farm* 188).

Yet the novel's status as 'unfinished' means that it is generally dismissed. Despite some compelling readings, *From Man to Man* has only sporadically been kept in print and has not been given the extensive readings it deserves. In their otherwise impressive literary biography of Schreiner, Ruth First and Ann Scott set a critical trend by giving the novel short shrift, seeing it as 'melodramatic and derivative' (170), and objecting to the frequent inclusion of long monologues. Karel Schoeman follows suit. Joyce Avrech Berkman and Carolyn Burdett give the novel more extensive and close readings (Berkman more so), although Berkman sees it as confused in its artistic aims (209), and Burdett says that it 'proved sadly unable to nourish the fictional representation to which it was supposed to give rise' regarding sexual relations (*Progress* 98). In the only book-length study entirely on Schreiner's fiction, Gerald Monsman devotes a chapter to *From Man to Man* (*The Story of an African Farm* has two), and, oddly, judges the novel positively on account of its optimism: the main female character 'transcends involuntary enslavement by becoming the one who chooses to serve' (136). Cherry Clayton's short book on Schreiner gives a chapter to *From Man to Man* and usefully notes the entanglement of 'gender norms' and 'racial norms' (73), although, like Burdett, Clayton sees the novel as doing no more than representing 'the furthest point to which the novel was capable of serving Schreiner's developing feminist vision' (73). Essays devoted entirely to *From Man to Man* are rarer. *Inter alia*, Anthony Voss sees it not as Schreiner's

---

1 For the first articulation of intersectionality studies, in 1988, see Teresa de Lauretis.
2 Schreiner was a socialist (although, for her, socialism needed tempering by individualism) and, generally speaking, the articulations of her social vision were more often focused on class than on race.

classic, but nonetheless as heroically striving to become the epic of its time; Murray Steele — who finds its neglect 'difficult to understand' (103) — sees it as a humanist bible; whereas Rose Lovell-Smith argues that it positions itself as a revisionist Biblical Genesis. Paul Foot's introduction to the Virago reprint in 1982 is, perhaps not surprisingly, unambiguously enthusiastic.

In anticipation of a new edition[3], this chapter aims to open discussion on what is felt to be the novel's major literary contribution; its narrative and poetic treatment of what Schreiner saw as the human ideal, and its relation to what Schreiner called 'the copy within' (*From Man to Man* 472)[4] in the context of evolutionary process. In this regard I turn to more positive effect the idea of the 'unfinished', considering comparatively another unfinished work in Schreiner's oeuvre: her introduction to an edition of Mary Wollstonecraft's *A Vindication of the Rights of Woman*. Nowhere else in Schreiner than in these two texts does one have so strong an impression of her struggle with writing and with the existential space created in the journey towards the ideal. Schreiner's strong interest in Plato and Charles Darwin adds to existing readings of *From Man to Man*, for critics have been — respectively — altogether or mostly neglectful in this regard, while nonetheless immensely productive in tracing lines of connection with John Stuart Mill, Herbert Spencer, Ralph Waldo Emerson and others.

Schreiner started reading Darwin during her period as a governess in the 1870s, and Plato during the 1880s. Her reading in Darwin was massively influential. Specifically, his *The Variation of Animals and Plants Under Domestication* and *On the Origin of Species* gave her an understanding of the theory of reversion, latency and the interdependence of all organic beings, which deeply informed her notion of history (for her, evolution was part of history) and the development of the individual subject. And then her reading in Plato gave her a way of understanding evolution as progress, for she introduced the notion of progress into an evolutionary science that was generally non-teleological, and also of pursuing a quasi-divine 'copy within', for it was this 'copy' or 'ideal' which served as both an origin and an end for the human subject.

---

3   Forthcoming from University of Cape Town Press, 2014; edited by the present writer, with introduction and notes.

4   All quotations are from the Virago text unless otherwise stated.

Changing the Victorian Subject

From Man to Man was first drafted under different titles — 'Thorn Kloof', 'Saints and Sinners'[5] — during the mid-1870s, while Schreiner was employed as a governess in the Cape Colony. She continued working on it during the 1880s, which she spent in England with short visits to Italy, and then also in her second South African period, 1889-1913. Her letters return time and again to both the exhilaration and despair she felt while rewriting it, but when she died in 1920 the revisions remained incomplete, the final chapter consisting of no more than a few lines. The upshot, then, was that the typescript and manuscript fragments of *From Man to Man* were edited by her husband, Samuel Cronwright-Schreiner, after her death.

There were various reasons for Schreiner's not seeing the novel into print. Other writing had taken up her time: the allegories, 'dreams' and short stories she seemed to dash off with such ease; the allegorical novel, *Trooper Peter Halket of Mashonaland*, which was a critique of Cecil John Rhodes; numerous political and sociological essays, many of which would later be collected in *Thoughts on South Africa* (1923); and *Woman and Labour*. In England she was kept busy with informal social work among female sex workers, and with generous acts of friendship — she spoke of friends sometimes seeming to suck out the 'life-blood' she needed for her writing (to Havelock Ellis, 10 March 1886, l. 11).[6] She likened herself in 1886 to 'a watch with the spring broken ... nothing to set me in motion' (to Karl Pearson, 10 July 1886, ll. 192-3), too exhausted to re-write particular scenes in *From Man to Man*, where her sarcasm and bitterness about middle-class morality and its petty-minded materialism now seemed to her to require an attempt to represent it from the inside. In both England and South Africa her writing time was curtailed by increasing ill-health — primarily asthma, the effects of which seemed to be worsened by ill-advised medication. Whereas popular novelists, she suggested, 'write in water, three novels a year', she felt she was writing 'with my blood' (to Havelock Ellis, 1890, ll. 8-10). But perhaps one of the strongest

---

5 See Schoeman 386-7; he disagrees with the account given in Cronwright-Schreiner's *Life*.

6 All letters quoted in this essay are available online, from www.oliveschreiner.org. These are verbatim transcriptions; they include in-line symbols noting additions and deletions, and retain original line lengths. Line lengths are not retained in my quotations, but line numbers are noted after the date in the in-text references, conforming to a request made in the website.

reasons for her not completing *From Man to Man* was the despair she felt during her last years on account of the increasingly oppressive political environment created by white South African rule and rampant capitalism, and added to by World War I[7], which she understood as a trade war that had nothing to do with ideals (to Havelock Ellis, 1914, ll. 6-11). Her despair had taken a global reach. In 1916 she wrote: 'And behind all, for me lies the great shadow — the future of our human race on earth during the coming centuries' (to Will Schreiner, 1916, ll. 20-1). Her short essay, 'The Dawn of Civilisation', written in 1917 and part-published in 1921, includes a litany of local and global horrors which lie so heavily on her that she is tempted even to cry out, '"Is it not possible to put out a sponge and wipe up humanity from the earth? It is stain!"' (213).

The story of *From Man to Man* centres on two white South African women, Rebekah and her sister, Bertie, in a double plot that allows Schreiner to explore the degraded position of women whose only social function is a sexual one, and who are socially constrained from achieving a higher human ideal. Rebekah marries and has children, but the sister is seduced against her will and — in psychological distress and a near outcast in colonial society — winds up as a kept woman in London. Rebekah, meanwhile, remains in the Cape Colony, looking after her husband and children, and spending her free time as an amateur naturalist as well as in reading and self-to-self philosophising. She makes friends with an explorer and collector called Drummond, who treats her as an equal and takes seriously Rebekah's continuing anxiety about her sister, who Rebekah feels may have returned to the Cape. Rebekah's husband, in contrast, dismisses Bertie as beyond help, treats Rebekah as his 'little woman', and has various extramarital sexual liaisons. One of these is with a young domestic servant who stays in their outside room. This woman will later bear his child.

In the ending that Cronwright-Schreiner remembers[8], Rebekah decides not to run off with Drummond (the physical desire between them is made

---

7 In a letter to John Merriman, the last Prime Minister of the Cape before the formation of the Union of South Africa in 1910, Schreiner voiced her despair at the current political climate, including the materialism, the withdrawal of educational advantages to Africans and their dispossession of land (to John X. Merriman, 1912).

8 In his introduction, Cronwright-Schreiner notes that his wife had told him how the novel was to end (15) and he therefore appends to the main text his summary of what she said (see Unwin edition 481-3).

evident in the text, but they do not so much as kiss), but stays instead with her husband and children. Cronwright-Schreiner explains that Rebekah did not want to 'degrade' her love for Drummond (482). His use of the word 'degrade' in this context betrays Schreiner's complex project about the social degradation of both women and men under a regime of marital prostitution, a situation all the further from her social ideal given its entanglement in the racial hierarchies of the time. Considerably more true to the spirit of the novel than the ending Cronwright-Schreiner recalls is the summary of the ending Schreiner wrote out in a long letter to her friend and colleague, Karl Pearson (10 July 1886, ll. 14-180). In terms of the plot, it cannot stand as definitive, for it is superseded by some later revision, but it clarifies Rebekah's situation by referring repeatedly to her 'life's work' and 'life of work' (ll. 177, 104) as the reason she does not leave her family. Certainly, below the surface, there lies a tumultuous story about the immense difficulty of balancing intellectual friendship with sexual love, but the novel steers Rebekah's decision to stay with her family in the direction of this 'life's work': to educate her children as best she can *out of* the race-class-sex/gender system of the time, and to take one more step for women and the human race in pursuit of the human social ideal.

Schreiner's project is both facilitated and deepened by Rebekah's adoption of her husband's mixed-race child, a plot development Schreiner described to her brother in 1908:

> [O]ne of the centre points of the story is that the wife has adopted & brings up as her own among the legitimate children a little half-coloured child who is her husbands [*sic*] by a coloured servant. He never suspects the child is his till the end of the book, when he attacks his wife with bringing up a coloured child with his white children. You will of course see how this opens up the whole question of our relation to the ~~unreadable~~ ^darker^ races, & the attitude which says 'they are here for *our* interest for our *pleasure*, & to hell with them when they aren't that!' If only I could live to finish that book, I would feel satisfied, though it was perfect failure. (To Will Schreiner, 1908, ll. 29-39)

This 'centre point' of the novel — involving, as she says, 'the whole question of our relation to the ... darker races' — allows Schreiner to investigate the entanglement of gender and racial subordination (which is crucial in her exploration of what women and men need to undergo before human equality might be achieved), and hence the impact on feminism of racial difference. The continuing regime of marital and extra-marital prostitution was degrading to both women and men, and effectively constituted incomplete human subjects in which the physical and intellectual, or the material and spiritual, were either out of balance or not interfused.

Near the end of the novel Rebekah offers Drummond the fossil of a winged reptile, which he recognises as 'the crown of her collection' (462) and which for her (and Schreiner) is an object that resonates with the possibility of creative change. As Drummond hesitates to accept it, Rebekah says, 'Someone might make use of it. I never will' (463). The self-conscious self-limitation of this statement aside, the act of exchange and the fossil's overall symbolic significance keep the notions of process, change and fruitful human connection in place. The winged reptile appears on the one hand to be the sign of a life-form which natural selection did not select; and in this sense it stands for those whose natures, lives and potentialities have been truncated by what evolutionary theorists called 'brute force' — 'Nature, red in tooth and claw', to use the phrase from Tennyson's *In Memoriam* (lvi). On the other hand, the winged reptile resonates in this novel as a signifier of change: it is one among a set of objects Schreiner uses, all of which, despite being dead, nevertheless metaphorically throb with life, pulsing into the present and helping create a better time to come. And so, too — knowing that Schreiner did not 'live to finish that book', as she put it to her brother — might we see Schreiner's own 'unfinished' writing as reflecting upon itself as *process*. It not only makes a subtle statement about the 'unfinished' aspect of human relations which remains to be 'finished', but also paradoxically places itself in an economy of exchange that keeps in motion the endless journey towards the social ideal (hence the title of the novel itself, *From Man to Man*).

Rebekah's own change in racial attitude is one of the themes of the novel. Readers of *The Story of an African Farm* have rightly criticised Schreiner's use of racial stereotypes and the restriction of Schreiner's black characters to servant roles. *From Man to Man* continues to be insensitive to the implications of certain racial terminology, neglects to give black South Africans active, extensive and significant roles in the main plot and is uncritical of Rebekah's patronising attitudes. But Rebekah begins to understand what black South African culture can offer European modernity, and what difference is made by the inclusion of a black perspective, as well as the fundamental importance to social harmony of autonomy for all subjects in a nation. Rebekah's change bears on Schreiner's conception of South Africa's possible progress towards an ideal.

Much of Schreiner's non-fiction writing after *The Story of an African Farm* makes clear a similar maturation in racial attitudes, as in her opposition to colonial racial politics and her foreboding about white domination. In 1896 she co-authored a book with her husband called *The Political Situation* which identified a 'backwards' movement in the country on account of the way in which the speculation in mineral wealth had no thought for the 'sufferings and loss' of, in particular, black South Africans (21, 91, 106). Franchise reform was needed, the book continued, in order to put 'the Native … on an equality with the white man in the eye of the law' (109-10). Moreover, as the country moved towards unifying the two Boer republics and the two British colonies after the Anglo-Boer War — during which time it became clear that in the process of withdrawal the British were betraying indigenous rights — Schreiner wrote a series of letters urging the extension of the franchise to black South Africans, as well as economic and trade union reform. Among the statements in her 1908 letters, for instance, were a sympathetic reference to an African leader whom the British were charging with treason for involvement in a revolt against a poll tax (to Frank Colenso, 1908, l. 13); a plea for 'white working men' to stand with 'the native in the struggle of the coming years' in trade union activity (to Will Schreiner, 1909, ll. 12-13); a recognition of Africans' difficulty in staging protest: 'if they strike or move in any way' they 'will be shot down like dogs' (to Edward Carpenter, 1909, ll. 29-30); an insistence that '[i]f no one else will speak out for the natives I must' (to Mary Brown, 1908, ll. 3-4); and a forecast of 'hard & stern works [to do with the above] that calls to all the bravest souls in South Africa for many years to come' (to Emily Hobhouse, 1908, ll. 9-10). The book she published in 1908, *Closer Union*, spoke in the strongest terms of the costs to the overall political health of the land of alienating black South Africans — breaking up their social organisation, dispossessing them of their land, relegating them to a poorly paid labouring class and withholding 'the rights of citizenship' (29).

Also in 1908 Schreiner withdrew from the South African Women's Enfranchisement League (of which she had been elected vice-president) once the majority decided that their demand for the vote would not include the vote for black women. This decision, she said, ran counter to 'the general interests of the country' (to Minnie Murray, 1908, l. 38). And after the Act of Union in 1910, Schreiner noted the establishment of 'a little white Oligarchy' (to John X. Merriman, 1912, l. 159) — South Africa's 'dark ages' — that had 'only one idea, to crush & keep down the native' (to Edward Carpenter, 1911, ll. 18, 19-20). In 1913, she voiced her outrage at the Natives Land Act which moved Africans into reserves that constituted a tiny fraction of the available land: 'the worst bit of work we have done for years' (to Edward Carpenter, 1913, l. 11); and in 1918, she wrote in an open letter:

> [W]e shall have to learn the lesson Mill taught — that the freedom of all human creatures is essential to the full development of human life on earth. We shall have to labour ... for every subject race and class, and for all suppressed individuals. ('Letter on John Stuart Mill', 204)

Moreover, unusually for her time, and without succumbing to stereotypes of primitivism or the noble savage, Schreiner had also started turning to African culture for what it might offer European modernity. This turn is already suggested in the late 1880s in the draft introduction Schreiner wrote to Wollstonecraft's *A Vindication* (as will shortly be discussed), but is now more fully articulated in *Closer Union*. While she recognised the oppression and exploitation of women within African culture[9], as in peasant culture more generally, Schreiner spoke in this book of how African social cohesiveness might replace Western individualism and rampant materialism: these 'social instincts ... we have only with wisdom and patient justice to transfer ... to our own larger society' (*Closer Union* 27). As she explains:

> [T]he problem which this century will have to solve is the accomplishment of this interaction of distinct human varieties on the largest and most beneficent lines, making for the development of humanity as a whole and carried out in a manner consonant with modern ideals and modern social wants. (26)

'It will not always be the European who forms the upper layer', she takes care to add, for 'European, Asiatic and African will interlard' (26). The word

---

9 See, for instance, her rage in 1912 at an African politician voting against (white) women being allowed to join the Provincial Council, since 'their place was in the home' (to Will Schreiner, 1912, l. 20).

'interlard' indicates that Schreiner did not exhibit the kind of moral revulsion to 'miscegenation' that was being voiced by other social theorists of the time.[10] Her position was more nuanced, intelligent and historicised than this: she saw a social problem arising when intermarriage between the races arose in a situation of power differentials, for these power differentials were likely to produce in their children a complex of denial and repression which would not only perpetuate racism but also extend it in insidiously internalised forms. Significantly, Schreiner was sensitive enough to the difficulties surrounding this topic to voice an anxiety about being misunderstood. Referring in a letter to an essay she published in *The Fortnightly Review* in 1896 which would later reappear in *Thoughts on South Africa*, she stresses that she wished this essay to show 'the evil that springs from a mixture of races while the men of mixed race are ashamed of their darker ancestors' (to Minnie Murray, 1909, ll. 40-1). A society needed first to work for equality between the races before interracial marriage could be of true personal pleasure and social benefit.

As the quoted comments suggest, Schreiner's thinking on class and race was part and parcel of her thinking on gender; their intersections were what made up the complex of human oppression and exploitation, and the notion of the human subject could not be understood simply in terms of any one of these categories, nor indeed out of its historical context. What makes *From Man to Man* so different a book from *The Story of an African Farm* is in part the development of this line of thought, but even more crucial is Schreiner's acute sense of what a non-racial South Africa might both achieve as a nation and offer as a model to the world at large. The repression of the African had for her more than merely immediate political import, then, for what is thus extinguished is in effect one of the crucial evolutionary 'gemmules' (to use Darwin's term), or what Schreiner appeared to think of as a connecting bond between the 'little individual particle' and humanity's 'great high end' (to Edward Carpenter, 1888, ll. 18-20). In other words, through this failure to interlard with African culture, society as a whole was failing to enter a new stage in its evolution towards what Schreiner

---

10   While current Schreiner scholarship — notably by Burdett and Liz Stanley — now mostly takes care to read Schreiner's commentary on race with the contextualisation and nuance it deserves, one recent critic turns back to an earlier trend in Schreiner criticism, seeing Schreiner as producing some of South Africa's 'white scripts of "miscegenation"' (Graham 112; see also 26, 49, 79).

saw as the social ideal, and it was doing so by not allowing the 'interaction of distinct human varieties' (as previously quoted), and thus by not incorporating into European culture the social instincts characteristic of African peasant culture. In one of her last pieces of writing, 'The Dawn of Civilisation' (written in 1917, part-published posthumously in 1921), she clearly articulates the ideal as involving a constant 'struggle against the primitive, self-seeking instincts in human nature, whether in the individual or in the larger social organism ... a life-and-death struggle, to be renewed by the individual till death, by the race through the ages' (213). And, for Schreiner, it was Africans — and (as we shall see) specifically African women, with their combination of individual strength and sense of social duty — who offered a way *out* of the 'primitive' and 'self-seeking'.

As suggested earlier, this idea seems first to emerge in Schreiner's thinking in an essay she drafted between 1887 and 1889, intended for a new edition of Wollstonecraft's *A Vindication of the Rights of Woman* (first published in 1792). Schreiner was at this stage still in England and had started to work in earnest on *From Man to Man*; the introduction to Wollstonecraft's work foreshadows the novel's greatest contribution.[11] Schreiner was in certain respects well placed to write this introduction: Wollstonecraft's main underlying theme — 'the movement ... *of sex towards sex*' (190, emphasis in original) — had already informed *The Story of an African Farm*, and is exemplified in Lyndall's statement to Waldo: '"When I am with you I never know that I am a woman and you are a man; I only know that we are both things that think"' (210). For Schreiner, the only difference between women and men is their sexual physiology, and this difference does not have the meanings attributed to it by the social construction of gender. As she insists in a letter to her friend Havelock Ellis: 'human development has now reached a point at which sexual difference has become a thing of altogether minor importance' (1884, ll. 16-17). However, the movement of sex towards sex would inform *From Man to Man* in a more mature and complex way than in *The Story of an African Farm*, since Schreiner now needed to take account of

---

11   Carolyn Burdett edited Schreiner's draft introduction for publication in 1994, and this is the text referred to in the present essay. However, scholars should look also at the text edited by Gray (Schreiner, 'Introduction to *A Vindication*'), which corrects a couple of errors in Burdett's edition (correctly transcribing 'fate' for 'face' and 'god' for 'good'), although it makes other errors.

the impact of racial difference on gender relations. This means that when the movement of sex towards sex is exemplified in the later novel, in the growing relation between Rebekah and Drummond, it is also problematised, for the relation between the two characters only partly depends on Rebekah's autonomy and Drummond's appreciation of her intellectual aspirations.

Because Schreiner begins to complicate the question of the argument about gender equality in her draft introduction to Wollstonecraft's *A Vindication*, it is worth spending a little time on the introduction in order to draw out its contribution to *From Man to Man*. In the introduction, Schreiner's thinking appears to have two deep-seated, interconnected motivations. The first is to use the figure of an African woman as a model of the kind of femininity she felt beneficial to inject into modernity, and specifically into motherhood. The second is to draw from African agricultural life a model of social duty at risk of disappearing in modern European life. While the argument is roughly made (the draft was left unrevised), it becomes clearer when we read it through Schreiner's interest in evolutionary science. Unlike the eugenicists of the time, Schreiner held that the successful pursuit of the maternal function was entirely dependent on women's access to labour and its rewards. By labour she meant both physical and intellectual labour, and was thereby indicating women's equality with men. Such access would return maternality to the social rather than the merely familial, and would nurture future generations of women and men.

Although she strongly disagreed with Karl Pearson that there had once existed a matriarchal age, she retrieved from early agricultural life a model of femininity in which women had access to both familial and social power, and were not in all respects highly differentiated from men. Early agricultural life stood, for her, in contrast to two later models: 'agricultural, slave-supported' cultures, which made excessive use of 'human muscular force' ('Introduction to the Life' 192) even if they seemed otherwise to have 'a great degree of civilisation' (192), and highly civilised societies in which machinery replaces muscular labour. She saw 'agricultural, slave-supported' cultures as encouraging a certain class of women to live parasitically (Turkish life with its harems gave Schreiner her example) and said that here lay society's lowest point — the 'point of greatest differentiation between the sexes' (192). And then she saw in mechanised or industrialised cultures, exemplified by the modern European world, the tendency for males and females to become 'increasingly similar' (192). Her anxiety was, however, as would later be made so clear in *Woman and Labour*, that women were being encouraged to rely solely on their 'sex-function' (as exemplified in non-working wives and mothers, and in prostitutes). Moreover, in the modern world, advancement was generally seen in terms of personal advancement (advancing the family or the individual) rather than the society as a whole.

This is why Schreiner's Wollstonecraft introduction turns to rural African women, finding in them an aspect of femininity which should interact in evolutionary terms with the European: there is 'none of that intellectual inferiority in the women of the native races which we are accustomed to associate with the feminine form in our own' (footnote on p. 192). Even if the African male sees the female as property, '[the woman's] functions as builder, manufacturer, cultivator prevent any deterioration of her mental powers and her physical strength ... [She is] superior in some [ways]' (192).

All the more crucial to our understanding of *From Man to Man*'s contribution to the changing notion of the human subject, however, is the way Schreiner both exemplifies and complicates her image of the African woman. Having noted African women's recognition of their suffering, rather than their blind acceptance of it, in their 'desire' that 'it should be otherwise' (193), Schreiner then recounts a conversation she had as a child with an African woman whom she calls 'completely uncivilised' (but without the weight of moral judgment typically attendant on the term), and from whose lips came 'an outburst of passion and bitterness' and 'a sense of her own suffering and wrong, deeper than [in] any civilised woman' (footnote on p. 193). Adds Schreiner:

> The strange part of such an outburst is the dead hopeless calm with which it is spoken. It is as though one sat in a house with one's dead and looked at them, but did not dream they could be made alive again ... What lies behind this awful calm, this dead [? resigned] nature like that of man to death? I think it is even more than a mere perception, that, under her social circumstances it is as hopeless for her to strive against oppression, as it would be for one wave in the sea to rise up against the tidal current. I believe that, deeper yet than this, lies the perception that it is her *duty to submit*. I believe the social instinct which formulates right and wrong, distinctly acts within her, and that her 'moral sense', unable as she may

be to formulate it exactly, acts as a mighty force upon her urging her to submission. (footnote on p. 193, emphasis in original)

For Schreiner, then, female submission at this moment of history was necessary to the wellbeing and perpetuation of an agricultural economy, which is why the African woman is performing what she sees as her social duty. Given what she would later say in *Closer Union* about the well-developed social instinct in African culture, and the contribution it might make to European notions of progress, it is clear that Schreiner is intent not only on the woman's exemplification of duty but also on the defining context that gives rise to it: that is, the culture of non-individualism which Schreiner associated with Africans. In this culture Schreiner sees women flourishing physically and intellectually, despite the amount of work they had to perform and the violence to which they were subjected. What gives these women social value is not their 'enslavement to socially-useful labour' (Burdett, 'A Difficult Vindication' 183), but their physical and intellectual capability and the direction it takes. This is why Schreiner is at the same time so engaged by the woman's 'passion' for independence and autonomy, a passion that Schreiner feels to be strongly evident, albeit repressed. It is this kind of passion, I argue, that Schreiner is retrieving in *From Man to Man*: a passion for a world in which women remain physically and intellectually powerful but in which their social duty does not depend upon their subordination and self-sacrifice; a world in which gender equality facilitates women's fulfilment of their social instinct — or, to put it another way, a world in which the social instinct is in constant dialectic with the aspirations of the individual, but has no truck with either male dominance of women or with the materialist greed and lack of concern for others which Schreiner would speak of as haunting white South Africa's notions of progress.

In their biography of Schreiner, First and Scott write briefly of this complex essay fragment, referring usefully to the African woman's 'social instinct' but claiming, wrongly in my view, that Schreiner's sympathy was with the African woman 'as a woman rather than as a black' (288). Carolyn Burdett takes up the discussion in a more detailed and often brilliant analysis, first in her essay 'A Difficult Vindication', which draws on an earlier, also path-breaking, essay by Laura Chrisman, and then in her book *Olive Schreiner and the Progress of Feminism*. Arguing that the unfinished nature of the Wollstonecraft introduction 'bears witness to Schreiner's struggle to articulate an aesthetic, theoretic and subjective position within the discourses available to her during the 1880s', Burdett uses the essay to investigate Schreiner's preliminary foray into the 'difference that colonialism makes to the historical narrative of European feminism' ('A Difficult Vindication' 177). However, she sees Schreiner as reaching a limit in her draft introduction — signified by the 'atrocious resignation' experienced both by the African woman and by Schreiner to that state of '"dead hopeless calm"' (*Progress* 59). My own reading instead sees in the Wollstonecraft introduction a moment of breakthrough for Schreiner, which is later articulated in a set of allegorical moments incorporated into *From Man to Man*. While having built on some part of what Burdett says, then, my essay goes in a different direction, not only stressing Schreiner's incorporation into her thinking of what it is to be an African peasant woman — the complex entanglement of the desire for autonomy, the physical and mental power, and the social sense *as an African woman* — but also showing how deeply the thinking and wording of Schreiner's inspirational introduction informs *From Man to Man*.

I note in passing that I depart from Burdett in three other respects besides those noted above: not seeing the African woman as an 'originary' figure outside of history ('A Difficult Vindication' 188); not seeing in Schreiner's prose evidence of either a 'sadistic' or a 'masochistic' stance towards the beaten African woman (188); and not seeing the introduction as indicating through its interest in allegory the failure of realism that Burdett feels characterises *From Man to Man*. However, this essay could not have been written without Burdett's preliminary analysis, and I recall here Schreiner's repeated image of the kind of inquiry that builds on the research and reading of others (as in the 'Hunter' allegory in *African Farm*, and 'Three Dreams in a Desert' in *Dreams*).

Burdett's engagement with the remarkable difficulty Schreiner has in her essay, as flagged in Schreiner's use of the lexicon of 'dead' and 'alive', has been particularly useful to my own thinking, but what needs to be added is the infusion of this lexicon into *From Man to Man*. The book's project, we might then say, is of keeping alive what has seemed to be dead — keeping alive a human ideal that is being retrieved from past moments in what Schreiner, as befitting her time, would call 'the history of the race'. In using the exemplary position of an

African woman, Schreiner enters a threshold moment in her capacity to think about what it is to be a woman in a racially divided society, and thus also about the intersections of gender and race. Other wording in this draft introduction is also of particular interest to *From Man to Man*. Thinking of the movement of sex toward sex, Schreiner imagines herself standing at 'this, the point of greatest differentiation between the sexes, looking backwards or forwards' and from this point seeing 'them [the sexes] coming nearer to one another' (192). The double perspective that she stages here, in the phrase 'backwards or forwards', not only indicates her rejection of any hierarchical thinking about what we might term the 'primitive' versus the 'civilised', but also points to the way in which her writing in *From Man to Man* knits together past, present and future in an invocation of what should not be lost in the new sense of time and space opened up by nineteenth-century evolutionary science and exploration.

Into the novel, then, Schreiner draws several extraordinary moments from the Wollstonecraft essay which will help her develop her model of the human social ideal: the restoration of women to a social function beyond the familial; the importance of women's physical and mental labour; the contribution of African culture towards modern civilisation; the bringing back to life of the seemingly dead; and the knitting together of vastly disparate times and spaces. When she says in *Woman and Labour* that the 'highest sexual ideal haunts humanity' (12-13), we hear that other haunting, indicated in the turn she makes, with such difficulty, both in the Wollstonecraft essay and in *From Man to Man*: the fact that surmounting conventions of racial difference must come into the pursuit of the sexual ideal. This is not to say that the Wollstonecraft essay systematically articulates this idea. Nor does it systematically articulate the other ideas I have drawn from it. Its unfinished status keeps it, to a far greater extent than occurs in *From Man to Man*, in a permanent state of difficulty, but it does provide hints that one can see germinate and grow in the novel. The exemplary position of an African woman leads Schreiner into a preliminary understanding of how such a woman experiences not only being a women in a patriarchal society, but also being a black woman in a racially divided society, constrained to silence. One can see developing in *From Man to Man* not just the idea that racial as well as gender equality define the human social ideal, not just that any model of equality entertained by white women and men needs first to come to terms with its context of racial inequality, but also that what she called the 'life long strife after truth' (to Karl Pearson, 13 July 1886, ll. 11-12), which was also the fundamental struggle within the act of writing, has to do with the process of creation and its continual need to engage in protection rather than destruction. Schreiner's writing strives to protect, preserve and nurture what is lost in Western civilisation's notion of progress, including inchoate longings for change.

From Man to Man investigates the question of racial autonomy and equality in several ways. For one thing, Bertie's behaviour towards the black servants is exemplary as regards kindness, although it does not in any way disturb the status quo, and is not self-reflexive, as Rebekah's is. After Rebekah discovers her husband's visits to Clartje[12] in the outside room, Rebekah thinks to herself, 'Are *you* the only creature in the world who has suffered wrong?' (300, emphasis in original), and decides to make an enlightened approach, imagining that she will find what the earlier manuscript called 'woman, herself, humanity to love' (Ms. of *From Man to Man*, 92-3). Instead she lapses into a sequence of racist epithets. Clartje, meanwhile, stands with her hands on her hips, giving out a 'defiant' laugh but with an 'undertone of fear' (301). Clartje is positioned as black in relation to this more powerful white woman, and Rebekah is positioned as the white woman she did not want to be. Any potential solidarity or sympathy between the two women has dissolved. In this clash between idealism and realism, Schreiner shows us that Rebekah should have been able to behave in one way but in actuality behaves in another.

It is of great significance that the location for the dialectic between black and white is the outer room, which functions as the limit-space that inaugurates the novel's race-sex/gender theme. At the very end of the novel, when Rebekah and Drummond have finally established the intellectual equality on whose basis a sexual relationship can flourish, the location on offer is another 'outer room', this time Drummond's (481). Rebekah politely refuses his invitation to enter it, and this refusal brings the novel to its close. As the place where sexual

---

12 The young woman is unnamed in the published novel, but in an early manuscript lodged in the Harry Ransom Humanities Research Center, University of Texas, Schreiner used the name Clartje, which is the name I use here. See Ms. of *From Man to Man*, 89. The Olive Schreiner Collection MS-3734. Box 1, folder 1.3. This Ms. is discussed in an earlier essay (see Driver) which rehearses some parts of the present argument.

consummation might occur, the mention of an outer room loads the text (but almost imperceptibly) with the memory of earlier encounters in another 'outer room', which means that in Rebekah's 'No' lies the suggestion that truthful relations cannot exist between women and men until *all* society is founded on human equality.

This is a strong theme in Schreiner's writing, and massively provocative in a South Africa hell-bent on minority rule. No society, Schreiner says, can flourish through 'the blossoming of a minute, abnormally situated, abnormally nourished class, unsupported by any vital connection with the classes beneath them or the nations around'; such a culture is 'without ground and [has] no root' (*From Man to Man* 192, 190; see also *Woman and Labour* 86-90). Rebekah's 'No' denies the novel the possibility of a conventionally happy ending: any narrative closure on a happy union between a white South African man and woman would forget the foundation of inequality over which it is laid. While the sexual relationship between Rebekah and Drummond would seem in strictly personal terms to be 'true', it would be fundamentally 'untrue' in the social or impersonal terms of concern to Schreiner.

In the relation between Rebekah and Clartje, the rupture of race cannot be repaired, but Schreiner uses the scene between them to set in motion a new plot development in which another attempt can be made, again with massive difficulty. When Clartje bears a daughter, whom, the text tells us (somewhat belatedly and cursorily), she does not want, Rebekah adopts the child and calls her Sartje. Much later, when her son Charles offers to walk freely with Sartje in the street, whatever the social disapproval, Rebekah's implicit 'No' — 'for her own sake I will not let her' (443) — foreshadows that other 'No', in a double insistence that readers recall the context of racial discrimination and its insidious effects on gender. The entry of the mixed-race child has already functioned as the entry of a new perspective — or the disturbance of an old perspective — which the novel instantiates through a set of stories that Rebekah uses to re-educate her sons, Clartje's unwitting half-brothers, whom she hopes to make better men than their father. She tells them two stories that give them lessons in identification with black people in general, and with women in particular. One of the stories is about an African woman warrior in the midst of a hopelessly unequal battle with European forces, handing out weapons to her fellow (male) warriors. The other is about an African woman who comes out of hiding to warn her fellows of the enemy's approach, even though she knows this will cost her her life. This second woman, Rebekah tells her children, shows 'a quality higher and of more importance to the race than those of any Bismarck'; she should be seen as 'the root out of which ultimately the noblest blossom of the human tree shall draw its strength' (197). We are reminded here of the African woman in the Wollstonecraft essay, who appears to function similarly for Schreiner as 'the root out of which … the noblest blossom of the human tree' will develop, although the 'passion' for independence that lies innate within her does not relate explicitly also to the African nation's independence, as it does here.

While the retrieval of an African perspective is not the dominant feature of the last chapter of the novel, it is subtly interwoven into the allegorical imagery, and it is this chapter, too, that winds up the text's strategy — initially articulated in the Wollstonecraft essay, and evident through the novel largely via Rebekah's hand-gestures and thought processes — of making dead yearnings and tendencies come alive. The chapter is devoted almost entirely to a conversation between Rebekah and Drummond about the creative impulse. The mother's storytelling has earlier been suggested as an environment for social change; this chapter establishes the work of art as an enabling environment as well. Creativity has three stages. First, an idea shapes itself in the artist, in the kind of 'sudden flash' that Schreiner herself had, she said, when she was inspired to write 'The Prelude' to *From Man to Man*:

> I was sitting at my dear old desk writing an article on the Bushmen and giving a description of their skulls; — when suddenly, in an instant, the whole of this little Prelude *flashed* on me … My mind must have been working at it *unconsciously*, though I knew nothing of it — otherwise how did it come? (To Adela Villiers Smith, 1909, ll. 27-30, 39-41, emphasis in original)

The idea is thus both born within the artist and comes from elsewhere. Second, the artist makes an external image of that internal idea, always looking to that 'copy within', which is the 'only guarantee of truth and right' (472). In the third stage, the artwork is severed from the artist: 'The child is weaned' (473). This severance may or may not issue in some form of publication, but Rebekah, quoting the Bible[13] — "'Shall I call to the birth and not cause to bring forth? saith the Lord'" — stresses the artist's longing that the original idea, the 'copy within', 'should live on — completely reflected in another mind as once it lived in his' (474-5).

Rebekah and Drummond's discussion is indebted to Plato's understanding of inspiration as a mysterious anamnesic power held by the poet, who is able to recollect the knowledge that the soul attains when in the company of the gods.[14] This leaning towards the ideal is related, in Schreiner's thinking, to what she called in 1903 'the will within us'. She defined this as 'that other vast reality' which we 'know & feel more intensely' than anything else in the universe and yet which remains 'uncomprehensible in its ultimate essence' (to S.C. Cronwright-Schreiner, 1903, ll. 17-18, 20). Her understanding of the 'will within us' would have been honed by her reading in German literature and philosophy, with its moral idealism (her favoured writers were Goethe and Schopenhauer, although she also read Schiller, Kant and Heine — all of whom had been influenced by Plato). It was also developed through her interest in Darwin, and specifically in the discussion throughout his work of latency, reversion and the interdependence of all organic beings within the overall context of the role of the environment. Schreiner's sense that the evolutionary history of any organism was retained in that organism and might re-emerge gave *From Man to Man* a powerful set of images through which she could develop, in part, that earlier inkling of passion referred to in the Wollstonecraft essay, and in the process harness it firmly to a human tendency that had everything to do with the socially protective instinct and nothing to do with brute force.

In her allegorising of the ideal, Schreiner generally made extensive use of Platonic imagery. In Plato, where wings soar or droop depending on their proximity to perfection, human love is a soul that 'soars upward' on her wings. An imperfect soul, on the other hand, loses her wings and, 'drooping in her flight, at last settles on the solid ground' (Plato 497). So, too, in *Woman and Labour*: when Schreiner spoke of a prostituted love, that degraded ideal, she portrayed a 'tired angel', her 'feather-shafts broken ... wings drabbled in the mire of lust

---

13   The quotation from the King James Bible, Isaiah 66.9 reads as follows: 'Shall I bring to the birth, and not cause to bring forth? saith the Lord'.

14   For a reference to the impact Plato had on her, see Olive Schreiner to Isaline Philpot.

and greed' (28). Rebekah uses similar imagery in one of the allegories she creates in her philosophising: a powerfully winged creature swoops down to encourage and advise the wounded and fettered figure of Humanity, who is shackled to the ground, detached from her ideal (224-5).

Schreiner's imagery of wings suited the politics of the time, as is particularly clear in the image of the Winged Victory of Samothrace, which Drummond marshals to allegorise the creative force in pursuit of the ideal. In the late Victorian era the Winged Victory assumed a key role in the public imagination. Statues of Nike were installed in public places, and the goddess's name appeared on trademarks and labels. The image was also taken up by the Suffragist movement: the emblem of the weekly journal, *Votes for Women*, which Sylvia Pankhurst designed in 1908, was an angel in green, purple and white, blowing a trumpet from which the word 'Freedom' unfurled (see Warner 141-4). The angel's wings, meanwhile, already had their own iconic register. Elizabeth Barrett Browning's poem 'To George Sand: A Desire' spoke of Sand's 'strong shoulders' as 'two pinions, white as wings of swan' (Browning 8-9). Drummond also discusses the possibility of wings on humans, reminding us of that vulnerable winged reptile, a figure of life-forms selected out by evolution.

Another of the text's reminders of a life-form selected out is the dicynodont skull, something specific to Africa, which Rebekah herself dug from the ground, and which she now imagines as the living creature coming out 'into the sunshine', making all life 'knit together even across boundless time' (475). The sunshine recalls images from *The Story of an African Farm* — the bees with their 'dreamy lyric' in the 'yellow sunshine' (299), Waldo, who 'Goes Out to Sit in the Sunshine' (292) and the African woman who chants a song like 'the humming of far-off bees' (292). These and other African images in the text suggest that Schreiner in this 'unfinished' novel is 'unfinishing' Europe, is reaching for ways in which to write Africa into European modernity.

I have already hinted that the scenes involving the outside room, and the imagined street, 'unfinish' whiteness in a peculiar way: white womanhood is not all we need to speak of when we speak of gender equality. These scenes also 'unfinish' the process of gender equality itself, which needs to incorporate racial equality as a key part of its process. Schreiner draws from her African setting the transformative images Africa can use to deliver itself from European domination and, equally importantly, to register African ways-of-being as a potentially transformative force over the European. In an extraordinarily powerful moment in the novel, when Rebekah imagines herself in a state of intensely pleasurable and peaceful fluidity between male and female, adult and child, she feels herself to be 'lying on the earth, on mats in the hut' (226), as if Africa, soon to be designated the 'cradle of humanity', were the site of such re-birth.[15]

Gender transformation is also figured in the statue of Hercules which Rebekah keeps in her study. Schreiner describes it as a bearded male figure looking fondly at the child in his arms. Drummond is the statue's substantiation: a motherly man, but not merely familially so, for he is a man with a strong sense of social duty. Schreiner's use of this figure (the statue plus Drummond) offers a counter to brute force and to the way society displaces care and compassion onto the feminine. It also poses a sharp challenge to the Social Darwinist tautology of the survival of the fittest. In Schreiner's Platonic Darwinism, the statue is a social force that has come (back) to life, born or re-born into the physical world, for nature itself had a 'copy within' which is now re-emerging in Rebekah's world as her own ideal and in her own practice as well: 'When I finger it and feel its beauty, the throb in him lives, across all the centuries, as an actual throb in me' (475).

Rebekah is sensual: when she passes the statue she strokes it, or, to quote the passage, 'strokes it down' (190). Her use of the verb, and — here — the verb plus adverb, recalls the stroking and the stroking down that take place elsewhere in the novel and, in the register of protectiveness, promote Schreiner's vision of the relation between the individual and the social, and hence of social reform. This relation is a key aspect of the creative process that Schreiner, ever Platonic, sees in erotic terms. The text provides repeated references to Rebekah's protective, creative hand stretched out as she tells stories to herself or others. In addition, there are repeated references to her hand touching the two youngest children (white boy, black girl) and also being touched by them.

If she is continually receiving and passing on to the children the 'throb' that first came from the statue into her hand, it seems also that she may be receiving from them *their* anamnesic memory of an ideal. The 'throb' and its passage have

---

15 The British Empire Exhibition in 1925 hung a banner reading 'Africa, the Cradle of Humanity' (Dubow 44).

now turned less vague than being simply the mysterious 'will within us'; they have become the sign of more specific social and familial practices, given the racialised context of the mothering and storytelling. The imagery of the dead coming alive which Schreiner uses in the Wollstonecraft introduction not only enters *From Man to Man* in the form of a passionate 'throb' of desire for an ideal world, and not only makes the argument of the novel come alive, but it also imbues the act of writing with the awareness of those whose fulfilment has been sacrificed in the path to the present but who now come back to life, as it were, in the history that lies in the words on the page. Rebekah is often portrayed in the novel as a writer: letter-writing, note-taking, annotating the margins of books, and engaging in the solitary philosophising that Schreiner herself called 'writing' as opposed to the graphic 'writing out' that put words on the page. The text thereby suggests that this complex social force with its simple name, 'mother-love', passes from the statue into the writerly hand. The hand in *From Man to Man*, which is at once a connecting hand, a protective hand and a writing hand, also functions as a kind of evolutionary hand that stretches down, as it were, from either the past or the future into the present, for on two key occasions in the novel a great hand reaches down to, or arms fold themselves around, the two women characters at a time of their greatest anguish.

Enfolding arms, unfolding wings. At the start of this essay I referred to the fossil of the winged reptile that Rebekah passes on to Drummond, and that Schreiner in a sense passes on to us: a complex signifier, now, if we can gather into it what else has been throbbing in the novel: motherly love or the protective instinct, a duty towards social cohesiveness that allows for individual autonomy, equality across difference. These were the components of what Schreiner loosely defines as the human ideal, and which she sees as so crucial for her time and place. Only through protecting and nurturing this ideal could society hope to ward off the disasters consequent on white racism and capitalist greed. Schreiner converts futility and death into a connecting throb of life, and she uses the fossil and related images to establish connections between the past and the present, the dead and the alive, the so-called primitive and the so-called civilised, the Greek and the African. All these things she connects in her fictional quest for the human ideal, which she saw as a parity among all — a parity based in economic equality but also allowing for the kind of individual aspiration that would serve humanity rather than merely the individual.

Works Cited

Letters

Olive Schreiner Letters Online, www.oliveschreiner.org

>Olive Schreiner to Adela Villiers Smith née Villiers, October 1909, National Library of South Africa, Cape Town, Special Collections.

>Olive Schreiner to Edward Carpenter, 23 April 1888, Sheffield Libraries, Archives & Information.

>Olive Schreiner to Edward Carpenter, 19 February 1909, Sheffield Libraries, Archives & Information.

>Olive Schreiner to Edward Carpenter, 7 January 1911, National English Literary Museum, Grahamstown.

>Olive Schreiner to Edward Carpenter, 23 July 1913, National English Literary Museum, Grahamstown.

>Olive Schreiner to Emily Hobhouse, 3 October 1908, Hobhouse Trust.

>Olive Schreiner to Francis (Frank) Ernest Colenso, 23 September 1908, Bodleian Library of Commonwealth and African Studies, Rhodes House, University of Oxford.

>Olive Schreiner to Havelock Ellis, 18 December 1884, Harry Ransom Humanities Research Center, University of Texas, Austin.

>Olive Schreiner to Havelock Ellis, 10 March 1886, National Library of South Africa, Cape Town, Special Collections.

>Olive Schreiner to Havelock Ellis, 23 May 1890, Harry Ransom Humanities Research Center, University of Texas, Austin.

>Olive Schreiner to Havelock Ellis, 21 August 1914, National Library of South Africa, Cape Town, Special Collections.

>Olive Schreiner to Isaline Philpot, August 1887, National Library of South Africa, Cape Town, Special Collections.

>Olive Schreiner to John X. Merriman, 11 August 1912, National Library of South Africa, Cape Town, Special Collections.

>Olive Schreiner to Karl Pearson, 10 July 1886, University College London Library, Special Collections, UCL, London.

Olive Schreiner to Karl Pearson, 13 July 1886, University College London Library, Special Collections, UCL, London.

Olive Schreiner to Mary Brown née Solomon, 1 December 1908, National Library of South Africa, Cape Town, Special Collections.

Olive Schreiner to Minnie or Mimmie Murray née Parkes, August 1908, National English Literary Museum, Grahamstown.

Olive Schreiner to Minnie or Mimmie Murray née Parkes, 30 August 1909, National English Literary Museum, Grahamstown.

Olive Schreiner to S.C. ('Cron') Cronwright-Schreiner, 16 July 1903, National Library of South Africa, Cape Town, Special Collections.

Olive Schreiner to William Philip ('Will') Schreiner, 4 June 1908, University of Cape Town Manuscripts & Archives.

Olive Schreiner to William Philip ('Will') Schreiner, 24 April 1909, UCT Manuscripts & Archives.

Olive Schreiner to William Philip ('Will') Schreiner, 29 July 1912, UCT Manuscripts & Archives.

Olive Schreiner to William Philip ('Will') Schreiner, January 1916, UCT Manuscripts & Archives.

Other Sources

Berkman, Joyce Avrech. *The Healing Imagination of Olive Schreiner: Beyond South African Colonialism*. Amherst: University of Massachusetts Press, 1989.

Browning, Elizabeth Barrett. *The Poetical Works of Elizabeth Barrett Browning*. London: Smith, Elder & Co., 1897.

Burdett, Carolyn. 'A Difficult Vindication: Olive Schreiner's Wollstonecraft Introduction.' *History Workshop Journal* 37.1 (1994): 177-88.

———. *Olive Schreiner*. Tavistock, Devon: Northcote House, 2013.

———. *Olive Schreiner and the Progress of Feminism: Evolution, Gender, Empire*. Basingstoke, Hampshire & New York: Palgrave, 2001.

Chrisman, Laura. 'Allegory, Feminist Thought and the *Dreams* of Olive Schreiner.' *Prose Studies: History, Theory, Criticism* 13.1 (1990): 126-50.

Clayton, Cherry. Ed. *Olive Schreiner*. Johannesburg: McGraw-Hill, 1983.

———. *Olive Schreiner*. New York: Twayne, 1997.

Cronwright-Schreiner, S.C. *The Life of Olive Schreiner*. London: Unwin, 1924.

———. Introduction; and appended ending. *From Man to Man*, by Olive Schreiner. London: T. Fisher Unwin, 1926. 9-17, 481-3.

Darwin, Charles. *On the Origin of Species by Means of Natural Selection, or the Preservation of Favoured Races in the Struggle for Life*. 1859. In *The Works of Charles Darwin*. Ed. Paul H. Barrett & R.B. Freeman. Vol 15. London: William Pickering, 1988.

———. *The Variation of Animals and Plants Under Domestication*. 1868. Rev. 1875. 2 vols. In *The Works of Charles Darwin*. Ed. Paul H. Barrett and R.B. Freeman. Vols 19 and 20. London: William Pickering, 1988.

De Beauvoir, Simone. *The Second Sex*. Trans. H.M. Parshley. 1953. New York: Vintage Books, 1973.

De Lauretis, Teresa. 'Displacing Hegemonic Discourses: Reflections on Feminist Theory.' *Inscriptions* 3 & 4 (1988): 127-44.

Driver, Dorothy. 'Reclaiming Olive Schreiner: A Rereading of *From Man to Man*.' *South African Literary History: Totality and/or Fragment*. Ed. Edward Reckwitz, Karin Reitner & Lucia Vennarini. Essen: Die Blaue Eule, 1997. 111-20.

Dubow, Saul. *Scientific Racism in Modern South Africa*. Cambridge: Cambridge UP, 1995.

First, Ruth and Ann Scott. *Olive Schreiner*. London: André Deutsch, 1980.

Foot, Paul. Introduction. *From Man to Man*, by Olive Schreiner. London: Virago, 1982. ix-xvii.

Graham, Lucy. *State of Peril: Race and Rape in South African Literature*. Oxford: Oxford UP, 2012.

James, Henry. *The Art of the Novel: Critical Prefaces*. Ed. Richard P. Blackmur. New York: Scribner, 1934.

Kristeva, Julia. 'The Subject in Process.' *The Tel Quel Reader*. Ed. Patrick Ffrench and Roland-Francois Lack. London and New York: Routledge, 1998. 133-78.

Lovell-Smith, Rose. 'Science and Religion in the Feminist Fin-de-Siècle and a

New Reading of Olive Schreiner's *From Man to Man.*' *Victorian Literature and Culture* 29.2 (2001): 303-26.

Monsman, Gerald. *Olive Schreiner's Fiction: Landscape and Power*. New Brunswick: Rutgers UP, 1991.

Plato. *Phaedrus*. Trans. Benjamin Jowett. www.gutenberg.org. Produced by Sue Asscher and David Widger. Release Date: October 10, 2008 [EBook #1635]. Last Updated: 15 January 2013.

Schoeman, Karel. *Olive Schreiner: A Woman in South Africa 1855-1881*. Johannesburg: Jonathan Ball, 1991.

Schreiner, Olive. *Closer Union*. Cape Town: The Constitutional Reform Association, 1908.

——. 'The Dawn of Civilization'. 1921. *Words in Season*. Ed. Stephen Gray. Johannesburg: Penguin, 2005. 205-14.

——. *Dreams*. 1890. London: Wildwood House, 1982.

——. *From Man to Man*. London: T. Fisher Unwin, 1926.

——. *From Man to Man*. 1926. London: Virago, 1982.

——. 'Introduction to A Vindication.' 1994. *Words in Season*. Ed. Stephen Gray. Johannesburg: Penguin, 2005. 19-28.

——. 'Introduction to the Life of Mary Wollstonecraft and The Rights of Woman.' Ed. Carolyn Burdett. *History Workshop Journal* 37.1 (1994): 189-93.

——. 'Letter on John Stuart Mill.' 1918. *Words in Season*. Ed. Stephen Gray. Johannesburg: Penguin, 2005. 204.

——. Ms. of *From Man to Man*. Harry Ransom Humanities Research Center, University of Texas, Austin. The Olive Schreiner Collection MS-3734. Box 1, folder 1.3.

——. *The Story of an African Farm*. 1883. Harmondsworth: Penguin, 1995.

——. *Thoughts on South Africa*. 1923. Parklands, Johannesburg: Ad Donker, 1992.

——. *Woman and Labour*. 1911. London: Virago, 1978.

Schreiner, Olive and S.C. Cronwright-Schreiner. *The Political Situation*. London: Unwin, 1896.

Stanley, Liz. *Imperialism, Labour and the New Woman: Olive Schreiner's Social Theory.* Durham: Sociologypress, 2002.

Steele, Murray. 'A Humanist Bible: Gender Roles, Sexuality and Race in Olive Schreiner's *From Man to Man.*' *Gender Roles and Sexuality in Victorian Literature.* Ed. Christopher Parker. Aldershot: Scolar, 1995. 101-14.

Tennyson, Alfred. *In Memoriam.* 1849. London: C. Kegan Paul, 1880.

Voss, Anthony. '*From Man to Man*: Heroic Fragment.' *The Flawed Diamond: Essays on Olive Schreiner.* Ed. Itala Vivan. Sydney: Dangaroo Press, 1991. 135-45.

Warner, Marina. *Monuments and Maidens: The Allegory of the Female Form.* London: Pan, 1987.

8

Guy Boothby's 'Bid for Fortune': constructing an Anglo-Australian colonial identity for the *fin-de-siècle* London literary marketplace

Ailise Bulfin[1]

'Mr. Boothby seems ... almost as much of a traveller as the mysterious Dr. Nikola ... as familiar with the South Sea Islands, Australasian capitals, and Eastern towns as he is with London.' *The Times* (27 Dec 1895)

In 1891 the aspiring young Adelaide-born author Guy Boothby set sail from his native city seeking the wider opportunities of London. After several pitfalls along the way, he eventually arrived and made his name with the indecisively-titled *A Bid for Fortune, or Dr Nikola's Vendetta*, an international crime thriller which took the London literary marketplace by storm in 1895 and catapulted its author to overnight celebrity status. While the novel's subtitle 'Dr Nikola's Vendetta' is far more suggestive of its content, turning as it does upon the machinations of the criminal mastermind Dr Nikola (ultimately Boothby's best-known character), the main title, 'A Bid for Fortune', can be read as highly suggestive

---

[1] The author gratefully acknowledges that this research has been funded by a Government of Ireland Scholarship from the Irish Research Council for the Humanities and Social Sciences.

Figure 1: 'Guy Boothby: The Creator of Dr Nikola.' *The Windsor Magazine* 4 (December 1896: 129).[2]

of Boothby's outlook on novel writing. One of the new identities developing in the late-Victorian period was that of the 'popular novelist', as Boothby termed it (*Love Made Manifest* 25). Though there was nothing new about the celebration of the author, the well-documented burgeoning of the book and literary periodical trade in the late-nineteenth century increased the number and prominence of a new breed of celebrity author.[3] With the general boom in printing, far more column inches were available for the discussion and veneration of the author. Indeed, new book trade periodicals—such as *The Bookman*, launched in London in 1891 for 'Bookbuyers, Bookreaders and Booksellers' — required endless copy on popular authors in order to supplement their review pages and bestseller lists.[4] The literary magazines abounded with laudatory articles on the activities and opinions of popular authors, frequently those whose tales graced their own pages, such as the two *Windsor Magazine* interviews with Boothby referred to subsequently in this chapter. And this trend is mirrored in a new emphasis observable in contemporary non-literary periodicals such as the satirical *Punch* magazine, which from the late 1880s featured a spoof book review column, 'Our

---

2 All images from The Windsor Magazine are reproduced with the permission of the Board of Trinity College Dublin.

3 For an account of the development of the literary marketplace in the late-nineteenth century see Keating, ch. 1.

4 For more on the impact of *The Bookman* see Bassett and Walker 205-36.

Booking-Office' by the 'Baron De Book-Worms,' and increasingly targeted both popular fiction and its well-known producers, such as H. Rider Haggard, Arthur Conan Doyle and Rudyard Kipling, as subjects for lampoon.[5]

While the London literary marketplace had expanded to support growing numbers of celebrity authors, competition to achieve this coveted status had likewise increased making it progressively more difficult for new authors to make their name. Clearly the possession of a distinguishing attribute that would make a prospective author stand out would be hugely advantageous. This chapter will examine Boothby's bid to become a popular novelist, arguing that he seized upon his colonial background to construct a new and distinctive Anglo-Australian authorial identity for himself and thereby create a selling point for his work in the crowded metropolitan literary marketplace. His successful attempt makes him highly representative of this new breed of celebrity author, whose popularity, though intense, was often ephemeral, whose work often did not transcend its era of publication, and who emerged dramatically to occupy the columns of the literary periodicals for a time before fading equally quickly into obscurity. Tracking the trajectory of Boothby's now-forgotten career therefore provides fresh insight into the workings of the fin-de-siècle London literary marketplace, the experience of immigrant Anglo-Australian authors writing for it, and the operation of this new kind of authorial identity within it. Boothby, himself, though now almost completely forgotten by general readers and consigned to the margins of academic scholarship, was for a time a bestselling author whose work warrants critical attention for the very popularity it attained.[6]

Boothby was by no means the first author to fruitfully draw upon his colonial experience in his popular tales. It is no coincidence that of the authors listed above as targets of *Punch*, Haggard and Kipling are two whose works are characterised by a deep engagement with empire, and Haggard's forerunning

---

5   See, for example, the satirical rhyme from 1895, 'A Hopeless Case', which laments the proliferation of the 'monthly magazines' and sends up several authors including Doyle (113).

6   There is currently very little sustained academic engagement with Boothby; of the small extant body of research, Dixon includes an insightful chapter on Boothby's Dr Nikola novels as imperial crime fiction, Ouyang analyses his fictional treatment of the Chinese, and Weaver's article includes a discussion of the depiction of Aboriginal-settler conflict in his short fiction.

success had notably paved the way for such an approach. Haggard had spent a formative period as a young man in Britain's South African colonies and many of his most popular novels are characterised by exotic African locations and characters that contributed hugely to their appeal. In fact, Gerald Monsman, a recent literary biographer of Haggard, goes so far as to class him as an Anglo-African author, so heavily does he believe Haggard's African experience to weigh upon his texts (3). The Anglo-Indian Kipling was another flourishing hyphenated author of the day and one who may have had a direct influence on Boothby's career, as this chapter will discuss. There is a substantial body of research into the impact of their respective African and Indian experiences upon these major and enduring authors of the period, and even on Doyle, whose Irish descent allows him to be examined from this perspective.[7] It is useful to likewise examine Boothby, although he is not of similar stature, because it facilitates an elucidation of the comparable Anglo-Australian experience.

In Australia, at the same time that authorial coloniality was driving the success of the imperial romance in the metropolis, the well-documented development of a new, distinctive Australian identity constructed against that of metropolitan Britain was entering a crucial phase. And many cultural historians and literary critics have analysed the role of Australian popular fiction in the delineation and dissemination of this mythic 'rugged' settler identity during the period of Boothby's youth in the 1880s and 1890s.[8] Less research has been undertaken on the subject of defining and exploiting this Australianness in order to market fiction in the imperial centre at this time, and it is the intention of this chapter to partially address this gap by examining Boothby's successful bid to do so.[9] Boothby's hyphenated identity, moreover, seems not only to have been a rich vein to be tapped for the metropolitan market but also a source of

---

7 See the Monsman biography of Haggard and the Allen and Lycett biographies of Kipling; see also Wynne on Doyle.

8 See Rickard, who tracks the development of the new identity and the settler myth of bush life in the 'ballad[s] and slice-of-life' stories promoted by the influential *Bulletin* newspaper (64, 70, 129). See also Dixon, who examines the parallel process of narrating the nascent Australian nation in the Australian colonial adventure novel.

9 The exploitation of Australianness is touched on in aspects of Trainor on the relationship between Australian writers and British publishers, and White ('Cooees') on the touristic performance of Australian identity in London.

conflict for him, producing a sense of dislocation from both his birth colony and his new metropolitan home. This conflict is apparent in the public Anglo-Australian authorial persona Boothby constructed, which alternately valorises his outré colonial background and his acquired status of English country squire. Likewise, it pervades his fiction, manifesting itself in some idiosyncratic representations that ultimately seem to favour his Australian heritage, as this chapter will explore.

On examination, Boothby's colonial youth bears some interesting similarities to Kipling's. Just as Kipling considered himself Anglo-Indian rather than purely English, Boothby thought of himself as Anglo-Australian, though each author in fact spent the majority of their lives outside their colonial birthplaces. Born within two years of each other, both authors were sent at an early age to school in England before returning at sixteen to their home colonies for a formative period of their early adulthood during which they both began writing. Likewise, each man, after a period of extensive travel, returned within five years of each other (between 1889 and 1894) to London as the appropriate place to launch their literary careers. While Kipling's success and biographical details are well-known, Boothby has long since fallen into obscurity and the little-known details of his life require some elaboration. He was born in Adelaide in 1867 to a leading family of the then British colony of South Australia. However, when he was aged approximately seven his English-born mother, whom he held in great regard, separated from his father and returned with her children to England. After a traditional English grammar school education, Boothby returned alone to South Australia at sixteen, where, following the family tradition, he entered the colonial administration, as a clerk. His natural inclinations ran more to the creative than to the administrative, though, and he soon began writing for the theatre. When his melodramas failed to gain him suitable acclaim in Adelaide and when severe economic collapse hit most of the Australian colonies, he followed the well-beaten path to London in December 1891.

Many cultural historians note the limited opportunities for authors in small colonial societies such as Adelaide and the ever-present lure of London as the cultural capital of the empire (Rickard 93-5, 129; Trainor 140-55). Boothby himself acknowledges this situation via the experiences of the struggling young protagonist of *Love Made Manifest* (1899) who has failed to have a 'book …

published, [or] a play produced' in Australia, causing the novel's narrator to lament: 'The Colonies, ever ready to claim talent when it has been thoroughly recognised elsewhere, were almost stoical in their firmness not to encourage him in his endeavours' (21). Correspondingly, it is then revealed that the young author 'had all his life entertained a desire that was almost a craving to see and know for himself the life of the greatest city in the world' (23). Boothby, however, was thwarted in his first bid for recognition as lack of funds forced him to disembark en route in Colombo, Sri Lanka, and begin making his way homewards through South-east Asia. According to family historians Robinson and Spence, the dire poverty he faced on this journey led him to accept any kind of work he could get: 'This meant working before the mast, stoking in ocean tramps, attending in a Chinese opium den in Singapore, digging in the Burmah Ruby fields, acting, prize fighting, cow punching' (qtd in Depasquale, *Boothby* 17). All this occured before he arrived at Thursday Island off the north Queensland coast, where he worked briefly as a pearl diver and then made an arduous journey overland across the Australian continent home to Adelaide (partly by buggy as shown in Figure 2). While this account of his travels may be somewhat glamorous, Boothby certainly travelled extensively in South-east Asia and Australia at this period, collecting a stock of colonial experiences and anecdotes that were to inform most of his later writing.

Boothby 'the novelist-merchant': selling the Australasian periphery

In 1893, approximately two years after his first failed journey, Boothby set off again for London. He finally arrived early in 1894 and succeeded in having an account of his previous peregrinations, *On the Wallaby, or Through the East and Across Australia*, published that year. This travelogue met with reasonable success, which was matched later that year by Boothby's first novel, *In Strange Company*. This text, which was set variously in England, Australia, the South Seas and South America, established a pattern that was to characterise the succeeding Boothby oeuvre: the use of exotic, international and particularly Australasian locales that frequently function as an end in themselves superfluous to the requirements of plot.

By October 1895, the prolific Boothby had completed three further novels, including the bestselling *A Bid for Fortune* — and an outline of its narrative

Figure 2: 'Across Australia.' Guy Boothby, *On the Wallaby* (London: Longmans, Green & Co., 1894): ii.

itinerary provides a useful example of Boothby's use of place. Opening in London, the novel introduces international master-criminal Dr Nikola and his host of colonial misfit henchmen, all recently arrived from exotic locations. The scene abruptly shifts to Sydney, introducing the protagonist, Richard Hatteras, who is about to embark for London. Onboard ship he meets the heroine — this representative in-transit encounter highlighted in the novel's cover detail — but soon after arriving in London she returns abruptly to Sydney under threat from the devilish doctor. After a brief interval Hatteras himself sets sail again for Sydney, stopping in Port Said to allow Boothby to indulge in a little orientalism. Here he also showcases Nikola's exotic secret headquarters (Figure 3) where Hatteras is detained while Nikola furthers his scheme against the heroine's family. Once back in Sydney, after tracking Nikola to a seedy Chinatown lair, Hatteras must set off for a Melanesian island in pursuit of Nikola and the now-kidnapped heroine. On successfully securing his ransom, Nikola makes good his escape. And the happy couple, reunited in Sydney, embark at once for England

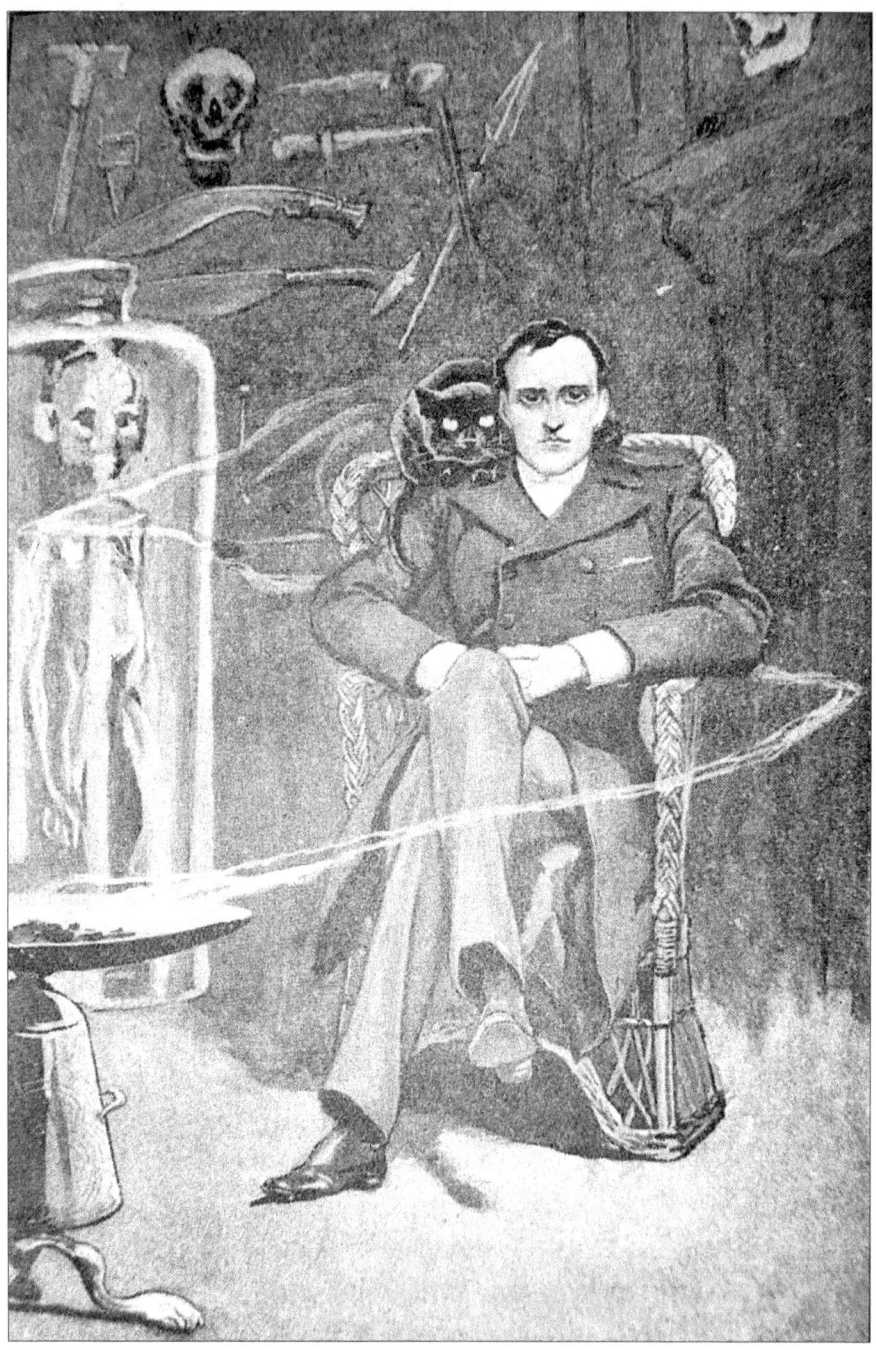

Figure 3: Frontispiece. Guy Boothby, *A Bid for Fortune* (London: Ward, Lock & Bowden, 1895).

and retirement to a country estate where presumably their hitherto constant motion can finally cease.

Robert Dixon, one of the few critics to write extensively on Boothby and who characterises him as the 'model of a popular romance writer of the day', considers travel to be the dominant motif of *A Bid for Fortune*. He aptly reads travel as 'a definitively modern, though profoundly disorienting experience' which in Boothby's usage reveals a crisis in the imperial identity (162-3). However, focusing on the places themselves rather than the motion between them, what the use of locale also reveals is Boothby's superlative manipulation of his colonial background and experience to create a compelling selling point for his work. As I argue elsewhere, it was the new international dimension assigned to Boothby's master-criminal Nikola character that differentiated him from forerunning exemplars of the type such as Doyle's Moriarty and contributed greatly to his appeal (Bulfin, 'Sherlock Holmes'). In the frontispiece to *A Bid for Fortune* (Figure 3) Nikola is situated in an exotic location designed to accentuate the menacing alterity upon which his character is predicated, a device replicated textually and illustratively across the Nikola series. Certainly, the *Times* reviewer of *A Bid for Fortune* was convinced by Boothby's cosmopolitan strategy, announcing: 'Mr. Boothby seems ... almost as much of a traveller as the mysterious Dr. Nikola ... as familiar with the South Sea Islands, Australasian capitals, and Eastern towns as he is with London' ('Recent Novels' 1895, 10).

A major factor which may have influenced Boothby in the production of this brand of Australasian adventure fiction was an encounter with Kipling, master of the colonial tale, while Boothby was still a struggling melodramatist. Paul Depasquale, author of the only Boothby biography, has amassed convincing evidence that Boothby was prompted to make the transition to novel writing by a brief meeting with Kipling while the latter was passing through Adelaide in 1891 (*Boothby* 115-20).[10] Kipling, by then a major literary phenomenon, did Boothby the invaluable service of putting him in touch with his literary agent, the renowned A.P. Watt, who helped Boothby break into the London literary

---

10 Depasquale notes that no known papers exist for Boothby, which leave the details of his life sketchy at best. Therefore, in this article I have extensively used commentary pertaining to Boothby from contemporary periodicals, particularly the literary review magazines, to provide further insight into his work and his place in the literary world.

marketplace.¹¹ Luke Trainor has established that by the 1890s a small Australian niche had developed in the British literary market, partly in response to the success achieved there by the tales of a forerunning producer of Australian colonial adventure fiction, Rolf Boldrewood (146-53), a circumstance that Boothby was more than likely aware of. That Boldrewood had previously secured Watt as his agent is significant: it would have ensured Watt's awareness of the interest in this type of fiction, and possibly encouraged him to take on the unknown Boothby, who, via his relocation to London, was better positioned to raise the profile of Anglo-Australian fiction there than the Melbourne-based Boldrewood. The acquaintance Kipling and Boothby struck up continued when Boothby moved to London: Kipling's endorsement was used by Boothby's publishers to boost his sales, and their friendship was frequently noted in the literary magazines. *The Bookman*, for example, in January 1895 mythologises their initial encounter in Australia, reiterating a much-touted claim that Kipling called to Boothby from aboard ship on his departure, 'Stick to it, and put your trust in Watt' ('News Notes' 105).

Just as Kipling's success derived in part from a popular perception of his privileged position as Anglo-Indian insider, able to decode the enigmas of Britain's Far Eastern empire for the domestic audience, so Boothby may have hoped to establish himself as a corresponding Anglo-Australian authority. Gail Ching-Liang Low exposes what she considers Kipling's affectation of this interpretive role in *Kim* (1901): '[Kipling's] task is to make people "see"; to become the authoritative voice on native affairs — the interpreter that would seek to translate native terms into English ones' (Low 234). And it is plausible to argue that Boothby was likewise trying to set himself up as a new mediator of all things Australasian for the metropolitan reader. *On the Wallaby*, for example, opens with the author's note that the title is 'a slang Australianism for "On the march" … generally applied to persons tramping the bush in search of employment'. And this is quickly followed by the author's assertion in the introduction that he and his travelling companion had 'experienced almost every phase of colonial life … from Government officials and stock-brokers, to dramatists, actors, conjurors, ventriloquists, goldminers and station hands' (xvi). In the same vein,

---

11 Watt's role in launching Boothby's career is acknowledged in a grateful 1894 letter from Boothby to Watt (qtd in Depasquale, 'An Incomplete Essay' 53-4).

the two other novels Boothby wrote in 1895, as per *A Bid for Fortune*, featured antipodean backdrops that showcased his intimate knowledge of the Australian territories — *A Lost Endeavour* being set solely on Thursday Island and *The Marriage of Esther* ranging across several Torres Strait islands.

Boothby's chief outlet at the time, *The Windsor Magazine: An Illustrated Monthly for Men and Women*, was a new, middlebrow *Strand Magazine* imitator which broke into the literary market place with good success in January 1895, its opening issue featuring the first instalment of *A Bid for Fortune*.¹² The *Windsor*'s opening foreword states that its 'chief purpose' is 'to widen ... [the] outlook' of 'the family hearth' with tales of 'the glamour of the world and the great mysterious movement beyond the borders of the home' ('A Foreword' 2). Its pages are correspondingly filled with exotic colonial tales, of which Boothby's are highly representative, and equivalent lightweight, informative non-fiction articles. The *Windsor* published eight Boothby short stories between 1895 and 1897, all of which were situated in Australia even though the location was not

Figure 4: 'The new Jackeroo.' Guy Boothby, 'The Reformation of the Jackeroo.' *The Windsor Magazine* 6 (1897): 280.

---

12   For a description of the magazine see Sullivan 453. Boothby's Nikola character was heavily marketed in conjunction with the magazine's launch and was influential in establishing the magazine's success. A series of eye-catching, intriguing advertisements were run in the literary classifieds worded simply 'Who is Dr Nikola?' and large pictures of the character graced the hoardings to the extent that they warranted frequent comment (see, for example, *The Times* 11 May 1895: 2 and 27 December 1895: 10).

always relevant to the plot. Representative of the tales that turned upon their Australian setting is 'The Reformation of the Jackeroo' (1897) (or 'colonial experiencer' as Boothby translates), who is depicted arriving at an outback station in Figure 4.

In this tale, Boothby, the insider, knowingly sends up metropolitan preconceptions of Australia, which as all knew was 'populated only by savages and squatters, with a few goldminers and convicts thrown in for the sake of picturesqueness ... of necessity ... barren in the wants of civilisation' (279). In fact, the colonial experience turns out to be the making of the profligate young English protagonist, a recurrent theme in the Boothby oeuvre. Many of these stories were re-issued in the 1897 collection *Bushigrams*, the intriguing Australianism of the title again designed to suggest a certain kind of colonial tale, and the suggestion reinforced by the stereotyped outback scene of swagmen sitting around a billycan depicted in the cover detail (Figure 5). Interestingly, the *Bookman* review of the collection observes both the catchiness of the 'truly wonderful title' and the sometimes superfluity of the Australian settings: 'The common belief that Bushigrams deal with the bush is entirely erroneous ... Many Bushigrams are merely histories of mild flirtations in a colonial ballroom' ('Novel Notes' 132).

An interview with Boothby published in the *Windsor* in December 1896, entitled 'The Creator of "Dr Nikola": An afternoon with Guy Boothby', reveals not only the success of the Nikola novels but also that Boothby was already noted for his Australian expertise. The interviewer admiringly remarks:

> With every phase of Australian life Mr Boothby is acquainted ... The pathos of the Australian solitudes has entered into [him]. He tells, as one who understands, how men ... live apart — three hundred miles perhaps from the next neighbour ... The humour, too, of the life — the rough and ready pungent humour — he has made his own. (Hyde 132)

In the interview Boothby's carefully-worded, knowing descriptions of this life, while glossing over other questions, reveal what seems to be a considered effort to establish an experienced Anglo-Australian identity for himself to act as a foundation for his fiction. Analysing accounts of nineteenth-century Australian travellers to London, Richard White observes that the experience of the metropolis seemed to heighten their awareness of national differences. He

Figure 5: Cover detail. Guy Boothby, *Bushigrams* (London: Ward, Lock & Co., 1897).

holds that this frequently led them to engage in a self-conscious 'performance of Australian identity', as it differed from metropolitan British identity, based on attributes such as the 'cooee' bush call that were popularly construed as Australian ('Cooees' 112). While White's conclusion — that this performance of difference was ultimately co-opted for nationalist purposes to legitimate Australian calls for self-government — is not applicable to Boothby, it is arguable that the aspirant author engaged in a similar self-conscious performance for marketing purposes. Interestingly, Graham Huggan, in his 2007 survey of Australian literature, observes the 'marketability of nationality' in the context of contemporary Australian emigrant authors spinning Australian 'yarns' for their new metropolitan audiences, demonstrating the ongoing effectiveness of this kind of transnational literary approach (2). The efficacy of Boothby's pose is apparent in a positive *Athenaeum* review of the third Nikola novel, *The Lust of Hate* (1898). In actuality a poorly constructed work, the review sets it above other similar adventure novels due to its 'sketches of life in Australia' which are 'evidently based on personal knowledge and observation' ('Tales of Adventure' 498). Boothby's ongoing maintenance of this new authorial identity is evident in a subsequent 1901 *Windsor* feature on Boothby 'At Home', throughout which he repeatedly ignores questions concerning professional authorship in favour of reiterating 'anecdotes of the times he had spent "on the wallaby"' or tramping across Australia (Klickman 299). That he is still harking back to a single trip, undertaken nearly a decade ago, emphasises the import he continued to attach to projecting this experienced colonial-Australian persona.

Boothby's style of writing, given that he averaged five novels a year, is superficial to say the least, and briskly summed up in his *Times* 'Obituary' as 'frank sensationalism carried to its furthest limits' (10). Speed and plagiarism typified his method, a contemporary review observing admiringly 'the facility of style with which Mr Boothby throws off novel after novel apparently without effort', and noting that as a matter of course '[h]e borrows ideas but adapts them to his purposes with ... deft ingenuity' ('Recent Novels' 1898, 10). Boothby borrowed unreservedly from current events, prevailing theories and contemporary popular works, linking elements of each together within a blur of action, and writing at such a speed that his output could almost be considered stream-of-consciousness. For this reason, while frequently making poor reading, his fiction is pertinent not only for the insight it provides into his Anglo-Australian identity but also as a veritable index of fin-de-siècle social and cultural concerns. Depasquale, who may be the only person in recent years to have read the entire Boothby oeuvre, claims that Boothby deliberately adopted an unchallenging popular style and wrote at such a breakneck pace in order to maximise sales (*Boothby* 30, 42, 92). And as well as exploiting his Australian experience, Boothby cynically exploited popular racial and social prejudices, populating his novels with an array of foreign and deformed villains whose obvious degeneracy was designed to titillate his readers and encourage identification with his simplistic, undemanding protagonists. In using his colonial knowledge he never challenged the preconceptions of his sedentary metropolitan readership, writing rather, as he claims in the dedication of *The Marriage of Esther*, of the 'queer places and still queerer folk (the like of which must necessarily lie outside the ken of the stay-at-home Englishman's experience)'. This reveals the Boothbian pose of appearing well-travelled, while pandering to the common prejudice of English superiority. As Edward Said complains of the earlier oriental traveller Alexander Kinglake, rather than gaining any real insight from his travels, Boothby's colonial experience seemed to act merely to 'solidify' his 'anti-Semitism, xenophobia, and general all-purpose race prejudice … [m]any of the attitudes he repeats are canonical, of course, but it is interesting to see how little the experience of actually seeing the Orient affected his opinions' (193).

For Boothby, as well as in the reiterated reviews lauding his colonial savvy, strong evidence for the effectiveness of his Anglo-Australian performance was his spectacular financial success. The first *Windsor* interview of 1896 is testament to Boothby's comfortable establishment as a new celebrity author. Here he made the startling revelation that after only two years as a professional writer, he was now working on his seventeenth novel, and gave tips to aspiring young writers. The article was illustrated with photographs which show Boothby at work in his 'pretty residence in Surbiton', and mentions an impending move to a larger property which would better reflect his improved status. The subsequent 1901 *Windsor* interview is accompanied by photos of a stouter and more affluent Boothby engaged in country pursuits in his impressive, new forty-acre Thameside residence. This pattern of moving from grander to grander residence fits with Depasquale's assertion, from his reading of the Boothby oeuvre, that Boothby's ultimate goal is retirement to an English country estate (*Boothby* 29). This assertion is certainly borne out both in the conclusions of many of Boothby's narratives and by this interview, during which Boothby not only reiterates his Australian tales but also takes great pains to show off his new model farm. These two aspects of the interview also provide an insight into the conflict in Boothby's Anglo-Australian identity in that he laboriously emphasises both the exotic colonial background which differentiates him from mainstream English experience, and his new, privileged status as English country squire which conforms to the domestic ideal.

Boothby's accomplishment as professional author is apparent from his constant presence on the contemporary bestseller lists between 1894 and his early death in 1905 (Bassett and Walker 205-36).[13] At the height of his career, he was earning an estimated £20,000 a year ('Boothby, Guy Newell'), and Nick Rennison considers him 'one of the ... most financially successful novelists of his time' (210). This is borne out by the fact that when the *Academy* magazine ran a spoof article in 1900 claiming that he had installed a solid gold bath in his latest mansion, it was credible enough to be reiterated across nine British periodicals, even crossing the Atlantic to feature in a couple of US magazines ('Old Par's Wanderings' 579-80). However, all this success was not enough to sustain the lavish lifestyle Boothby had adopted. His series of impressive residences were rented, and he was forced to keep writing at a tremendous rate to maintain them, while the quality of his output steadily declined.[14] He worked long, unsociable hours, dictating his novels onto a phonograph for transcription by a team of secretaries. And his career was cut short when in February 1905, at the early age of thirty-seven, he died suddenly of pneumonia, quite possibly brought on as a result of overwork. He had completed a staggering fifty-three novels over the previous ten years, not to mention dozens of short stories and plays (Sutherland xiii). The following satirical poem of 1899 attests to the impression Boothby had made upon the literary profession during his short career:

---

13   This article also observes that Boothby was the eighth most popular author in Scotland at this time.

14   His obituary in the *Academy and Literature* concludes that 'the vein of invention which, in the days of "Dr Nikola", promised to be rich, had been worked out some time before his early death' ('Notes' 187).

> The old order passes, the new order comes,
> And Fiction to-day as a trade simply 'hums,'
> So that Grub Street's inhabitants, once on the rates,
> Are now to be found at their country estates.
> The public, who pay, name the tunes of their choice,
> And the novelist-merchant, by heeding their voice,
> By pouring his tales in the phonograph's ear,
> At the rate of four six-shilling thrillers a year,
> And by trusting to Watt (who is Muse number ten)
> Attains the ideal of good business men:
> A mansion (by Maple), with everything fitting,
> And once every week a photographer's sitting;

Lamenting the declining interest in more serious work, it wryly concludes:

> Nor do I presume to suggest which is greater:
> George Meredith — King, or Guy Boothby — Dictator.
> ('The Literary Week' 76)

The double-voice of the hyphenated author

According to John Sutherland, in his introduction to the only recent scholarly reprint of *A Bid for Fortune*, Boothby's early transnational experience led him to develop the feeling that he belonged to two countries (viii), which passing observation provides a clue to assessing the impact of Boothby's Anglo-Australian identity on his literary work. His sense of identity was constituted not just by what Said terms 'the peculiarly compelling fact of residence in, actual existential contact with, the Orient [or colonies]' but also by his sense of being both English and Australian (156). The colonial-born Boothby grew up in a settler society that adhered doggedly to British traditions, was conditioned to consider himself a loyal subject of the empire and was clearly attracted to London as its metropolitan heart. However, he was also irrevocably the product of his home colony — a hybrid, in the sense articulated in Homi Bhabha's influential theory, which stresses the reciprocal construction of the identities of coloniser and colonised at the colonial peripheries ('Signs taken for Wonders'). Boothby's identification with England was unavoidably inflected by his encounters with the realities of colonial life beyond the confines of white Adelaide society, with indigenous peoples, other ethnic groups of settlers, and with terrains and landscapes, societies and cultures that diverged widely from the domestic English experience. This conflicted state of dual nationality was common to many of Boothby's contemporary colonial-born Anglo-Australians, but in Boothby it was aggravated by his movement back and forth between the colonial peripheries and the metropolis. This produced a dislocated sense, observable in the work of many other contemporary colonial-migrant authors, of belonging fully neither to his home colony nor his adopted metropolitan British abode, a kind of 'doubled hybridity' as Robert Young puts it (24). Stephen Arata, for example, observes that Kipling never felt at home in England, viewing it merely as a 'wonderful foreign land' (151). Writing specifically of Australia, John Rickard observes a kind of 'cultural schizophrenia' affecting early Australian authors stemming from the dilemma engendered by attempting to forge a distinctive Australian literature in the face of 'the continuing cultural ties with the metropolitan society' and the widespread belief 'that cultural standards had their ultimate source and legitimation there' (132). A close analysis of Boothby's texts discloses evidence of this cultural schizophrenia and to his doubly-hybrid state can be attributed a contradictory double-voice that pervades his fiction.

The contradiction most evident in the Boothby oeuvre is that which is signalled in the divergent emphases noted in the 1901 *Windsor* article: the recurrent valorisation of the 'Coming Man' of the colonies versus the simultaneous idealisation of the life of the English country gentleman above all others. According to the imperial myth of the 'Coming Man', the renewal of the English race was taking place in the tougher conditions of the imperial frontiers.[15] Thus the degeneration and weakness feared endemic in the cosseted metropolitan English population would be cured by the development of an active, competent colonial type produced by such colonies as Australia. Boothby's protagonists accordingly tend to divide into what may be termed 'strong colonial' types who can, for example, withstand the mesmeric power of his exotic villains, and 'weak metropolitan' types whose will is entirely subsumed to them; occasionally, as in the 'Jackeroo' story, the strenuous life of the colonial frontier can reinvigorate the weaker English-born. In Boothby's 1896 novel, *The Beautiful White Devil*, the English doctor De Normanville, who repeatedly

---

15 For an account of the Australian version of the Coming Man, see White, *Inventing Australia* 63-84.

faints at key moments, represents the weak, homegrown type, and Walworth, the product of Britain's Far Eastern colonies, who almost single-handedly defeats a mutinous crew of Chinese sailors, exemplifies the strong colonial. One of the least competent of Boothby's metropolitan protagonists is the gentleman artist Cyril Forrester of the gothic extravaganza, *Pharos the Egyptian* (1899). '[T]he usual idiot of these stories' as *The Athenaeum* reviewer scathingly adjudges him ('Historical Romances' 368), Forrester shows a passivity that is one of the novel's defining motifs. Nor is it a coincidence that Boothby assigns the profession of artist to him as most schools of fin-de-siècle art were targeted by Max Nordau in the exposition of degenerate phenomena presented in his influential 1890s articulation of degeneration theory (27-31).

The articulation of the strong colonial type accords with and supports Boothby's own assumption of a savvy Anglo-Australian identity, and this is particularly evident in the delineation of the Australian protagonist of *A Bid for Fortune*. Hatteras, epitomising the Australian version of the Coming Man, is a self-made success forged in the challenging (not to mention racially charged) conditions of the north Queensland frontier, as his bluff, hearty introduction attests:

> Richard Hatteras, at your service, commonly called Dick, of Thursday Island, North Queensland, pearler … and South Sea trader generally. Eight-and-twenty years of age … six feet two in my stockings, and forty-six inches round the chest; strong as a Hakodate wrestler … And big shame to me if I were not so strong, considering the free, open-air, devil-may-care life I've led. Why, I was doing man's work [*sic*] at an age when most boys are wondering when they're going to be taken out of knickerbockers. (14)

This testimonial is vindicated by repeated demonstrations of Hatteras's physical superiority, such as in Figure 6 where he ably dispatches some unruly natives in Port Said.

Hatteras's strength is further emphasised by repeated juxtaposition with versions of the weak metropolitan, as for instance in Boothby's sweeping characterisation of 'new arrivals [to Australia] from England' as 'weak-brained young pigeons with money' (18). But nowhere is the contrast more starkly drawn than between Hatteras and the examples of the homegrown English aristocracy that populate the text. The English branch of Hatteras's family are minor

Figure 6: 'We must fight our way out.' Guy Boothby, *A Bid for Fortune* (London: Ward, Lock and Bowden, 1895): 151.

nobility, and on paying a visit to the ancient family seat, Hatteras encounters his cousin Gwendoline: incapable of speech, bearded and dwarfish in stature, she is a crude caricature of the most excessive nineteenth-century theories of physical and mental degeneration. The message is obvious — in the same family one cousin, Hatteras, the product of the colonial frontier, is hale and hearty; the other, Gwendoline, product of the home counties, is degenerate to a shocking degree. Similarly, Hatteras's subsequent travelling companion, the Marquis of Beckenham, seems a typically effete aristocrat, as first impressions attest: 'His voice was very soft and low, more like a girl's than a boy's, and I noticed that he had none of the mannerisms of a man — at least, not of one who has seen much of the world' (90). However, Beckenham, though initially weak, is not as degenerate as his peers (with whom his father had forbidden contact), and is thus capable of regeneration through his contact with Hatteras and ensuing travels. The message again is straightforward — colonial experience can reinvigorate the weakened home stock.

In Boothby's work the contrast between the two types of Englishman, strong colonial and weak metropolitan, is frequently highlighted by the differing effects of mesmerism upon subjects of each type. Thus, in *A Bid for Fortune*, Beckenham describes Nikola's successful mesmeric attack on him as follows:

> 'I could not get away from those terrible eyes. They seemed to be growing larger and fiercer every moment. Oh! I can feel the horror of them even now. As I gazed his white right hand was moving to and fro before me with regular sweeps, and with each one I felt my own will growing weaker and weaker. That I was being mesmerised, I had no doubt, but if I had been going to be murdered I could not have moved a finger to save myself.' (154)

This description of an irresistible mesmeric hold reads like a textbook account of the powers of many fin-de-siècle villains. However, it pales by comparison with the lasting and total hold in *Pharos the Egyptian* of the villain Pharos over the hapless Forrester, a control so complete Pharos can use Forrester to spread a lethal plague across Europe killing millions, while Forrester's main hope for escape seems to lie in suicide (82, 216). These acts of subjection contrast markedly in their total success with Nikola's attempts on Hatteras, during which, despite his evident potency, Nikola must resort to either the use of narcotics or weaponry to ensure his control of Hatteras. Another son of the colonies, the

Hon. Sylvester Wetherell, Colonial Secretary of New South Wales and object of Nikola's plot in *A Bid for Fortune*, also experiences a failed attempt at hypnosis:

> 'He laid himself back in his chair, and for nearly a minute and a half stared me full in the face. You have seen Nikola's eyes, so I needn't tell you what a queer effect they are able to produce. I could not withdraw mine from them, and I felt that if I did not make an effort I should soon be mesmerised. So, pulling myself together, I sprang from my chair, and, by doing so, let him see that our interview was at an end.' (318)

Thus it is made clear that all the strong colonial type has to do to thwart the mesmeric powers of the foreign villain is to 'pull himself together', a course of action clearly unavailable to his metropolitan counterpart.

Hatteras's fortune is ultimately secured in *A Bid for Fortune* via the early death of Gwendoline, which allows the family title and property to pass to him (her degeneracy being far too extreme for personal salvation through contact with him). He then ensures the renewal of the family line through his marriage to another vigorous colonial, the heroine Phyllis, daughter of the strong-minded Colonial Secretary. That she is born and bred in Australia is a point Boothby belabours at the novel's opening when Phyllis refers to herself jokingly as 'an Australian native' explaining that she 'mean[s], of course, as you know, colonial born?' (30-1). However, the lifestyle that these two exemplars of Australian vitality choose in *A Bid for Fortune* is not a return to the supposedly invigorating atmosphere of north Queensland but rather seclusion in the sheltered environs of Hatteras's English county seat, a choice echoed, or aspired to, by many others of Boothby's hardy colonial protagonists. Yet this ultimate rejection of the colonial heritage that is presented as the source of their strength is only mentioned in a throwaway remark concerning the 'mother country' in the novel's concluding paragraphs, a pattern which is repeated in some of the subsequent Nikola novels. Thus, while throughout the bulk of his narratives and in the authorial persona he constructed, Boothby seems to favour the Australian aspect of his identity, in practice, like many of his protagonists, he poured the fruits of his labours into the pursuit of the English squirely ideal.

Recognition of his ideal is evident in the *Academy and Literature* magazine's obituary of Boothby, which also bears out my opening contention concerning his monetary attitude toward novel writing: 'Mr. Boothby, a man of exuberant vitality', it observes lightly, 'found story-writing not only easy and pleasant, but a rapid means of providing for the hobbies of a country gentleman' ('Notes' 187). Boothby's own pithy description of his method would concur: 'I give the reading public what they want … in return my readers give me what I want' (qtd in 'Boothby, Guy Newell'). This attitude comes across most clearly in what reads like the semi-autobiographical account of the young writer's journey from colonial obscurity to hard-won success in London in *Love Made Manifest*: '"Yes, my friend," he said to himself, as he watched a smart mail phaeton driven by a *popular novelist* go by, "some day you are going to drive in this park in exactly the self-same style; and perhaps another poor literary devil … may see you and derive some sort of encouragement from the look of fatted contentment upon your face"' (25, emphasis added). The flippancy of the obituary writer's tone seems to imply both an awareness of and derision for the new breed of transient celebrity author Boothby represented. In a fuller account of his method, Boothby too seems cognisant of, and quite content with, the dubious status accorded to his carefully crafted 'novelist-merchant' persona: having divulged the surprising number of novels he could work on simultaneously, he smilingly explained: 'You see, I don't take literature seriously … Not … literature as I make it … Suppose I choose to spend two years on a book, like some of my esteemed contemporaries … perhaps I'd be an artist too; but it would bore me to death' (qtd in 'Mr Guy Boothby' 5).

Works Cited

Allen, Charles. *Kipling Sahib: India and the Making of Rudyard Kipling 1865-1900*. London: Little, Brown, 2007.

Arata, Stephen. *Fictions of Loss in the Victorian Fin de Siècle*. Cambridge: Cambridge UP, 1996.

Bassett, Troy, and Christina Walker. 'Books and Bestsellers: British Book Sales as Documented by *The Bookman*, 1891-1906.' *Book History* 4 (2001): 205-36.

Bhabha, Homi K. 'Signs taken for Wonders: Questions of ambivalence and authority under a tree outside Delhi, May 1817.' *The Location of Culture*. London: Routledge, 1994.

Boothby, Guy. *The Beautiful White Devil.* London: Ward, Lock, 1896.

———. *A Bid for Fortune, or Dr Nikola's Vendetta.* London: Ward, Lock & Bowden, 1895.

———. *Love Made Manifest.* New York: Herbert Stone, 1899.

———. *The Marriage of Esther: A Torres Straits Sketch.* London: Ward, Lock & Co., 1895.

———. *On the Wallaby, or Through the East and Across Australia.* London: Longmans, Green, and Co., 1894.

———. *Pharos the Egyptian.* London: Ward, Lock, 1899.

———. 'The Reformation of the Jackeroo.' *The Windsor Magazine* 6 (August 1897): 279-83.

'Boothby, Guy Newell (1867-1905).' *Australian Dictionary of Biography.* Vol. 7. Melbourne: Melbourne UP, 1979: 347-8. http://www.adb.online.anu.edu.au/biogs/A070352b.htm, accessed 23 January 2011.

Bulfin, Ailise. 'Sherlock Holmes and Dr Nikola: Too much at home in the underworld.' *Sherlock Holmes: The Man and His Worlds.* Ed. Sally Sugarman. Shaftsbury, VT: Mountainside Press, 2013.

Depasquale, Paul. *Guy Boothby: His Life and Work.* Seacombe Gardens, SA: Pioneer Books, 1982.

———. 'An Incomplete Essay on Guy Boothby and the London Theatre.' *The Pioneer Books Magazine* 1 (Spring 1994): 53-61.

Dixon, Robert. *Writing the Colonial Adventure: Race, gender and nation in Anglo-Australian popular fiction, 1875-1914.* Melbourne: Cambridge UP, 1995.

'A Foreword.' *The Windsor Magazine* 1 (January 1895): 1-3.

'A Hopeless Case.' *Punch* 108 (9 March 1895): 113.

'Historical Romances.' *The Athenaeum* 3726 (March 1899): 368.

Huggan, Graham. *Australian Literature: Postcolonialism, Racism, Transnationalism.* Oxford: Oxford UP, 2007.

Hyde, John. 'The Creator of "Dr Nikola": An afternoon with Guy Boothby.' *The Windsor Magazine* 4 (December 1896): 129-33.

Keating, Peter. *The Haunted Study: A Social History of the English Novel 1875-1914.* London: Secker & Warburg, 1989.

Klickman, Wilfrid. 'Guy Boothby At Home.' *The Windsor Magazine* 13 (February 1901): 297-302.

'The Literary Week.' *The Academy* 57.1420 (July 1899): 75-8.

Low, Gail Ching-Liang. *White Skins/Black Masks: Representation and Colonialism.* New York: Routledge, 1996.

Lycett, Andrew. *Rudyard Kipling*. London: Weidenfeld & Nicolson, 1999.

Monsman, Gerald. *H. Rider Haggard on the Imperial Frontier: The Political and Literary Contexts of His African Romances.* Greensboro, NC: ELT Press, 2006.

'Mr Guy Boothby.' *The Advertiser* (Adelaide) 1 March 1905: 5. http://trove.nla.gov.au/ndp/del/article/5039806, accessed 13 March 2013.

'News Notes.' *The Bookman* 7.40 (January 1895): 103-6.

Nordau, Max. *Degeneration*. 1892. Lincoln: University of Nebraska Press, 1993.

'Notes.' *The Academy and Literature* 69.1713 (March 1905): 187-9.

'Novel Notes.' Rev. of *Bushigrams* by Guy Boothby. *The Bookman* 13.76 (January 1898): 132.

'Obituary. Mr Guy Boothby.' *The Times* (London) 28 February 1905: 10.

'Old Par's Wanderings.' *The Academy* 1492 (December 1900): 579-80.

Ouyang, Yu. *Chinese in Australian Fiction, 1888-1988*. New York: Cambria Press, 2008.

'Recent Novels.' Rev. of *A Bid for Fortune* by Guy Boothby. *The Times* (London) 27 December 1895: 10.

'Recent Novels.' Rev. of *The Lust of Hate* by Guy Boothby. *The Times* (London) 10 August 1898: 10.

Rennison, Nick. *The Rivals of Sherlock Holmes.* Herts, Harpenden: No Exit Press, 2008.

Rickard, John. *Australia: A Cultural History.* 2nd edn. London: Longman, 1996.

Robinson, Philip M. and Leslie A. Spence. *The Robinson Family of Bolsover and Chesterfield.* Chesterfield: Robinson & Sons, 1937.

Said, Edward. *Orientalism*. 1978. London: Penguin, 2003.

Sullivan, Alvin. Ed. *British Literary Magazines: The Victorian and Edwardian Age, 1837-1913*. London: Greenwood Press, 1983.

Sutherland, John. Preface to *A Bid For Fortune, or Dr Nikola's Vendetta* by Guy Boothby. New York: Oxford UP, 1996.

'Tales of Adventure.' Rev. of *The Lust of Hate* by Guy Boothby. *The Athenaeum* 3677 (April 1898): 498.

Trainor, Luke. 'Australian Writers, British Publishers, 1870-1902: Talking to the Nation.' *Australian Historical Studies* 37.127 (2006): 140-55. http://www.tandfonline.com/doi/abs/10.1080/10314610608601208, accessed 5 May 2011.

Weaver, Rachael. 'Colonial Violence and Forgotten Fiction.' *Australian Literary Studies* 24.2 (2009): 33-53. *Academic Search Complete*, accessed 25 May 2011.

White, Richard. 'Cooees across the Strand: Australian Travellers in London and the Performance of National Identity.' *Australian Historical Studies* 32:116 (2001): 109-27. www.tandfonline.com/doi/abs/10.1080/10314610108596150, accessed 14 May 2011.

———. *Inventing Australia: Images and Identity 1688-1980*. London and Sydney: Allen & Unwin, 1981.

Wynne, Catherine. *The Colonial Conan Doyle: British Imperialism, Irish Nationalism, and the Gothic*. Westport, Connecticut: Greenwood, 2002.

Young, Robert J.C. *Colonial Desire: Hybridity in Theory, Culture and Race*. London: Routledge, 1995.

9

The scenery and dresses of her dreams: reading and reflecting (on) the Victorian heroine in M.E. Braddon's *The Doctor's Wife*

Madeleine Seys

In Mary Elizabeth Braddon's 1864 novel, *The Doctor's Wife*, heroine Isabel gazes into the looking glass 'to see if she really were pretty; or if her face, as she saw it in her day-dreams, was only an invention of her own, like the scenery and the dresses of those foolish dreams' (155). Throughout *The Doctor's Wife*, Braddon explores the mirror's dual capacity to fashion fantasy and register reality. In the mirror, Braddon fashions a new symbolic relationship between reading and dressing and, thereby, metafictionally negotiates Isabel's dual position as reader and heroine, subject and object in the novel. Dressing, reading and dreaming in front of the looking glass, Isabel self-consciously acts out the construction and representation of the heroine in the Victorian novel. At the same time, Braddon negotiates shifts in conceptions of feminine and literary subjectivity in *The Doctor's Wife* and fashions a form of highly self-conscious and culturally receptive authorship and readership in the genred literary climate of the mid-nineteenth century.

The Doctor's Wife traces the life and reading of Isabel Gilbert (née Sleaford) from naïve adolescence to wisdom and maturity. Like many female members of 'the poorer middle classes', Isabel has received a 'half-and-half education' (Braddon 27). The narrator advises us that she

> knew a little Italian, enough French to serve for the reading of novels that she might have better left unread, and just so much modern history as enabled her to pick out all the sugarplums in the historians' pages ... She played the piano a little, and sang a little, and painted wishy-washy-looking flowers on Bristol-board. (27)

After the cessation of her formal education at the age of sixteen, the narrator continues, Isabel 'set to work to educate herself by means of the nearest circulating library ... and read her favourite novels over and over again' (27-8). Despite her voracity, Isabel is neither a critical nor discerning reader. The narrator states that she

> was not a woman of the world. She had read novels while other people perused the Sunday papers ... She believed in a phantasmal world created out of the pages of poets and romancers. (253)

She dreams of inhabiting this world and being 'really, truly sentimentally beloved, like the heroine of a novel' (247). Isabel's position as a literary subject in the novel is defined both by her status as a reader and as a heroine.

Isabel's 'small delicate features', pale face, dark eyes and purple-black hair 'invested her with a kind of weird and melancholy beauty ... which could only be fully comprehended by a poet', the narrator states (167, 25). Her suitor, George Gilbert, thinks she is 'fitted to be the heroine of a romance' (30). Sigismund Smith, within the novel an author of popular fiction, uses Isabel as his muse: 'I do her for all my dark heroines', he says (30). Roland Lansdell, a poet of Byronic character, is also attracted to Isabel's beauty, innocence and impressionability. He thinks of her as a 'beautiful piece of animated wax-work, with a little machinery inside' onto which he can impose his fantasies of seduction (151). In the course of the novel, however, Isabel resists seduction and transcends these models of dangerous and corruptible femininity. Through a process of reading, reflecting and self-fashioning, Isabel transforms herself into a model of feminine respectability.

This chapter explores the significance of the mirror as a tool for reflection, both literal and figurative, in M.E. Braddon's *The Doctor's Wife*. It examines Braddon's use of the mirror as both a physical tool and self-conscious metaphor for Isabel's transformation as reader and heroine. Standing in front of her looking glass, novel in hand and reflection before her, Isabel muses on her subjectivity. She gradually refashions her appearance and identity in light of contemporary ideas about gender, genre and reading. At the same time, Braddon uses the mirror to refashion her own literary subjectivity. In *The Doctor's Wife*, she self-consciously and playfully employs elements of sensationalism and realism whilst also critiquing the legitimacy of these generic distinctions (P. Gilbert, *Disease* 9). In this way, Braddon addressed her public authorial persona as 'The Sensation Novelist' and defended herself on the charge that she was a 'slave' to popularity and sensationalism (P. Gilbert, *Disease* 92; Rae 197). This chapter explores the various ways in which the narrative of *The Doctor's Wife* brings together and reflects on the self-consciousness of heroine, reader and author in the mirror and uses them to fashion a series of conscious, comprehensible and culturally relevant literary subjectivities. In *The Doctor's Wife*, the mirror is a site for changing literary, feminine and authorial subjectivities and subjects. This chapter draws on this and uses the mirror to a shape a reading practice which itself changes the critical subject and repositions Braddon's novel within debates about women as heroines, readers and authors in the mid-Victorian period.

During the 1860s, the British literary field was dominated by the genres of realism and sensationalism (Brantlinger 15). These were socially-, morally- and politically-, as well as artistically-driven categories (Phegley 27). Contemporary critics such as H.L. Mansel, W. Fraser Rae and Margaret Oliphant criticised sensation fiction as a 'wildly popular and artistically dubious upstart genre' and 'a crisis in ... literary realism' (Phegley 113; Brantlinger 27). According to Rae, realism is premised on the understanding that 'a novel is a picture of life, and as such ought to be faithful' (203). Sensation novels, alternatively, were defined as 'fancy portraits of repulsive virtue and attractive vice' (Mansel 499). The forthright narratives and morals of realism were 'punctuated with question marks' in sensation fiction (Brantlinger 2). A deficiency of verisimilitude yet penchant for describing frivolous details was identified as the genre's main artistic fault and the point on which it differed, most markedly, from realism (Rae 189). However, the sensationalism/realism dichotomy is not a simple one. As a genre, sensation fiction is defined by its instability: generic, narrative and thematic. Patrick Brantlinger furnishes us with the most succinct definition of the genre when he states that it is governed by the idea that 'innocent appearances cloak evil intentions; reality functions as a mystery until the sudden revelation of guilt' (14). Whilst this was unsettling, it was the genre's themes, characterisation and setting which Victorian readers and critics considered particularly problematic.

Sensation fiction broaches subjects that many Victorians thought inappropriate: it depicts murder, adultery, bigamy, insanity, fraud and impersonation (Brantlinger 5-6). Its heroines are women of ambiguous and unstable identities and secret histories who transgress accepted models of gender, class and morality (Brantlinger 5-6). Most shocking, however, is that they commit their crimes, 'not in the worst rookeries of Seven Dials' but in the 'sweet … calm' of the middle-class Victorian home (Braddon, *Lady* 54). It was not just within the world of the novel that sensation fiction and the sensation heroine were considered to threaten the sanctity of the home, however. Sensation fiction was also perceived to threaten the Victorian cult of the domestic in appealing to a large and enthusiastic female readership.

According to contemporary critics and reviewers, sensation fiction was primarily consumed by women readers (Phegley 113). In *The Doctor's Wife*, Braddon addresses contemporary concerns about this readership through the observations of an inhabitant of Graybridge (the fictional setting of the novel). This critic states that 'a young person who spent so much of her time in the perusal of works of fiction could scarcely be a model wife' (117). Female readers were depicted as uncritical and easily corrupted by the genre's transgressive and immoral narratives (Phegley 111-13). By appealing to female readers' latent 'dislike of their roles as daughters, wives and mothers' and their repressed 'fantasies of protest and escape,' sensation fiction was considered to threaten the sanctity of the Victorian home (Showalter 130). It was also perceived to appeal to women's sexual passions and 'eagerness … [for] physical sensation' (Oliphant 259).

In 1867, Margaret Oliphant wrote that the heroines of sensation novels are

> women driven wild with love for the man who leads them on to desperation … women who marry their grooms in fits of sensual passion;[1] women who

---

[1] This is an obvious reference to M.E. Braddon's 1863 novel, *Aurora Floyd*, in which the passionate and impulsive Aurora elopes with a groom employed by her father.

pray their lovers to carry them off from husbands and worlds they hate; women, at the very least of it, who give and receive burning kisses and frantic embraces, and live in a voluptuous dream. (259)

This model of femininity, she states, 'is held up to us as the story of the feminine soul ... [and] state of mind' (Oliphant 259). In *The Doctor's Wife*, M.E. Braddon questions this model of dreaming, corruptible, dangerous and uncritical female readership. In the course of the novel, heroine and reader Isabel Gilbert awakes from her 'voluptuous dream' of being a heroine and transforms herself into an active and mature reader (Oliphant 259). Braddon uses this redemptive narrative to defend sensation fiction and its female readership and to refashion her own authorial subjectivity.

Mary Elizabeth Braddon was known as the 'queen of the sensation novel' (Phegley 23) and was amongst the most prolific and popular authors of the nineteenth century (Tromp, Gilbert and Haynie xv). She was also one of the most frequently and vehemently criticised. Her novels *Lady Audley's Secret* (1862) and *Aurora Floyd* (1863) are considered definitively 'sensational' in their depiction of women who subvert the Victorian ideal of angelic and passive femininity (Showalter 130-5; Brantlinger 1; Pykett, '*Improper*' 84). Of Lady Audley, the eponymous heroine of Braddon's first sensation novel, Rae states that

> [w]henever she is meditating the commission of something inexpressibly horrible, she is described as being unusually charming. Her manner and her appearance are always in contrast with her conduct. All this is very exciting, but also very unnatural. (186)

Rae considered Lady Audley's crimes to be both moral and narrative (186). Her 'horrible' actions breach ideas about innocent and passive femininity. Simultaneously, the fact that she maintains her 'charming' looks whilst perpetrating such transgressions upsets the established realist equation of signifier and signified (Rae 186). Sensation fiction, therefore, engenders instability on both thematic and narrative levels. Amongst the most common criticisms of sensation fiction was that it violated the carefully constructed boundaries between high art and popular culture and combined elements of both (Phegley 113). Because of this, it is unclear where exactly 'the boundaries of sensation fiction begin and end' (Knight 325) and critics continue to grapple to define and identify the genre. A review of the existing critical literature on Braddon's *The Doctor's Wife* makes evident this struggle.

The Doctor's Wife was published in 1864, during Braddon's most 'sensational' period.² However, as the novel's narrator states, it 'is *not* a sensation novel' (358, emphasis in original). Because of this tension, *The Doctor's Wife* has proved a point of contention for critics from Rae in 1865 into the twenty-first century. Analysis of this novel defines it as either self-consciously sensational or unsuccessfully realist. Writing in the *North British Review* in 1865, Rae stated that *The Doctor's Wife* was Braddon's attempt to write a realist novel but that she remained a 'slave ... to the style which she created. "Sensation" [was] her Frankenstein' (197). This argument still has credence for critics in the twenty-first century (Pykett, 'Introduction' xx; Sparks 208). Golden argues that in this novel Braddon attempted (unsuccessfully, it is implied) to censor her sensationalism in pursuit of critical, rather than popular, acclamation (30). Sparks accords and states that the novel is a 'confused compendium of three types of popular Victorian literature, sensationalism, sentimentalism, and realism' (198). Pamela K. Gilbert attributes Braddon with greater control over the style of her text, suggesting that *The Doctor's Wife* signalled a decisive break with sensationalism (*Disease* 106). Braddon, she states, deliberately establishes *The Doctor's Wife* 'in the high-culture genre of realism by positioning ... [it] through internal textual cues, against sensation fiction' (*Disease* 9).³

The Doctor's Wife, as these divergent readings attest, cannot be easily accommodated within Victorian models of genre. Rather than constructing her text within the strictures of realism or sensationalism, Braddon critiques the legitimacy of these generic distinctions (P. Gilbert, *Disease* 9). As Jennifer Phegley argues, in this novel Braddon 'hoped to show that she could write

---

2   *Lady Audley's Secret*, Braddon's most famous sensation novel, was serialised from 1861 to 1862 and the equally sensational *Aurora Floyd*, *John Marchmont's Legacy* and *Eleanor's Victory* were published between 1862 and 1863.

3   P. Gilbert goes on to say that *The Doctor's Wife* was a response not only to sensation fiction but also to Gustave Flaubert's *Madame Bovary* (1856) (*Disease* 9). Golden agrees, stating that in *The Doctor's Wife* Braddon was 'laundering the sensationalism' of Flaubert's novel (30). It seems undeniable that the plot of Braddon's novel is influenced by *Madame Bovary* (Flint 288). In fact, Braddon admitted to 'borrowing' from Flaubert's text (Wolff, *Sensational* 162). However, she places Isabel's story firmly within British social, generic and literary conventions. Braddon's reflections on and refashioning of these conventions are the focus of this chapter and, for this reason, it will not undertake an intertextual analysis of *The Doctor's Wife* and *Madame Bovary*.

realistically even while playfully engaging with elements of sensation' (136). *The Doctor's Wife* is 'tempered with a certain self-consciousness' of its own generic position (P. Gilbert, *Disease* 106). Our reading of the novel, then, must be similarly playful and self-conscious; it must be alert to the ways in which Braddon manipulates genre through her depiction of Isabel reading, dressing and acting in front of the mirror. Writing on Braddon's later but similarly self-conscious novel *Vixen*, Albert Sears argues that in order to understand Braddon's 'simultaneous engagement and resistance to the sensation fiction marketplace, we need a reading practice ... that reads for generic expectation but also attends to the ways her narratives surpass generic boundaries' (51). Reading through the mirror, this chapter takes up this challenge; it draws on the work of P. Gilbert, Phegley and Sears and considers the way in which *The Doctor's Wife* sets up and then transcends prevailing generic structures.[4]

The ideas of reading and reflecting inform this chapter in all of their literal and metaphoric senses. The image of Isabel pontificating on the relative fantasy or reality of her appearance, dress and status as the heroine of the novel in front of her looking glass connects the actions of reading, dressing and reflecting in *The Doctor's Wife*. It also foregrounds Braddon's consciousness of the complex codes that surrounded these activities for women in the 1860s. Braddon uses the mirror as a surface on which to cognitively and visually reflect

---

4   Although best known for her sensation novels of the 1860s, Mary Elizabeth Braddon continued to publish until her death in 1915; much of her later work is yet to have sustained critical attention. Braddon's later novels are marked by their contemporaneity. Her narrative style and subject matter continually evolved, keeping pace with the multifarious literary, cultural, social and political changes of the late-Victorian and Edwardian periods. Many of her later novels mediate between popular genres, self-consciously and playfully examining their poetics and politics. Scholarship on *The Doctor's Wife* has begun to explore this generic instability and self-consciousness. Albert C. Sears's examination of *Vixen* and Pamela K. Gilbert's reading of *Joshua Haggard's Daughter* similarly explore these novels' generic instability. Such readings provide a model for examining Braddon's later work in light of generic expectation, whilst also attending to the ways in which these novels interrogate or transgress generic conventions (Sears 51). This also opens up the possibility of returning to her better-known novels, *Lady Audley's Secret*, *Aurora Floyd* and *Eleanor's Victory* and reconsidering their relationship to sensationalism and its antithesis, realism, rather than reinforcing these strict distinctions. A similar approach could be taken to other sensation novels and novelists. This also has implications for the wider study of Victorian genres and generic anomalies.

on the 'restrictive nature and devious possibilities that underwrote accepted class behaviours and gender roles' during this period (Phegley 137). Thus we begin to see the mirror as a site for the changing literary subject within and without the sensation novel. The literal use of the mirror as a tool for reflection also prompts self-consciousness of other, more figurative, sorts in *The Doctor's Wife*. The image of Isabel reading in front of the mirror, then, becomes a metaphor for literary self-consciousness in the novel.

Braddon's positioning of *The Doctor's Wife* within contemporary debates about realism and sensationalism, reality and fantasy, and women's writing and reading is deliberately self-conscious. The novel uses the mirror to reflect on notions of genre and gender and interrogate the ways in which they are employed, in contemporary literature and associated critical commentary, to fashion feminine literary subjectivities. This emphasises the status of the narrative and its heroine as works of fiction and, therefore, identifies Braddon's *The Doctor's Wife* as a work of metafiction. Patricia Waugh defines metafiction as literature that self-consciously and systematically draws attention to 'its own status as an artefact in order to pose questions about the relationship between fiction and reality' (2). Metafiction re-examines

> the conventions of realism in order to discover — through its own self-reflection — a fictional form that is culturally relevant and comprehensible to contemporary readers. (18)

However, Waugh also argues that nineteenth-century literature is not metafictional (31-2). The characterisation of Isabel as reader-heroine refutes this claim. In her role as reader, Isabel reflects on the fictionality of the heroine as a literary construct. As heroine, she consciously aspires to this ideal of literary femininity before finally refashioning and transcending it. In her self-conscious portrayal of the act of reading in the novel, Braddon unites Isabel with her favourite heroines and with the actual readers of *The Doctor's Wife*. Braddon fashions a narrative, then, which is culturally receptive and relevant, and comprehensible to contemporary readers in the way that Waugh describes.

In employing the mirror as a space in which Isabel fashions, inhabits and ultimately transcends the 'phantasmal world created out of the pages of poets and romancers' (253), Braddon provides a unique metaphor for thinking about the intersection of reality, fantasy and ideality in representations of the heroine in Victorian fiction. When Isabel stands in front of the mirror she is reflecting not only on her literary and readerly subjectivity but also on her appearance. She peers into the looking glass to see if she is as pretty as the heroine of a romance or if her appearance is only an invention of her own, like the dresses of her foolish dreams (155). In the mirror, fantasy (and fiction) are acted out and realised by Isabel. She fashions a new wardrobe and identity for herself in the styles of the novels she reads (155). The imagery of Isabel's appearance and a range of possible symbolic meanings borrowed, by both heroine and readers, from other texts to interpret it, coalesce at the reflective surface of the mirror. This captures the dual function of mirror (and of reflection) to create, distort and refashion the signification of the visual and written codes of Victorian genres. It also provides the tool with which Isabel and Braddon refashion how they are read within these codes as the novel progresses. Together, these forms of reflection and refashioning typify Braddon's self-conscious approach to representation and narrative in *The Doctor's Wife*.

In Victorian literature, a heroine's subjectivity is developed through her dress; the fabrics and style of a woman's clothing attest to her wealth, class, morality and respectability as well as to current tastes and fashions (Kortsch 55; Reynolds and Humble 59). Dress also frames the woman's body within prevailing ideas about gender and sexuality (P. Gilbert, *Disease* 68). In her study of fashion and modernity, *Sex and Suits: The Evolution of Modern Dress*, Anne Hollander speaks to the power of dress in fashioning notions of femininity and female subjectivity. She argues that throughout the modern period, the 'form of the actual woman' was replaced by the fictional 'image of the Dressed Woman … shaped … according to shifts in the erotic imagination' (47).

The Victorian Dressed Woman and heroine of contemporary literature was, and continues to be, defined by a pair of antithetical and erotically charged images. She is either the virginal domestic angel of realism (Talairach-Vielmas 9), the 'ideal woman in feelings, faculties and [white muslin] flounces' (Eliot 301-2), or the sexual and sensational 'demon' in 'a ruby-velvet gown that *wouldn't* keep hooked' (Braddon, *Doctor's* 199, emphasis in original). She is bound to her narrative fate by the symbolic threads of her dress. There are two narrative alternatives available to her:

> [S]he will either get virtue's earthly reward, a rich husband, or be seduced and die ... The conscious heroine must work out a view of this absurdly simple pair of alternatives by which to transcend them. (Brownstein 81)

By reflecting on her appearance in the mirror, Isabel becomes a 'conscious heroine' (Brownstein 81). She 'stitches up' a new identity out of the stuff of Victorian literature and admires her fictional effect in the looking glass. In doing so, she works out a view of these genred alternatives of Victorian 'heroine-ship' and transcends her potential as a corruptible reader and seducible heroine.

When we first meet Isabel 'she [is] sitting in a basket-chair ... with a book on her lap ... She [is wearing] a muslin dress, a good deal tumbled and not too clean' (23). In the first part of the narrative, Isabel struggles to negotiate her individual subjectivity and agency with the literary codes which would cast her as a passive and fated heroine-reader. The book in her lap in this scene is a potent symbol of this struggle. She is discovered in the garden, not only by readers, but also by author Mr Sigismund Smith and his friend Dr Gilbert. Smith and Gilbert attempt to engage Isabel in conversation; however, she keeps one finger shut in the novel she is reading, indicative of her desire to plunge back into its fictional world as soon as possible (23-4). Isabel's struggle to tear herself away from her romance reading mirrors Braddon's struggle to distance herself, as an author, from such popular and sensational literary genres. As Braddon narrates these struggles in *The Doctor's Wife*, she knowingly enters contemporary debates surrounding female subjectivity and reading.

'Miss Sleaford's a very good little girl', states Sigismund Smith in the first volume of the novel, 'but she's got too much Wonder, and exaggerated Ideality' (66). Smith, we are told, is 'the author of about half a dozen highly-spiced fictions, which enjoyed an immense popularity' amongst the reading public (11). As well as being an author of sensation fiction within the narrative — although, as the narrator notes, 'that bitter term of reproach ... had not [yet] been invented' (11) — Smith also functions as the author-by-proxy of *The Doctor's Wife*. In casting Smith in this role, Braddon metafictionally dramatises the act of writing and the construction of femininity and female subjectivity in Victorian literature. She uses Smith as a mirror to her own authorship and, therefore, symbolically distances herself from the writing of the novel.

As Braddon's fictional authorial *alter ego* (Pykett, 'Introduction' ix), Sigismund Smith orchestrates and chronicles the action of *The Doctor's Wife*. He introduces Isabel to Dr Gilbert and then to Roland Lansdell and chronicles their romances in his letters and, though indirectly, his fictional writing. Through his narrative commentary and description of his own literary efforts for the penny press, Smith establishes the normative way of reading Isabel as a sensational Braddonian heroine. Readers versed in Braddon's sensation fiction (namely *Lady Audley's Secret* and *Aurora Floyd*) see Isabel, slovenly in her limp white muslin gown, as an ill-fated *femme fatale*. 'Pretty and inexperienced' and with purple-black hair, red lips and a clinging gown, Isabel is easy prey to a profligate (Braddon, *Doctor's* 167). With a novel in her lap, she is simultaneously represented as the corrupted (or eminently corruptible) reader of such fiction; Isabel is thought to be prey to a profligate because she is 'dreadfully romantic' and 'reads too many novels' (30). The tension between reading Isabel as a corruptible reader and a corruptible heroine forms the basis of the metafictional reflection on and refashioning of feminine and literary subjectivity which Braddon undertakes in this novel.

Whilst Isabel has every appearance of a typical sensation heroine, Braddon suggests that her husband, Dr George Gilbert, belongs to the realm of the 'real' rather than the sensational, phantasmal or romantic. Dr Gilbert, the narrator notes, 'had those homely, healthy good looks which the novelist or poet in search of a hero would recoil from with actual horror' (6). When cast together, Isabel and George symbolise the genres of sensationalism and realism which Braddon plays with in this novel (Pykett, 'Introduction' xii). Smith introduces Isabel Sleaford and Dr Gilbert and, befitting his role as the 'author' of the novel, is the means of communication between them. Smith, therefore, symbolically traverses the space between reality (realism) and fantasy (sensationalism): he authors the letters that keep George informed of Isabel's life, and George falls in love with the 'heroine' of these epistles. Meanwhile, a mysterious misfortune befalls the Sleaford family and Isabel leaves her family and seeks work as a governess. She is reunited with George Gilbert whilst thus employed and accepts his proposal of marriage. Isabel is wooed by the 'pretty story' of his confession of love (Braddon 87) and by her desire to be 'really, truly sentimentally beloved, like the heroine of a novel' (247). Prior to this, she has lamented her role as governess, the marginal female figure who haunts the glamorous and beloved heroine in the novels she reads.⁵ Furnished with her library, a wardrobe of new gowns and 'a card-case with a new name on the cards contained in it' (110) Isabel fashions a new subjectivity as the wifely heroine.

Isabel believes, according to the narrator, that upon her marriage '[her] story had begun, and she was a heroine' (90). The narrator states that 'although Isabel amused herself by planning her wedding-dress … she had no idea of a speedy marriage. Were there not three volumes of courtship to be gone through first?' (99). However, Isabel's life does not follow the structure of the three-volume romance novel and she is fashioned into the model Victorian wife without the narrative climax of the joyful wedding. This shift in narrative emphasis changes the subject of the romance from the wedding to its outcome. The wedding is a quiet affair and her gown is not of the light elegant stuff as she planned, but, rather, 'a somber brown-silk' chosen by George because of its homely usefulness (105). Through this change in dress, Isabel is fashioned as an object of Dr Gilbert's fantasy of ideal domestic femininity; she is expected to be 'handy with her needle, and clever in the management of a house and the government of a maid-of-all-work' (36). As the narrator states, though, 'Isabel could scarcely be that, since her favourite employment was to loll in a wicker-work garden-chair and read novels' (36). Her life (and wardrobe) as the 'doctor's wife' does not fit her literary fantasies of wifehood. In order to satisfy her yearning for romance, Isabel retires more regularly to her 'garden-chair' and ventures further into the world of popular romance where 'reality and fantasy mingle' (36; Wilson 228) and where the scenery and dresses of her dreams take on the vividness of reality.

Longing to be a heroine in the fashion of the novels she reads and dissatisfied with married life, Isabel falls in love with Roland Lansdell, a poet of works which are 'a sort of mixture of Tennyson and Alfred de Musset' (Braddon 130). Isabel and Roland meet in secret to exchange and discuss books of poetry. In her romance with Roland, Isabel appears to have fulfilled expectations of her as a corruptible reader. Her imminent seduction also indicates her fall as a sensation heroine. The role of printed literary stuff in their relationship echoes

---

5   There is much scholarship on the figure of the governess in the Victorian novel. Helena Michie describes this representation of the governess as 'the heroine's shadow-double, the figure in muted grey or brown who follows the gaily dressed heroine … and is always one step behind her in her progress through the novel' (46).

that played by Smith's letters in Isabel's courtship with Dr Gilbert. There is, however, a subtle change in the metafictional tone of the novel and in Isabel's form of heroine-ship. Braddon casts Isabel as an active reader of, rather than passive object in, the written stuff; she is transformed from objectified heroine to active reader in her relationship with Roland. This shift is captured in the mirror. Standing in front of her looking glass, Isabel fashions a new literary and feminine subjectivity which eclipses both Gilbert's and Smith's notions of the 'heroine'. Isabel becomes a more conscious (and self-conscious) and discerning reader. She exchanges Dickens's *Dombey and Son* — she had wished to be Mrs. Dombey 'sublime in scornful indignation and ruby silk velvet' (357) — for *The Revolt of Islam* (402) and the works of Shakespeare. The narrator tells us that Isabel

> took a dingy volume of the immortal William's from the dusty row of books ... and went up to her room and locked the door, and pleaded for Cassio, and wept and protested opposite the looking-glass. (155)

Throughout *The Doctor's Wife*, there is an ongoing symbolic connectedness between the form of self-consciousness evoked by the mirror and that (though fantastic) encouraged by reading, acting and dressing-up. Kate Flint argues that reading played an important role in the Victorian woman's construction and assertion of her sense of self (330). At the same time, reading provided the means for the Victorian women to abnegate the self, withdrawing into passivity (Flint 330). Helena Michie describes the same juxtaposition of passivity and self-consciousness in her discussion of the mirror; the reflection, Michie argues, 'is an image of the body (vanity/surface) and of an attempt to move beyond the body (reflection/contemplation)' (8). Dressing and dressing-up allow the Victorian woman to fashion herself in order to adhere to or transcend the archetypal images of femininity and heroine-ship; this is a literal manifestation of the process of moving beyond the body which Michie describes. In *The Doctor's Wife*, Braddon stages this process in detail: Isabel reads with her workbox, scissors, needles and looking glass at hand, recutting and reshaping her dresses, and her sense of self, as she reads. Christine Bayles Kortsch argues that the Victorian woman reader's workbox was equipped not only with scissors and a needle but with something more invisible and intangible — a knowledge of the significance of cloth and clothing (55).

Isabel is acutely aware of the literary significances of the cloths and clothing she wears. She imagines her devotion to stereotypically Byronic hero Roland Lansdell in the symbolic ethereal terms of the passive white muslin-clad angel. In anticipation of a visit to the Lansdell estate, Isabel unpicks and refashions 'a soft transparent' gown of white muslin and lace with a 'white muslin mantle to match' (165). This gown is a significant departure from the homely brown silk that symbolises her role as the doctor's wife. Dressed in muslin, Isabel '[fancies] herself as a perpetual worshipper in white ... kneeling at the feet of her idol' (357).

While Sigismund Smith sees Isabel as one of his corruptible sensation heroines, Roland sees her as the virginal, passive feminine ideal of nineteenth-century realism. He imagines her as a silent and 'slender white-robed figure on the moonlit terrace' (214). During the Victorian period, white muslin at once symbolised virginity, innocence and passivity, and ghostliness and blankness (Hughes 70). This duality underpins the narrative of Wilkie Collins's 1860 novel *The Woman in White*, which Braddon metafictionally refashions in *The Doctor's Wife*. Collins's heroine, Laura Fairlie, is the image of the archetypal Victorian feminine ideal: fair, pretty, demure and modest (Reynolds and Humble 52). Her 'sexual nullity' is symbolised by the textural and chromatic nullity of her gowns (53). Laura Fairlie is the feminine ideal because garbed in white, 'her body functions as a blank canvas on to which the observer's desires and fantasies can be sketched' (53). In *The Doctor's Wife*, Isabel appropriates this objectification. Through refashioning her white muslin and lace gown (164) Isabel sketches her own fantasies and desires (to be a beloved heroine) onto the surface of her appearance. This is symbolic of Braddon's metafictional 'involvement in — and mediation of — reality through ... pre-existent texts' (Waugh 14) in this novel.

Evocatively garbed in white muslin, Isabel occupies a space between the real and the imaginary, the realist and the sensational for both characters in and readers of *The Doctor's Wife* (P. Gilbert, *Disease* 110). Vainly gazing at her image in the looking glass, Isabel traverses the fictional (fantastic) and the real, thereby playing out her own literary fantasies and those of the readers. Likewise, through this image Braddon plays out her metafictional manipulation of the norms of genre in this novel. Braddon employs such subtle yet critical metafictional and intertextual techniques in order 'to cue reader's expectations — expectations that will be overturned one by one, as "reality" is not the stuff of novels' (P. Gilbert, 'Braddon' 185). In the mirror, Isabel refashions the 'stuff' of reality just as she refashions her plain stuff gowns. The actual function of women's dress to hide and reshape their 'natural' forms and replace it with prevailing fictional verities of femininity (Hollander, *Sex* 47) is analogous with this, as Isabel performs.

In Volume II of *The Doctor's Wife* Isabel goes to the looking glass. The narrator says that she

> rested her elbows on the mantelpiece and looked at herself, and pushed her hair about, and experimented with her mouth and eyes and tried to look like Edith Dombey [from Charles Dickens's *Dombey and Son*] in the grand Carker scene, and acted the scene in a whisper. No, she wasn't a bit like Edith Dombey, She was more like Juliet or Desdemona. (155)

In this strikingly metafictional and intertextual scene, Braddon illustrates the use of the mirror and dress to alter feminine and literary subjectivity and exhibits her awareness of the visual codes that surround these. The mirror functions as a link between the human, and literary, subject and their external representation (Hollander, *Seeing* 391). Anne Cranny-Francis suggests that the 'real' body is inscribed by prevailing discourses and material practices (2); the body is the 'real material fact' and representations thereof a 'reflection' of current ideas and fantasies (13). The looking glass literalises this process of 'reflection': it symbolises the idea that female identity is not only created but also distorted in the mirror (P. Gilbert, *Disease* 66). Through internalised literary fantasies of femininity, heroine-ship and genre (symbolised by the gazes of Sigismund Smith, Dr Gilbert and Roland Lansdell) Isabel's subjectivity is distorted and refashioned.

Through her reading, self-fashioning and acting, Isabel oscillates between the 'angel in the house', the seduced fated heroine considering an Ophelia-like suicide (Braddon, *Doctor's* 222), and the plain doctor's wife darning coarse grey socks (189). She ultimately transcends these limiting narrative alternatives and refashions the stuff and dresses of her dreams. The mirror and the self-contemplation it facilitates are integral to this process. Braddon expresses this transformation from a fantastic dreamlike notion of femininity to a 'realistic' one through the symbolism of dress and cloth. The narrator states that:

> The sweet age of enchantment is over; the fairy companions of girlhood, who were loveliest even when most they deluded, spread their bright wings and flutter away; and the grave genius of common-sense — a dismal-looking person, who dresses in grey woollen stuff, warranted not to shrink under the ordeal of the wash-tub, and steadfastly abjures crinoline — stretches out her hand, and offers, with a friendly but uncompromising abruptness, to be … [Isabel's] guide and monitoress. (277)

This scene has a dual function. It signals Isabel's journey through the mirror from the phantasmal world of romance and poetry to the narrative world of *The Doctor's Wife*. It is also the moment of reformation and redemption for Isabel and, therefore, for the novel from the realm of the sensational. Through this imagery Braddon raises questions about literature's capacity to hold a mirror up to social life. She addresses readers who, like Isabel, 'think that their lives are to be paraphrases of their favourite books' (30) and critics who charged her with being 'unnatural' and unrealistic (Rae 201). In this scene of sartorial and narrative transformation, Braddon interrogates this distinction between fact and fantasy, reality and fiction, and realism and sensationalism and their depictions of femininity through the distortion of the metafictional mirror. She questions the assumptions and the symbolic 'stuff' (written and 'clothy') which underpin realism and sensationalism as genres through viewing their self-reflections in a highly metafictional fashion.

The multiple acts of (genred) reading, acting, gazing and dressing are played out in this novel through the characters of Sigismund Smith and Roland Lansdell. Roland is the author of Byronically cynical poetry and 'delightful melodrama[s] which hold the mirror up to nature so exactly' to life (85). Smith, on the other hand, 'is compelled to avail himself of the noses, eyes, ruby lips, and golden or raven tresses … of every eligible young lady he meets, for the decking out of numerous heroines' (404). Through the voices (and gazes) of these two figures, Braddon draws attention to the impossibility of the mirror (in both its literal or literary manifestation) reproducing an image that is undistorted by engrained ways of reading and seeing (Michie 10). Whilst Roland assumes his literature to be a true depiction of 'real life', Smith makes no effort to disguise the fact he collects and refashions the features and details of the social world (and its female inhabitants) in writing sensation fiction for the penny press.

Through literalising the gaze of the alternatives of Victorian genre, Braddon reflects on the role of the visual in objectifying the woman, as both heroine and author, in Victorian fiction. Through sewing and dressing, however, Isabel takes control of this. The fabrics and dresses of her dreams finally float away from her like cobwebs in a sudden wind (*Doctor's* 276). Through self-reflection and refashioning, Isabel transcends her subordinate position as an object of reading and the gaze by becoming an agent in her own representation and plot.

This transformation is made manifest when Roland proposes that she run away to France to be his mistress. He imagines Isabel as the feminine ideal: 'I went there, Izzie', he passionately declares, 'and set up your image in the empty rooms, and fancied you hovering here and there in your white dress, upon the broad marble terrace' (270). Roland again conjures the image of the passive and angelic heroine in white. This time, however, it connotes the ghostliness of fantasy and absence. In contrast, Isabel sees the image of another feminine archetype of Victorian literature at this suggestion — she is shocked that Roland would think of her as 'like those wicked women who run away from their husbands' (273). Conscience forbids her final refashioning into the ultimate beloved (and seduced) heroine: the Fallen Woman. 'If she had been Clotilde or the glittering Duchess', Isabel reflects, she would have been better suited to this role (276). However, her 'fairytale was finished now', the narrator states, 'with an abrupt and cruel climax; the prince had vanished; the dream was over' and she is left only with a 'vague sense of her own wrong-doing' (225, 275).

This realisation is indicative of a new consciousness, of world and self, which Isabel realises in the final chapters of *The Doctor's Wife*. In a vivid image of hindsight (couched in the language of the mirror) the narrator tells us that Isabel sees 'herself again as she had been; "engaged" to the man who lay dead upstairs [Dr Gilbert]; and weaving a poor little web of romance for herself even out of that prosaic situation' (374). When she gazes into this metaphoric looking glass, she recognises the fantasy of 'the scenery and the dresses of [her] foolish dreams' and realises that she has been 'the dupe of her own fancies, her own dreams' of heroine-ship (155, 271).

The novel concludes in a frenzy of incident. Dr Gilbert falls victim to typhoid. Mr Sleaford returns to the narrative and, recognising Roland as the 'swell' (353) who gave evidence at his fraud trial, beats him to death. Roland bequeaths his fortune to Isabel and she lives on it modestly, donating large sums to charitable and benevolent causes in the town of Graybridge (353). With this, the narrator states, she 'passe[d] away from me into a higher region than that in which my story has lain' (402). This 'higher' region is both a moral and a cultural one. Morally, Isabel achieves the highest ideal of femininity as the 'angel in the house'. She is modest and demure and thinks only of the comfort and happiness of others. With this, she also graduates from the realm of sensationalism into the 'higher' literary form of realism. Sigismund Smith, too, leaves behind the genre of sensation fiction and sets to writing 'three volumes of the quiet and domestic school' (404). In his position as author-by-proxy of the novel, Smith's transition into the 'quiet and domestic school' of fiction holds a metafictional mirror up to Braddon's desire to change the fashion and subject of her authorship in writing *The Doctor's Wife*.

Whilst writing the novel, Braddon wrote to Edward Bulwer-Lytton of her intention of leaving behind sensationalism and 'going in a little for the subjective' in her writing (qtd in Wolff, 'Devoted' 19). She articulated her desire to change the subject of her fiction and, thereby, to alter the way in which she was perceived as an author by the Victorian reading public (qtd in Wolff, 'Devoted' 19). Her tools in doing so were the mirror and the yards of fabric with which Isabel fashions herself. In this novel, Braddon performs these changes by narrating Isabel reading, acting, dressing and self-fashioning in the mirror. The looking glass is a symbol of heightened self-consciousness and subjectivity for Isabel; it allows her to transcend the fantastic and erotic images of Victorian women as heroines and readers and move beyond them into autonomy.

In the closing chapters of *The Doctor's Wife*, the narrator describes Isabel as a woman (not a heroine, as she was previously referred to) governed by the higher feelings of sympathy and tenderness rather than the phantasm of fiction and dream (403). She refuses to be seduced by Roland Lansdell and retires to a life of respectability, domesticity and benevolence. That the corruptible female sensation reader resists actual seduction and, therefore, a moralising death, in the final chapters of the novel is highly significant. In this resolution, Braddon overturns the myth of the uncritical and corruptible female readers and fashions a positive image of women as heroines, authors and consumers of popular literature in the mid-Victorian period.

In their influential work on nineteenth-century women's fiction, *The Madwoman in the Attic*, Gilbert and Gubar state that

> [b]efore the woman writer can journey through the looking glass toward literary autonomy ... she must come to terms with the images on the surface of the glass, with, that is, those mythic masks males have fashioned over her human face both to lessen the dread of her inconstancy and — by identifying her with the 'eternal types' they have themselves invented — to possess her more thoroughly. (17)

In *The Doctor's Wife*, Braddon uses the mirror as a place of reflection, literal and figurative, in which to refashion the 'eternal types' of femininity which dominated mid-Victorian debates about popular literature. She refashions the seducible heroine of sensation fiction, transforming her into a sensible and grey-clad matron. Braddon also refashions her own subjectivity as an author. She refashions the image of 'The Sensation Novelist' which is held up by critics as a true reflection of her subjectivity (P. Gilbert, *Disease* 92). Instead, she celebrates the generic inconsistency of her metafictional novel and shows herself to be an intelligent and witty author, autonomous of the thrall of the 'style which she created': sensationalism (Rae 197). Using metafictional and intertextual techniques, Braddon makes this autonomy available to her readers.

Patricia Waugh argues that

> [a]lthough the intrusive commentary of nineteenth-century fiction may at times be metalingual (referring to fictional codes themselves), it functions mainly to aid the readerly concretization of the world of the book by forming a bridge between the historical and the fictional worlds. It suggests that the one is merely a continuation of the other, and it is thus not metafictional. (31-2)

Through the narrative commentary of Sigismund Smith in *The Doctor's Wife*, Braddon holds a metafictional mirror up to the writing of the novel. She reflects its intricate influences, references, patterns and techniques for the readers and emphasises the narrative's status as a work of fiction. This breaks down the typically realist continuity between the world of fantasy and fiction and that of history and reality in a way that can fittingly be described, despite Waugh's statement, as metafictional. This is emphasised when Isabel's daydreams give way to reality and she comes to the realisation that '"reality" is not the stuff of novels' (P. Gilbert, 'Braddon' 185). In this way, Braddon gives readers the tools with which to read critically and intelligently and, therefore, resist the fate of corruptible readers, harbingered by contemporary reviews, who 'think that their lives are to be paraphrases of their favourite books' (*Doctor's* 30). Braddon, therefore, invites her heroine and readers through the looking glass into a more self-conscious readerly subjectivity.

When Isabel puts aside her novels and fantasy of being a heroine and turns away from her looking glass toward the real world, she performs a significant symbolic action for women as authors, heroines and readers in the 1860s. She resists corruption and seduction and, by coming to terms with the eternal types of femininity reflected in the mirror, transcends them and achieves autonomy as a reader. Through a similar process of reading and reflection Braddon also refashions her authorial subjectivity as 'The Sensation Novelist' (P. Gilbert, *Disease* 92). In *The Doctor's Wife*, she incorporates elements of both realism and sensationalism whilst also critiquing the artistic and moral bases of these generic distinctions. She therefore demonstrates that she is neither a slave to sensationalism nor to her reputation as a sensation novelist.

Nevertheless, critics were quick to identify *The Doctor's Wife* as another Braddonian sensation novel in the fashion of *Lady Audley's Secret* and *Aurora Floyd*. Braddon's reputation as 'The Sensation Novelist' or 'queen of the sensation novel' functions as a mask, denying her versatility as an author and forestalling any reading of her novels as outside the conventions of the 'style which she created' (Rae 197; P. Gilbert, *Disease* 92; Phegley 23). In the final chapters of *The Doctor's Wife*, Braddon's narrator addresses these critics, stating that 'this is *not* a sensation novel. I write here what I know to be the truth' (358, emphasis in original). This claim to veracity and reality adds another layer of complexity and playfulness to Braddon's already self-conscious engagement with the literary codes surrounding reality, realism and sensationalism in this novel. By making this statement within the frame and mirror of the narrative, Braddon shows that all claims to reality are fictional and premised on particular, genred, ways of reading and reflecting. In *The Doctor's Wife*, Mary Elizabeth Braddon not only changes her subjectivity and that of her heroine and readers, then, she also changes the subject. She changes the literary subject by refashioning the sensation novel and its seducible and transgressive heroine. She also changes the authorial subject by actively addressing her reputation as a sensation novelist. Lastly, she changes the readerly subject by providing her audience with the tools with which to read attentively and critically.

This chapter takes up these tools and, in doing so, reassesses the claims that nineteenth-century literature cannot be metafictional, that Braddon is a slave to sensationalism and that sensationalism and realism are mutually exclusive (Rae 197; Waugh 31-2). This self-conscious critical approach provides a way of thinking about the construction of narratives of Victorian gender and genre, not only in contemporary literature, but also in subsequent scholarship. Braddon's reputation as a sensationalist may have its roots in the 1860s, but it has been continually reinforced by subsequent critics. In reading for generic instability as well as generic expectation, we are holding a mirror up to our own critical practices, and continuing Braddon's process of reading and reflecting (on) gender and genre in representations of the Victorian heroine, novelist and reader.

Works Cited

Braddon, Mary Elizabeth. *Aurora Floyd*. 1863. Ed. P.D. Edwards. London: Oxford UP, 2008.

———. *Lady Audley's Secret*. 1862. Ed. David Skilton. Oxford: Oxford UP, 1987.

———. 'Letter to Edward Bulwer-Lytton.' 17 January 1864. Letter 7 qtd in Robert Lee Wolff. 'Devoted Discipline: The Letters of Mary Elizabeth Braddon and Sir Edward Bulwer-Lytton, 1862-1873.' *Harvard Library Bulletin* 22.1 (1974): 5-35.

———. *The Doctor's Wife*. 1864. Ed. Lyn Pykett. Oxford: Oxford UP, 2008.

Brantlinger, Patrick. 'What is "Sensational" About the "Sensation Novel?"' *Nineteenth-Century Fiction* 37.1 (1982): 1-28. JSTOR, http://www.jstor.org.proxy.library.adelaide.edu.au/stable/3044667, accessed 4 July 2010.

Brownstein, Rachel M. *Becoming a Heroine: Reading About Women in Novels*. New York: The Viking Press, 1982.

Collins, William Wilkie. *The Woman in White*. 1860. Ed. Harvey Peter Sucksmith. London: Oxford UP, 1975.

Cranny-Francis, Anne. *The Body in the Text*. Melbourne: Melbourne UP, 1995.

Eliot, George. 'Silly Novels by Lady Novelists.' 1856. *Essays of George Eliot*. Ed. Thomas Pinney. London: Routledge and Kegan Paul, 1963. 300-24.

Flint, Kate. *The Woman Reader, 1837-1914*. Oxford: Clarendon Press, 1993.

Gilbert, Pamela K. 'Braddon and Victorian Realism: *Joshua Haggard's Daughter*.' *Beyond Sensation: Mary Elizabeth Braddon in Context*. Ed. Pamela K. Gilbert, Aeron Haynie and Marlene Tromp. New York: State University of New York Press, 2000. 183-95.

———. *Disease, Desire, and the Body in Victorian Women's Popular Women's Novels*. Cambridge: Cambridge UP, 1997.

Gilbert, Sandra M. and Susan Gubar. *The Madwoman in the Attic: The Woman Writer and the Nineteenth-Century Literary Imagination*. 2nd edn. New Haven and London: Yale UP, 2000.

Golden, Catherine J. 'Censoring Her Sensationalism: Mary Elizabeth Braddon and *The Doctor's Wife*.' *Victorian Sensations: Essays on a Scandalous Genre*. Ed. Richard Fantina and Kimberly Harrison. Columbus: The Ohio State UP, 2006. 29-40.

Hollander, Anne. *Seeing Through Clothes*. New York: The Viking Press, 1978.

———. *Sex and Suits: The Evolution of Modern Dress*. New York: Kodansha, 1995.

Hughes, Clair. *Dressed in Fiction*. Oxford and New York: Berg, 2005.

Knight, Mark. 'Figuring out the Fascination: Recent Trends in Criticism of Victorian Sensation and Crime Fiction.' *Victorian Literature and Culture* 37.1 (2009): 323-33. *Cambridge Journals Online*. http://journals.cambridge.org, accessed 12 August 2010.

Kortsch, Christine Bayles. *Dress Culture in Late Victorian Women's Fiction: Literacy, Textiles and Activism*. Farnham: Ashgate Publishing, 2009.

[Mansel, H.L.] 'Sensation Novels.' *The Quarterly Review* 113 (January and April 1863): 481-514.

Michie, Helena. *The Flesh Made Word: Female Figures and Women's Bodies*. New York and London: Oxford UP, 1987.

[Oliphant, Margaret.] 'Novels.' *Blackwood's Edinburgh Magazine* CII.DCXXIII (September 1867): 257-80.

Phegley, Jennifer. *Educating the Proper Woman Reader: Victorian Family Literary Magazines and the Cultural Health of the Nation.* Columbus: The Ohio State UP, 2004.

Pykett, Lyn. 'Introduction.' *The Doctor's Wife.* Mary Elizabeth Braddon. 1864. Oxford: Oxford UP, 2008. vii-xxviii.

——. *The 'Improper' Feminine: The Women's Sensation Novel and New Woman Writing.* London: Routledge, 1992.

[Rae, W. Fraser.] 'Sensation Novels: Miss Braddon.' *The North British Review* 43 (1865): 180-204. http://books.google.com.au, 10 November 2006, accessed 4 September 2010.

Reynolds, Kimberley and Nicola Humble. *Victorian Heroines: Representations of Femininity in Nineteenth-Century Literature and Art.* Hemel Hempstead: Harvester Wheatsheaf, 1993.

Sears, Albert C. 'Mary Elizabeth Braddon and the "Combination Novel": The Subversions of Sensational Expectation in *Vixen.*' *Victorian Sensations: Essays on a Scandalous Genre.* Eds Richard Fantina and Kimberly Harrison. Columbus: The Ohio State UP, 2006. 41-52.

Showalter, Elaine. *A Literature of Their Own: From Charlotte Brontë to Doris Lessing.* Revised and Expanded Edition. London: Virago Press, 2009.

Sparks, Tabitha. 'Fiction Becomes Her: Representations of Female Character in Mary Braddon's *The Doctor's Wife.*' *Beyond Sensation: Mary Elizabeth Braddon in Context.* Ed. Pamela K. Gilbert, Aeron Haynie and Marlene Tromp. New York: State University of New York Press, 2000. 197-209.

Talairach-Vielmas, Laurence. *Moulding the Female Body in Victorian Fairy Tales and Sensation Novels.* Aldershot: Ashgate Publishing Limited, 2007.

Tromp, Marlene, Pamela K. Gilbert and Aeron Haynie. 'Introduction.' *Beyond Sensation: Mary Elizabeth Braddon in Context.* Ed. Pamela K. Gilbert, Aeron Haynie and Marlene Tromp. New York: State University of New York Press, 2000. xv-xxxviii.

Waugh, Patricia. *Metafiction: The Theory and Practice of Self-Conscious Fiction.* 1984. London and New York: Routledge, 1988.

Wilson, Elizabeth. *Adorned in Dreams: Fashion and Modernity.* London: Virago Press, 1985.

Wolff, Robert Lee. 'Devoted Discipline: The Letters of Mary Elizabeth Braddon and Sir Edward Bulwer-Lytton, 1862-1873.' *Harvard Library Bulletin* 22. 1 (1974): 5-35.

——. *Sensational Victorian: The Life and Fiction of Mary Elizabeth Braddon.* New York and London: Garland Publishing, 1979.

10

The woman artist and narrative ends in late-Victorian writing

Mandy Treagus

The character of Elfrida in Sara Jeannette Duncan's *A Daughter of Today* is a representation of a figure increasingly seen in late-Victorian writing: the woman artist. The novel is a *Künstlerroman*, a significant form for the period, not only for the new narrative possibilities it seems to provide for female characters, but also because of its prominence in the rise of Modernism (Pykett 135). *A Daughter of Today* is one of the earliest examples of the form to feature the artistic development of a female protagonist, but it goes further than others in its exploration of new subjectivities for the heroine. Not only does the novel feature Elfrida's development as an artist, but it also depicts her as a confirmed egoist, preoccupied above all with her own development as both woman and as artist. This requires an abandonment of the dominant mode of being depicted in most nineteenth-century heroines, at least those endorsed by their narrators. Even in fiction in which the passion of the protagonist utterly drives the plot, most heroines are constrained by a finely tuned conscience and sense of duty that dominates their own desires for vocation, romantic fulfilment or both. This sense of self-sacrificing duty does not guarantee fulfilling fictional ends for such heroines, though, even when their narrators position readers to side with them. In *A Daughter of Today*, however, there is no such sense of sublimation or submission of self. Rather, the central character follows her quest for artistic success by projecting a new kind of subject, the desiring ambitious heroine, whose cultivation of ego is her most defining mode. Whether the narrative closure of death forecloses the possibilities presented by this new kind of heroine is an issue that the novel raises; another is the question of how Duncan came to conceive of such a heroine in the *fin-de-siècle* context, when even first-wave feminists depicted self-sacrifice as the ultimate mode for women.

I argue that by taking her inspiration from the memoir that 'caused a sensation in Europe and more so in America' (Parker and Pollock vii), Duncan was able to move outside of the models already present in the Victorian novel. She was, I suggest, inspired by *Le Journal de Marie Bashkirtseff*, published in France in 1887 and translated into English by the poet Mathilde Blind in 1890. Though there is no known record of Duncan acknowledging this debt, the similarities in milieu, names and minor characters, and most of all in the core drive of both heroines, show that Duncan used *Le Journal* as a source. I agree with Michelle Gadpaille when she asserts that 'Bashkirtseff provided Duncan with more than merely the names of streets and the Bohemian atmosphere of the Latin Quarter. Bashkirtseff furnished Duncan with a model for representing interiority for a woman artist' (3). *A Daughter of Today* was published in London in 1894 and in North America the following year. Both novel and journal offer the strong narrative closure provided by the death of their heroines, yet both transgress late-nineteenth-century codes of femininity in ways that seem to overflow the bounds placed on them by such closure. Marie Bashkirtseff, a young Ukrainian noble who studied painting in Paris, kept a journal for most of her life (Konz 3). In it she wrote of her eclectic education, her developing illness, artistic aspirations and self-preoccupation. Bashkirtseff died of tuberculosis in her mid-twenties, just as she was beginning to achieve some fame as a painter. The heroine of Duncan's novel, Elfrida, also begins her artistic career as a painter, eventually becoming a novelist and self-absorbed bohemian who, despising the conventional paths open to her, suicides artistically in the face of apparent artistic and romantic disappointment.

Describing Elfrida as an egoist requires some clarification. I use this term in its nineteenth- rather than twentieth-century psychological sense. The idea of the egoist had been brought to literary attention in George Meredith's *The Egoist*

(1879), in which it is applied to a man only concerned with gratifying his vanity through the pursuit of his own desires, though the term had been in use since the previous century. Meredith's novel is another obvious precursor to Duncan's. Not only does it foreground the male protagonist's egoism, but Meredith is presumably the model for the famous author, George Jasper, before whom Elfrida expresses, embarrassingly for those around her, public adulation (151).

On the publication of the English translation of Bashkirtseff's journal in 1890, Marion Hepworth Dixon wrote, 'It is this journal with which the world is ringing now, and which it is hardly too much to say is likely to carry the fame of Marie Bashkirtseff over the face of the civilised globe' (Dixon 276). Dixon was especially well placed to assess the journal, as she and her sister Ella had studied in the Académie Julian in Paris with Bashkirtseff herself. She claims that 'In it we find a woman self-revealed, a woman who, almost for the first time in history, has had the courage to present us with a real woman, as distinguished from the sham women of books' (276). Dixon was prompted to write her defence of Bashkirtseff following negative responses to the French edition which reflected the commonly held attitude that anything less than self-abnegation in a female was undesirable. W.E. Gladstone, in *The Nineteenth Century*, reacts to the French edition and what were seen as the more shocking of its characteristics: Bashkirtseff's ambition and hence her transgressive gender performance. Gladstone allows her some femininity, but only the worst sort: 'Womanish she was in many of woman's weaknesses', he wrote, 'and she did not possess the finer graces which we signify by the epithet feminine' (605). Instead, he notes that 'If there was an idea at the root of all her aspirations, that idea was power' (606). Gladstone was not entirely condemnatory, though. He acknowledges the one characteristic that might provide some justification for her apparent faults: 'indeed there is one remark, obvious enough to make, which seems to cover the whole case of this extraordinary person. She was a true genius, though some of her judgements in letters and in art seem to be eccentric' (604). The admission that a woman might be characterised as a genius is quite a concession, however crowded about it might be with qualifications and criticisms.

In his own journal, *The Review of Reviews*, W.T. Stead similarly complains of Bashkirtseff's lack of feminine virtues, writing, 'there is more pathos in the evidence with which every page abounds of the life poisoned at its source by vanity, egotism, and absolute indifference to the welfare of others' (549). Despite having begun his article with the statement that 'In all the world there is nothing so interesting, or so little known, as woman', Stead goes on to deny Bashkirtseff's womanhood (539). He does this in response to her statements regarding her apprehension of her own beauty, her lack of romantic feelings for any of the men who professed to love her, and her overwhelming desire to succeed as a painter. In marked contradiction with Dixon's view, Stead writes, 'She was very clever, no doubt, very fascinating, but woman she was not' (546). Though often sympathetic, it is the quality of ambition that Stead finds hardest to accept: 'Ah, what did she not want? Her ambition was insatiable' (543). It is this same quality that appealed to others, though, and allowed critique of those reviewers who found her performance of gender alarming. The anonymous reviewer for *The Century*, 'D', canvasses two extremes of responses to Bashkirtseff that were circulating, making the observation that 'the generality of men do not easily pardon an egoism which encroaches upon their own, an ambition which measures itself with theirs, and an absence of reserve which seems the very abdication of womanhood' (28).

Reading responses to the journal in terms of gendered power relations provides an antidote to, and powerful analysis of, the condemnatory yet pruriently fascinated reviews the journal was receiving. Arthur Symons reported on its popularity: 'A few years ago one only knew of two or three people here and there who had ever heard of the Journal — to-day everyone has read it or is reading it. No doubt this is to a large extent the result of Mr. Gladstone's article' (5). But while there was fascination, even voyeurism, for many in reading the inner thoughts of a young woman, others were excited by the aspirations it voiced. Like Dixon, 'D' greets the journal as a significant intervention, with the revelations it contains momentous: 'Marie Bashkirtseff has shot like a flame across the sky' (28). What excites 'D' the most, though, is that it seems to announce 'a whole world of possibility and suggestion' (28). It is this quality that connects it with Duncan's novel and the wider trajectory of the female *Künstlerroman*. Even if the narrative of the woman artist is cut short in death, as occurs in memoir and novel, both recount lives in which women pursue, discuss and produce art, whatever their personal and romantic ends might be.

All responses to the journal demonstrate to some extent the problem late-nineteenth-century culture had with the juxtaposition of these two very different and generally separate categories: 'artist' and 'woman'. Bashkirtseff was acutely aware of the restraints that had an impact on her own career. In the 'Introduction' to her translation, Blind somewhat theatrically suggests that the journal represents 'the drama of a woman's soul; at odds with destiny, as such a soul must needs be, when endowed with great powers and possibilities, under the present social conditions' (695). What Blind is asserting is not the inherent individual problem of being female with aspirations — a form of gender failure — but rather the social problem that women lacked equality of opportunity. The material circumstances of training to become a painter were quite different for men and women, as were the opportunities for functioning artists. The *atelier* in which Bashkirtseff trained, the Académie Julian, run by Rodolphe Julian, was one of few that admitted women and it was also the only one at which women could paint from the nude, and hence develop their skills more accurately from living models rather than from statuary (Bashkirtseff 275). Julian was remarkably democratic in his approach to gender, encouraging female students when they were 'excluded from studying at Ecole des Beaux Arts' and allowing them to compete for the same internal prizes (Zimmermann 169) at a time when women could not compete for the Prix de Rome, which was the case until 1903 (Zimmermann 170). Despite these moves toward equality, the studio still expressed a structural hierarchy. The male studio was regarded more seriously and male students had access to cheaper training, 'as it was generally believed that women would be able to find a family member or an outside sponsor who would pay their expenses' (Weisberg 14). More significantly, style itself was seen to be gendered.

The women artists in training were under no illusions that their work was considered equal to that of the men. Bashkirtseff recorded that when she painted well she was told 'it looks like a man's work', and she knew she was being complimented when told, 'the others said at the men's studio that I had neither the touch, nor the manner, nor the capabilities of a woman' (Bashkirtseff 464, 292). Of the male artists she writes: 'These gentlemen despise us and it is only when they come across a powerful, even brutal piece of work, that they are satisfied; this vice is rare among women. It is a work of a young man, they said of mine' (350). Because some forms of painting were considered to be female accomplishments, Bashkirtseff also had to fight off the impression of amateurism that clung to women training at the Académie, as 'The spectre of the wealthy amateur, dabbling in drawing as she might in singing or reciting, infuriated those women who were ambitious and serious about their work' (Garb, 'Men of Genius' 128). Her class background worked against others perceiving her serious artistic intent, and she sometimes expressed envy at what she supposed were the 'simpler lives, the more artistic *milieu*' of her fellow pupils (Dixon 279, emphasis in original). Similarly, if she looked conventionally feminine for her class, she knew this would go against her reception as a committed artist: 'But I (was) so pretty and so well dressed that they (will) be convinced that I don't paint my pictures alone' (Bashkirtseff 674, parenthesis in original). In a very early review, Helen Zimmern noted the day-to-day conditions undertaken by the young upper-class Bashkirtseff in the studio. She would 'work for eight or nine hours a day in a small, close, ugly studio, with a fervor not to be surpassed by those whose art was their bread' (314). Such smelly cramped conditions were also emphasised by Dixon: 'closed windows, a fierce charcoal stove, the indescribable smells of oil paints, turpentine, rags … could hardly have conduced to the health of the strongest; yet I cannot recall one word of complaint that ever fell from Marie Bashkirtseff' (280). It was rare for someone of her class to even enter such a space; that Bashkirtseff gave it such serious attention made it even more remarkable, and contributes to Dixon's view that she worked with 'a kind of ferocious joy' (279). The conflict between the roles of woman and artist, outlined briefly here, provide the greatest source of disequilibrium in both of these texts, a disequilibrium that reaches narrative resolution in the death of the heroine in both cases.

Bashkirtseff's apprehension of such inequalities led to involvement in one of the suffrage groups of her day. From 1880, Bashkirtseff had become involved in *Les Droits des Femmes*, visiting its leader wearing a brunette wig to disguise herself. Not only did she help fund their journal, *La Citoyenne*, but she also wrote for it under the pseudonym Pauline Orell (Konz 101). One of her pieces, 'Les Femmes Artistes', was published in 1881. In it she outlines the difficulties encountered by female artists, especially in training and opportunities, and she argues strongly for equal chances at prizes and exhibitions:

> All women are not artists, just as not all want to be politicians. There is a very small number who take action, taking nothing away [from] the famous hearth; you well know it. We have schools of drawing in the truly artistic point of view, or, well, two or three fashionable studios where young rich girls amuse themselves in making paintings. But what we need is the possibility to work like men and not have to carry out amazing feats to attain what men easily have. You ask us with indulgent irony the number of great women artists. Well, messieurs, there have been some, and it is astonishing, in view of the enormous difficulties they have encountered.
> (Qtd in Konz, 102)

Bashkirtseff is clear here that women's underrepresentation in the ranks of great artists is societal and structural, rather than something intrinsic in women themselves. That she had to assume a pseudonym in order to make such criticisms publicly indicates her perception of the restrictions she still negotiated, even if she managed to transcend many in gaining access to the studio. Tamar Garb affirms such ongoing restrictions, noting that '[i]n the multiple identities and disguises which Bashkirtseff assumed lies a clue to the duress under which she and other assertive women lived' (*Sisters* 53).

Seeking to be an artist would be enough to incur condemnation from some, but Bashkirtseff compounded this by expressing sheer driving ambition throughout her journal. She consciously follows her own desires, is expressly aware of her will to succeed over any rival — fellow artist Louise Breslau being the chief of these (Becker 69-114) — and is confident, even vauntingly so, of her own capacity. It is this aspect of the narrative which provides a clear reason for the journal's sensational response, but her youth and beauty add a piquancy, even a heightened eroticism to this, for her beauty was of a very specific type. While challenging the apparently immutable boundary between woman and artist, Marie Bashkirtseff also confirmed the age's association of femininity with sickness, death and tubercular beauty. She presents herself as a romantic heroine, with 'bewitching pallor' and perfect dress sense (Dixon 278). While apparently challenging conventional femininity, she also reinscribes it, provoking Gladstone's mixed response: 'Mlle. Bashkirtseff attracts and repels alternately, and perhaps repels as much as she attracts' (603). However, this mixture possibly made the journal even more titillating than it might otherwise have been, had she only expressed the conventional.

Changing the Victorian Subject

Sara Jeannette Duncan's unacknowledged debt to Bashkirtseff seems indisputable, I suggest, in her descriptions of the Paris studio where her heroine studies. In many instances only the names have been changed. The understanding that women's and men's art is intrinsically different is made clear. Lucien, the Julian character of the novel, tells Nádie, the Russian girl, 'In you, mademoiselle … I find the woman and the artist divorced' and takes her painting to the other studio for the approval of the men (Duncan 21). When it comes to Elfrida, it is her lack of 'male' qualities which signals her lack of success: 'Your drawing is still lady-like, your colour is still pretty, and *sapristi!* you have worked with me a year!' (Duncan 23). Elfrida's pursuit of a career as a woman artist is thwarted by the practicalities of her parents' financial difficulties, and her own accurate assessment that her talents for painting are limited. She soon abandons the Paris *atelier* milieu to pursue one Duncan knows better: the London literary scene. The heroine's sense of the romance of being penniless is mitigated by the need to eat and pay the rent, so despite the fact that it is not her chosen 'art', she moves into journalism, though initially she views it as 'a cynical compromise with her artistic conscience' (Duncan 35). She is able to shift her ambitions from painting to writing, as 'her solemn choice of an art had been immature and to some extent groundless and unwarrantable' (Duncan 54). The *Künstlerroman*, after a brief setback, is once more on course. In this new setting, Duncan examines similar issues to those raised by the Bashkirtseff journal: the assertion of the existence of the female egoist, and the apparent impossibility of the existence of the female artist. Like Bashkirtseff, Duncan's heroine Elfrida admires herself in the mirror and is preoccupied with her effect upon others. While Bashkirtseff records, 'I spend my life in saying wild things, which please me and astonish others' (317), the reader has the opportunity to observe Elfrida at this pastime almost continually. However, in both these character portraits, self-consciousness is presented as an element of ego which feeds the artistic impulse and gives drive to its possessor. It may be repulsive to others but it is productive.

The sense that the male artist is the real arbiter of the value of women's art is caught in Elfrida's relationship with Kendal, a painter she had known in Paris and for whom she harbours romantic hopes. Though he takes great pleasure in her presence, his need to define her limits his emotional response, as he thinks 'eagerly of the pleasure of proving, with his own eyes, another step in the working out of the problem which he believed he had solved in Elfrida' (Duncan 204). His ultimate expression of this is in the portrait he paints, in which he feels 'an exulting mastery', and 'a silent, brooding triumph in his manipulation, in his control' (Duncan 246, 247). Her objectification is clear during her last sitting for the portrait, as his sense of control increases in line with her objectification. Finally, when they both view the finished portrait, it is Elfrida's egoism that seems to define her, resulting in her shame and his diminished interest, once he has captured her. The portrait's title — '*A Fin de Siècle Tribute*' — links the figure of the female artist and other preoccupations of the age: Aestheticism, the Decadence and the primacy of art (Duncan 151). Indeed, Kathryn Ready suggests that this portrait, like that of Oscar Wilde's Dorian Gray, shows Duncan's 'specific interest in analysing the implications of Aestheticism and Decadence for the female artist' (100). It also raises the narrative problem common to heroines: whether they will follow a fulfilling vocation, a *Bildung*, or the romance plot. Elfrida's response to Kendal, at least momentarily, is to offer him romantic submission in the place of her artistic ambition. However, Duncan does not let this triumph of romance over *Bildung* stand. Later, ironically rejecting this choice, Elfrida tells her confessor, the statue of Buddha she has in her room: 'It was a lie, a pose to tempt him on. I would never have given it up — never!' (Duncan 254).

In many ways, Elfrida's ultimate suicide is the result of the apparent collapse of both of these potential plots. When the romance with Kendal fails, and her novel is rejected, she makes a choice that links her with other nineties artists. Ready claims that her suicide is, in fact, 'the fullest expression of her Decadence, aligning her with famous Decadent heroes like George Moore's Mike Fletcher' (100). Elfrida considers it to be 'the strong, the artistic, the effective thing to do', but initially she does not go through with it (Duncan 253). She eventually destroys Kendal's painting, informing him in a note that 'I have come here this morning ... determined either to kill myself or IT' (Duncan 276, emphasis in original). Elfrida's end is raised even before her chic poison ring is introduced when the landlady comments on the propensity of female artistis to commit suicide: 'I only 'ope I won't find 'er suicided on charcoal some mornin', like that pore young poetiss in yesterday's paper' (Duncan 64).

Nineteenth-century literature, especially poetry, had been preoccupied with this link for much of the century. As Angela Leighton notes regarding representations of Sappho in the poetry of Felicia Hemans, 'Sappho's leap connects female creativity with death, in a pact which the Victorian imagination finds endlessly seductively appealing' (35). The choice presented to nineteenth-century heroines, to pursue either art or love, precluded the woman artist from romantic fulfilment. The artistic deaths portrayed in this poetry are predicated on the experience of romantic disappointment and the inadequacy of art as an alternative to it. When her potential lover chooses a more conventional woman, and shows his abhorrence for her egoism, the romance narrative is closed to Elfrida. However, more significantly in this *Künstlerroman* is the apparent failure of her artistic career. It is as though the tried and true romance plot has been abandoned, but the plot of the achieving female artist is just too radical for the author. Death becomes a means of escape for the author just as much as for the heroine. Death not only provides closure to the plot, then, but because of its association with female art it can be seen as almost a compulsion for Elfrida, a proof of artistic sensibility.

Egoism, as part of the late-nineteenth-century construction of genius, is necessarily part of the creation of a female artist but it adds to the already present conflict between the categories of 'woman' and 'artist'. This is probably Duncan's greatest debt to Bashkirtseff. In depicting the function of egoism in the development of her art, Bashkirtseff allowed Duncan to envisage a functioning female artist, not just the caricatures that had been brought into being previously. George Gissing had portrayed women writers in his 1891 novel *New Grub Street*, but they are pale and tired hacks who lead unnatural lives and have no real professional or artistic ambitions. Amongst the New Woman novels of the 1890s were many examples that sought to demonstrate the element of unnaturalness of any career for women other than that of wife and mother. Joanna Wood's *Judith Moore; or Fashioning a Pipe* is a Canadian example of this genre. The heroine, under the weight of her 'unnatural' life as a famous singer, collapses physically and is only restored by retirement under the care of a simple farming man whom she marries. The implication throughout is that although she has an astounding voice, the pursuit of a career actually makes a woman sick, because it is not her purpose in life. As a reminder of her mistake, this heroine is unable to have children, but is more than content with her husband. In the reception of Bashkirtseff's journal there is also this sense that her life, ambition and choices have been unnatural, and that her death is the only possible outcome for them. At least her death solves this dilemma of what to do with the contradiction of the functioning woman artist.

In Duncan's *A Daughter of Today*, this dilemma is played out at the level of plot, as the narrative turns on just this question. When her egoism is highlighted, in the revelatory portrait, Elfrida comments ironically on this plot device as the narrator rejects it: 'Don't think I shall reform after this moral shock, as people in books do' (Duncan 250). The course of *this* heroine's plot will be different from previous ones, but the author's ambivalence about her heroine is finally revealed in the closure she imposes on her narrative. Duncan also demonstrates an ambivalence about the association of the female artist with sickness and death, though ultimately she reinforces it. Consumption will not provide Elfrida's end, but she can create her own tragedy. Suicide, as a way out, has been toyed with by Elfrida throughout the novel. The question in this novel is what it signifies. Is it the martyrdom of true genius, or the impossibility of the woman artist? Or does Elfrida's suicide merely demonstrate the excesses of bohemian values, and the thwarted self-will of a spoilt young woman? Adorno later described Bashkirtseff as 'the patron saint of the *fin de siècle*' (qtd in Molloy, 12), and perhaps it is the fact of Elfrida's death, whether by suicide or disease, that also marks her as emblematic of the era. Dixon described her friend's characteristics thus: 'Her very faults are an epitome of the age. All the restlessness, the fever, the longings, the caprices, the abnegations, the fervours, the belief, and the scepticism of the nineteenth century are here' (282). In imbuing her heroine with this same spirit, Duncan highlights the inherent contradictions between her aspirations and her opportunities and the romantic ends to which these contradictions are put.

If there is any consensus about the fate of the *fin-de-siècle* woman artist, it is that she cannot succeed. She cannot have both romantic *and* artistic fulfilment within the life of the novel, but must give up one for the other, or even both, in a denouement that often belies the life of her creator, the woman writer, working at bringing her to light in the world of literature. In her depiction of the woman artist, Duncan finds herself in this same dilemma, despite going beyond the models of fiction in English for her character's inspiration. Some reviewers were shocked by Duncan's heroine. The reviewer in *The Athenaeum* claims that 'Her creator touches her with an almost malignant hand, illuminating her egotism, her affectation, her heartlessness, the ill-breeding of her gospel of art and life, in letters of flame' (705). But dissatisfaction with the narrative possibilities of the 1890s novel also resulted in decidedly disappointed responses. The reviewer for *The Nation* sees the denouement as 'a wasteful and ridiculous excess of consideration for the requirements of a novel as understood by literary Philistia' (473), while *The Review of Reviews* bemoans 'One feels now and then like beseeching our tender fiction writers to let one of these Bohemian and charmingly bold young women live to find forty years and a little happiness' (114). But not until the novel moved beyond the closed ending would such narrative ends be possible.[1]

The figure of the female artist certainly expanded the range of potential roles for the heroine in English fiction, even if her creators often seemed to view her with ambivalence. Such woman artists appear as part of a range of new feminine roles, especially in the New Woman fiction of the 1890s. In fact, Lyn Pykett claims that 'New Woman fiction is littered with would-be literary artists, painters and musicians' (136), most of whom were writers (Pykett 135) — although as Penny Boumelha points out, 'it is difficult to think of any such female character who actually *wants* to be a journalist or to write in this way' (165, emphasis in original). These female characters generally begin to write when other options fade or their circumstances compel them to make a living. Often they must provide for others and so they work in order to do so. They are shown as finding their occupations wearisome and debilitating; they 'break down or give in under the pressures of the various circumstances which conspire against them' (Pykett 136). Apparently physically unsuited for such roles, these characters find them to be fatiguing, enervating and, tellingly, unnatural. Even more significantly, they express little ambition as artists. Boumelha also outlines a specific figure within the range of woman artists, the woman of genius, who similarly lacks obvious ambition. Despite Galton's claims that 'women lack the

---

[1] For a broader discussion of these issues, see my *Empire Girls*.

capacity for genius'[2] (Boumelha 168), some writers used the category in order to provide a justification for heroines pursuing an artistic role:

> The concept of innate genius also enables the representation of achievement without conscious ambition — then as now a problematic quality in feminist reconstructions of the feminine. If the power of genius simply resides within, then it becomes only another form of destiny to which women must assent, without challenge to the conventional womanliness of self-forgetfulness. (Boumelha 172)

The woman of genius could therefore succumb to that higher power, rather than using her own ambition to take her own artistic space.

In a link between the 1890s and the early decades of the twentieth century, Duncan moves away from either of these models — the reluctant, obligated artist, working out of necessity, and the genius, forced by her talents to succumb to their powers — and changes the conversation about the woman artist by depicting her as ambitious *even if her 'genius' is not certain*. In doing so, she creates a new figure in fiction about the female artist, a woman ambitious for the role and prepared to put it above all else.

Works Cited

Bashkirtseff, Marie. *The Journal of Marie Bashkirtseff*. Trans. Mathilde Blind. 1890. Ed. and intro. Rozsika Parker and Griselda Pollock. London: Virago, 1985.

Becker, Jane R. 'Nothing Like a Rival to Spur One On: Marie Bashkirtseff and Louise Breslau at the Académie Julian.' *Overcoming all Obstacles: The Women of the Académie Julian*. Ed. Gabriel P. Weisberg and Jane R. Becker. New Jersey: Rutgers UP, 1999. 69-114.

Blind, Mathilde. 'Introduction.' Marie Bashkirtseff. *The Journal of Marie Bashkirtseff*. Trans. Mathilde Blind. 1890. Ed. and intro. Rozsika Parker and Griselda Pollock. London: Virago, 1985. 695-716.

---

[2] In the index to *Hereditary Genius*, he lists: 'Women: why their names are omitted here, transmission of ability through, influence of mothers, mothers of eminent men, wives of eminent men' (Galton).

Boumelha, Penny. 'The Woman of Genius and the Woman of Grub Street: Figures of the Female Writer in British *Fin-de-Siècle* Fiction.' *English Literature in Transition, 1880-1920* 40.2 (1997): 164-80.

D. 'Two Views of Marie Bashkirtseff.' *The Century Magazine* XL (1890): 28-32.

Dixon, Marion Hepworth. 'Marie Bashkirtseff: A Personal Reminiscence.' *Fortnightly Review* 47 (1890): 276-82.

Duncan, Sara Jeannette. *A Daughter of Today*. 1894. Ottowa: Tecumseh, 1988.

Gadpaille, Michelle. 'Aesthetic Debate in the *Fin-de-Siècle* Novel: A Canadian Perspective.' 2008. http://oddelki.ff.uni-mb.si/filozofija/files/Festschrift/Dunjas_festschrift/gadpaille.pdf, accessed 1 July 2012.

Galton, Francis. *Hereditary Genius: An Inquiry into its Laws and Consequences*. London: Macmillan, 1869.

Garb, Tamar. '"Men of Genius, Women of Taste": The Gendering of Art Education in the Late Nineteenth-Century Paris.' *Overcoming all Obstacles: The Women of the Académie Julian*. Ed. Gabriel P. Weisberg and Jane R. Becker. New Jersey: Rutgers UP, 1999. 115-34.

———. *Sisters of the Brush: Women's Artistic Culture in Late Nineteenth-Century Paris*. New Haven: Yale UP, 1994.

Gissing, George. *New Grub Street*. 1891. London: Penguin, 1985.

Gladstone, W.E. '*Journal de Marie Bashkirtseff.*' *The Nineteenth Century* Oct. 1889: 602-7.

Konz, Louly Peacock. *Marie Bashkirtseff's Life in Self-Portraits (1858-1884)*. Lampeter, Wales: Edwin Mellen, 2005.

Leighton, Angela. *Victorian Women Poets: Writing Against the Heart*. London: Harvester Wheatsheaf, 1992.

Meredith, George. *The Egoist*. 1879. Ware, UK: Wordsworth Classics, 1995.

Molloy, Sylvia. 'Voice Snatching: "De sobremesa," Hysteria and the Impersonation of Marie Bashkirtseff.' *Latin American Literary Review* 25.50 (1997): 11-29.

'More Fiction.' *The Nation* 21 June (1894): 472-3.

Parker, Rozsika and Griselda Pollock. 'Introduction.' Bashkirtseff, Marie. *The*

Journal of Marie Bashkirtseff. Trans. Mathilde Blind. 1890. Ed. and intro. Rozsika Parker and Griselda Pollock. London: Virago, 1985. vii-xxx.

Pykett, Lyn. 'Portraits of the artist as a young woman: representations of the female artist in the New Woman fiction of the 1890s.' *Victorian Women Writers and the Woman Question.* Ed. Nicola Diane Thompson. Cambridge: Cambridge UP, 1999. 135-50.

Ready, Kathryn. 'Sara Jeannette Duncan's "A Daughter of Today": Nineteenth-Century Canadian Literary Feminism and the *fin-de-siècle* magic-picture story.' *Canadian Literature* 173 (2002): 95-112.

'Recent American Publications.' *The Review of Reviews* 10 (1894): 114.

'Review of *A Daughter of Today*, Sara Jeannette Duncan.' *The Athenaeum* (2 June 1894): 705.

[Stead, W.T.]. '*The Journal of Marie Bashkirtseff:* The Story of a Girl's Life.' *The Review of Reviews* 1 (1890): 539-49.

Symons, Arthur. 'The Journal of Marie Bashkirtseff.' *Academy* 38.948 (1890): 5.

Treagus, Mandy. *Empire Girls: the colonial heroine comes of age.* Adelaide: University of Adelaide Press, 2014.

Weisberg, Gabriel. P. 'The Women of the Académie Julian: The Power of Professional Emulation.' *Overcoming All Obstacles: The Women of the Académie Julian.* Ed. Gabriel P. Weisberg and Jane R. Becker. New Jersey: Rutgers UP, 1999. 13-68.

Wood, Joanna. *Judith Moore; or, Fashioning a Pipe.* New York: J. Selwin Tait & Sons, 1898.

Zimmerman, Enid. 'The Mirror of Marie Bashkirtseff: Reflections about the Education of Women Art Students in the Nineteenth Century.' *Studies in Art Education* 30.3 (1989): 164-75.

Zimmern, Helen. 'Marie Bashkirtseff: A Human Document.' *Blackwood's Magazine* 146.1387 (1889): 300-20.

11

Miss Wade's torment: the perverse construction of same-sex desire in *Little Dorrit*

Shale Preston

The title of this chapter seeks in a 'tongue in cheek' way to wrest Miss Wade's torment away from its familiar self-imposed shackles to a torment that is at least in part connected to frustration with her less than sympathetic creator.[1] This is a small step but one that is nonetheless significant because perhaps of all Charles Dickens's characters, Miss Wade, from the serial novel *Little Dorrit*, has been locked up for far too long in walls that are thought to be entirely of her own making. Certainly, Miss Wade does offer up her confessional text 'The History of a Self-Tormentor' to a male auditor and this unfortunate piece of writing very conveniently gives readers the permission to dismiss her as a highly disturbed self-saboteur. But Miss Wade is not simply hoist by her own petard — her creator has had an active hand in making the poor quality fuse for the petard. So, whilst it may be 'a commonplace in criticism' (Barrett 200) to note that the primary metaphor of *Little Dorrit* is the prison, it is far from commonplace to

---

[1] Goldie Morgentaler writes: 'Miss Wade, the very epitome of the forsaken child Dickens once championed, elicits in this later work very little sympathy from her creator. She is presented instead as incapable of subduing her own tormented nature, and being responsible for her failure to do so' (98).

note that Miss Wade's particular blend of psychological imprisonment owes as much to her own distorted views as to Dickens's wish to figuratively lock her up and throw away the key. Accordingly, the title of this chapter also playfully alludes to Jeanette Winterson's comment on her book *Oranges Are Not the Only Fruit*: 'it dares to suggest that what makes life difficult for homosexuals is not their perversity but other people's' (xiii).

Just who and what is Miss Wade? This is a very vexed question. In the text, Miss Wade appears to defy description. Upon tracking her down, the highly conservative character Mr Meagles is reduced to spluttering:

> '... I must say it ... you were a mystery to all of us, and had nothing in common with any of us when she [Tattycoram] unfortunately fell in your way. I don't know what you are, but you don't hide, can't hide, what a dark spirit you have within you. If it should happen that you are a woman, who, from whatever cause, has a perverted delight in making a sister-woman as wretched as she is (I am old enough to have heard of such), I warn her against you, and I warn you against yourself.'[2]

Mr Meagles may have attained the state of maturity that has armed him with the knowledge that certain 'wretched' women derive pleasure from making other women as 'wretched' as themselves but he does not have a pejorative name at his disposal for this condition and, as a result, his only alternative is to send out warning signals to these apparently lost and out of control vessels of sister-womanhood. The inability to name the condition that Miss Wade suffers from puts Mr Meagles at a disadvantage because it means that Miss Wade effectively eludes his epistemological framework. Despite this, Mr Meagles is aware that he is in the presence of a new and different kind of subjectivity — a subjectivity that is so frightfully new that it does not even have a name.[3]

Mr Meagles is also aware that this nameless subjectivity is rooted in an exclusive relationship between two women. That Mr Meagles actively ties this relationship up with his own worldliness is significant. No babe in the woods, Mr Meagles is old enough to know that there are other women in the world

---

2   Charles Dickens, *Little Dorrit*, (379; bk 1, ch. 27). Subsequent references to this edition will appear in the text.

3   Piya Pal Lapinski notes: 'His use of "what" instead of "who" points to his sense of Miss Wade as something not quite human' (83).

who share Miss Wade's 'perverse' proclivities. Mr Meagles's words, then, quite obviously point to the fact that Miss Wade is attracted to her own sex. Indeed, Edwin B. Barrett definitively states: 'Mr. Meagles believes [Miss Wade] to be lesbian' (211). So, too, Merryn Williams writes: 'Mr Meagles is so shocked by the unnatural spectacle of two women running away together that he obliquely accuses Miss Wade of being a lesbian' (86).[4] Strangely, however, many critics have chosen to eschew the possibility that Miss Wade could be a lesbian or could have any place along a genealogy of lesbian desire. As Anna Wilson writes:

> [P]revious readings of Miss Wade … are, if anything, anti-lesbian readings … We are variously assured that Miss Wade is no lesbian because it is people she hates, not just men … or that Tattycoram is a surrogate daughter and hence in no eroticized relation to her companion. What is singularly consistent is the unanimity of feeling that there is nothing right and perhaps something faintly disreputable about looking at Miss Wade through a lesbian glass. (188)

For Wilson, these 'anti-lesbian readings'[5] serve the dual purpose of 'keeping both history and critics … safe from lesbian taint' (189).[6] Wilson's comments accord with Patricia Juliana Smith's observation:

> [T]here has heretofore been a continuing critical reluctance, if not refusal, to see lesbians and lesbianism outside those contemporary and generally demotic narratives clearly labeled "lesbian literature." This has, until very

---

4 Furthermore, Geoffrey Carter maintains that Miss Wade's response to Mr Meagles's warnings conveys her same-sex attraction: 'In reply Miss Wade, who has already "laid her hand protectingly on the girl's neck for a moment," now puts her arm about Tattycoram's waist "as if she took possession of her for evermore" (p. 379; bk. I, ch. 27). Here Dickens seems to be referring to lesbianism as clearly as he was able to' (145).

5 See Wilson for a discussion and overview of these readings. Not all commentators have produced anti-lesbian readings of Miss Wade. See the summation of lesbian readings that Janet Retseck provides (224). Retseck, however, takes an emphatically anti-lesbian stance: 'Miss Wade cannot and should not be read in terms of sexuality … Dickens succeeds in shaping Miss Wade into a paranoid, delusional woman, but he does not represent her as a lesbian' (217).

6 A similar critical fear of lesbian taint surrounded the reception of Henry James's 1886 novel *The Bostonians*. See Terry Castle's chapter 'Haunted by Olive Chancellor' (150-85). Whilst critics generally affirmed that the character Olive Chancellor was a repressed lesbian they denied that the novel could be viewed as a study in lesbianism.

recently, obscured what is very much in plain sight. As a result of this tendency … we find novelistic incidents … discussed only obliquely in literary criticism — when they are discussed at all. (4)

The assertions of both of these critics carry particular resonance considering that even as recently as 2008 the literary critic Robert Dingley (in a book chapter purporting to address 'the lesbian menace' in Victorian popular fiction)[7] made a point of quibbling over the nature of Miss Wade's relationship with Tattycoram in *Little Dorrit* because Dickens had made 'no reference whatever to love' (Dingley 112).[8] Writing ten years earlier than Dingley, Annamarie Jagose suggests that this critical practice of avoiding Miss Wade's sexuality is highly suspect:

> Homosexuality's open secret structure means there can be no direct rebuttal of homophobia's practice of neither confirming nor denying — which certainly does not allay but raises to the second power the suspicion of homosexuality. Not saying what the text itself does not say — usually the mark of scholastic integrity — can be read, in a field structured by homophobia's double bind, as collusive neglect. Attempts to go by the book are outflanked when everywhere the charge of homosexuality is already 'proved' not by hard fact but by suspicion and suggestion … ('Remembering Miss Wade' 433)

Given this persuasive argument, it is ironic that the most prominent Neo-Victorian novelist of lesbian desire, Sarah Waters, either avoids or downplays the significance of this character when fielding questions about lesbian subjectivity and Victorian literature. In one interview, for instance, when Waters was asked if her research had yielded any nineteenth-century literature that had focused

---

7   The chapter actually only addresses the lesbian menace in relation to literary examples of intense encounters between mistresses and maids or employers and employees.

8   Paradoxically, despite casting doubt on the nature of Miss Wade's relationship with Tattycoram, Dingley claims to be 'in substantial agreement' with Annamarie Jagose's 'historicisation' (112) of Miss Wade's relationship with Tattycoram in her book *Inconsequence: Lesbian Representation and the Logic of Sexual Sequence*. It should also be noted that Dingley's rather quaint objection invites at least two questions — just why is a narrative reference to love required to establish a same-sex relationship between women characters and would a narrative reference to love be required to establish a heterosexual relationship or a same-sex relationship between male characters?

on lesbians, she steered clear of *Little Dorrit*[9] and for that matter, literature, and instead placed emphasis on diaries[10] and other modes of discourse:

> It's tricky. There isn't really much in the way of novels and stuff like that. There's some poetry ... It's more though that you have to look for evidence of lesbian life. You have to look at other sorts of things, like medical writing or diaries, letters, and poetry to a certain extent ... ('BBC2' n.p.)

However, in another interview Waters cursorily referred to Miss Wade:

> Victorian writing doesn't have any explicit lesbian sex ... but it does have a lot about gender and sexuality, Miss Wade in *Little Dorrit* is queer in all sorts of ways, and there is a thing between a woman and her maid in Hardy. There are strange, erotic situations and power dynamics, with innocence and corruption counterpointed. ('Hot Waters' n.p.)

Waters is therefore aware of Miss Wade's significance in terms of the evidence that literature furnishes when considering female same-sex desire in the Victorian period.[11] Accordingly, it would appear that she does not wish to draw

---

9   It is worth noting that Sarah Waters appears to be very familiar with *Little Dorrit* because Margaret Prior, one of the main characters in her novel *Affinity*, actually reads *Little Dorrit* aloud to her mother (201). Added to this, the other main character in *Affinity*, Selina, happens to possess the surname of Dawes, which was the surname of a nurse that Miss Wade felt a strong antipathy towards in *Little Dorrit*.

10   In terms of diaries, Waters is likely referring to the discovery in the 1980s by historian Helena Whitbread of Anne Lister's diaries. These early nineteenth-century diaries of a Yorkshire gentry-woman contain accounts — mostly written in code — of the passionate sexual relationships that Lister engaged in with other women throughout her life. Indeed, in her diary entry of 29 January 1821, Lister wrote: 'I love and only love the fairer sex and thus, beloved by them in turn, my heart revolts from any other love than theirs' (qtd in Whitbread 161). Rebecca Jennings succinctly explains the historical importance of these diaries: 'The discovery of Anne Lister's diaries clearly refuted the argument that before the late nineteenth century women were unable to imagine sexual relationships with other women and forced historians to reassess the notion of romantic friendships as unquestionably non-sexual' (43). Notwithstanding the significance of these diaries and the other records that Waters cites, it is somewhat surprising that Waters glosses over the evidence of lesbianism from Victorian novels.

11   She would also, in all likelihood, be aware of the pivotal narrative significance that Dickens attached to Miss Wade and her 'History of a Self-Tormentor' narrative confession. As Mary A. Armstrong notes: 'There is no better evidence for the importance of Miss Wade's story than Dickens's own commentary on it: "In Miss Wade I had an idea, which I thought a new one, of making the introduced story so fit into surroundings

much attention to Dickens's portrait of Miss Wade in *Little Dorrit* or that her additional comments on the subject were edited out of the textual version of the 2002 interview ('BBC2').[12]

For anyone familiar with Victorian literature, Miss Wade would be one of the first characters that spring to mind when contemplating the question of Victorian literary examples of intra-female desire. As Mary A. Armstrong writes:

> In the Victorian pantheon of fictional female perversion, Miss Wade is arguably the character most widely recognized as lesbian, although that recognition has often taken place by means of a reverse discourse or a kind of definition by denial. (69-70)

In addition, Annamarie Jagose writes:

> Long after I had forgotten the fortuitous connections between characters seemingly remote, after I had forgotten even the 'specific scenes and details … [and their] almost emblematic or even visionary significance' that Peter Ackroyd claims haunt the reader of *Little Dorrit*, I remembered Miss Wade, not only her frighteningly intense — and no less intense because opaque — representation of same-sex desire but also the unspeakably pathological frameworks within which such representation is couched and which would very shortly in the history of sexuality be annexed for female homosexuality.
>
> I remembered Miss Wade. ('Remembering Miss Wade' 423-4)

Assuredly, Miss Wade is a searingly memorable character. As Michael Slater puts it, she is a 'vital creation, who stays in the reader's mind long after the minor role she plays in the novel's intricate plot has been forgotten' (269).[13]

---

impossible of separation from the main story, as to make the blood of the book circulate through both'" (72).

12 In relation to the latter possibility, it is useful to recall Philip Tew and Leigh Wilson's comments: 'Writers are, of course, interviewed a great deal, but primarily by journalists. Material used from spoken interviews with journalists is often very spare in the final article, and the emphasis is often either anecdotal, or centred on the latest novel just or about to be published' (ix).

13 Slater may speak of Miss Wade's role as being minor in terms of the novel's plot but Dickens did not view it that way. Significantly, he baulked at John Forster's suggestion that Miss Wade's 'History of a Self-Tormentor' narrative should be excised from *Little*

There is probably a very good reason that Sarah Waters does not always cite Miss Wade when reflecting on whether there is any nineteenth-century literature which features female same-sex desire. Miss Wade is a thoroughly unlikeable and dubious character. As such, she does not offer a particularly favourable historical model for lesbians. In one of her own scholarly works, Waters writes: 'With relatively few recognized or prestigious historical models and traditions of their own, lesbians have been frequent visitors to classical scenes of erotic male bonding' ('The Most Famous Fairy' 212). Far from presenting a prestigious model of lesbian desire, Miss Wade presents the kind of model which would turn most lesbians off. This is evident if one considers the reaction by lesbian viewers to the 2008 British television serial adaptation of *Little Dorrit*. In an online forum for a lesbian and bisexual women's website called AfterEllen, one post reads:

> [*Little Dorrit* is] on right now in the UK. They're not exactly being subtle about the lesbian subtext. I don't like it though, it feels really retro, what with Miss Wade being all predatory and sinister, like she's trying to tempt Tattycoram into her 'evil lifestyle'. ('Little Dorrit — Miss Wade and Tattycoram' n.p.)

Not always recalling the character of Miss Wade might therefore be viewed in the light of a marketing strategy. Miss Wade may appear in a 'prestigious' Victorian novel by a canonical writer whom Waters enthusiastically professes to admire — she claims to be 'a huge Dickens fan' ('Desire, betrayal' n.p.) — but Dickens's pathological depiction of Miss Wade is far from prestigious and therefore far from worth foregrounding.[14]

Dorrit and he defended its inclusion as being crucial to the overall scheme of the novel (see footnote 11). According to Anna Wilson, the paradoxical narrative position of Miss Wade's confession being 'somehow at the heart of things, and yet both excisable and having no natural place' arguably parallels her 'position in history' (188).

14   Perhaps this is why Waters also doesn't draw attention to the character, Bell Blount, from Eliza Lynn Linton's 1880 novel *The Rebel of the Family*. Bell Blount is quite an extraordinary character in terms of nineteenth-century literature because she actually takes another woman as her wife. Her depiction, however, is far from sympathetic (and therefore not at all prestigious) owing to Eliza Lynn Linton's virulently anti-feminist standpoint. For a fascinating article on the interactions between Charles Dickens and Eliza Lynn Linton see Nancy Fix Anderson's 'Eliza Lynn Linton, Dickens, and the Woman Question'.

There are really only three positive things to say about the depiction of Miss Wade. First, she is physically attractive. The narrator mentions her handsome features on a number of occasions.[15] Second, she displays a sharp intellect, as Peter Christmas states:

> It is as if Miss Wade stands for all the things Dickens knew about people, but which he was loath to confront directly, for artistic and moral reasons, so bound did he feel to the exigencies of lively caricature and resolved endings ... Yet, however seldom she appears, she shares more of the author's intelligence than any other character in the whole large cast. (144)

Third, she stands as one of the key examples of the kinds of new subjectivities that were adumbrated in the Victorian era. For Deidre David, this subjectivity is now quite clear. Bucking the anti-lesbian critical trend, she authoritatively states: 'Inevitably, Miss Wade must be read as a lesbian' (263). Nevertheless, any self-respecting lesbian would be less than enamoured with Miss Wade and this would be due, in no small measure, to the singularly repellent nature of her depiction. Not simply allowed to stand as an anomaly, Miss Wade is consistently cast by the narrator in an evil, sick light and her views are made to appear distorted and self-delusional. As to her implied same-sex desire, this is represented as predatory, repulsive, erroneous, deeply unsatisfying and even potentially murderous. Remembering Miss Wade, then, necessarily entails remembering the censorious and pathologising language in which she is constructed.

---

15   Holly Furneaux, in seeking to reconfigure Miss Wade as 'one of Dickens's queer travellers' (21) is attentive to the contextual conditions which allowed for Miss Wade's attractive appearance. According to Furneaux, 'Dickens's insistence on Miss Wade's accordance with ideals of female beauty' and 'his non-masculine rendering of [her] suggests the greater range of conceptual possibilities in a period before sexological accounts yoked homosexuality to gender inversion' (20). It is also worth noting that Dickens's insistence on Miss Wade's prepossessing looks may have been tied up with his wish to underscore the considerable threat that she posed to the heterosexual and reproductive values of mid-Victorian society. Beautiful women like Miss Wade might all too easily draw women away from men and consequently the social reproductive economy through their natural ability to inspire love and adoration. This is made manifest in Dickens's earlier novel *Bleak House* when the servant Rosa is completely taken in by her mistress's physical charms and aroused by her touch: '[Lady Dedlock] is so affable, so graceful, so beautiful, so elegant; has such a sweet voice, and such a thrilling touch, that Rosa can feel it yet!' (208) The inherent power of Miss Wade's good looks is therefore countered in a narrative sense by the thoroughgoing depiction of her repulsive nature.

Examining the representation of Miss Wade is a depressing task. When she first appears in the novel, she is described in ambiguous terms as

> a handsome young Englishwoman, travelling quite alone, who had a proud observant face, and had either withdrawn herself from the rest or been avoided by the rest — nobody, herself excepted perhaps, could have quite decided which. (60; bk 1, ch. 2)

Less than two pages later, these ambiguous terms are reinforced:

> She sat, turned away from the whole length of the apartment, as if she were lonely of her own haughty choice. And yet it would have been as difficult as ever to say, positively, whether she avoided the rest, or was avoided. (62; bk 1, ch. 2)

Narrative ambiguity, however, is all too quickly replaced by extreme generalisations and unfounded conviction:

> One could hardly see the face, so still and scornful, set off by the arched dark eyebrows, and the folds of dark hair, without wondering what its expression would be if a change came over it. That it could soften or relent, appeared next to impossible. That it could deepen into anger or any extreme of defiance, and that it must change in that direction when it changed at all, would have been its peculiar impression upon most observers. It was dressed and trimmed into no ceremony of expression. Although not an open face, there was no pretence in it. 'I am self-contained and self-reliant; your opinion is nothing to me; I have no interest in you, care nothing for you, and see and hear you with indifference' — this it said plainly. It said so in the proud eyes, in the lifted nostril, in the handsome but compressed and even cruel mouth. Cover either two of these channels of expression, and the third would have said so still. Mask them all, and the mere turn of the head would have shown an unsubduable nature. (62; bk 1, ch. 2)

By the end of this description the narrator has effectively put a sack and noose over Miss Wade's head. In a rhetorical sense, she is effectively judged, sentenced and very nearly executed before her actions are allowed to speak for themselves. In any contemporary creative writing course, writers are taught to show rather than to tell but telling is the option that Dickens immediately takes with Miss Wade.[16] Admittedly, Miss Wade does go on to act in repugnant ways

---

16   Janet Retsek takes an entirely different line and views Dickens's definitive description of Miss Wade as something of a skillful tour de force. See 'Sexing Miss Wade' (219-21).

but her portrait has been indelibly drawn from the outset by the omniscient narrator and consequently there is very little chance that she will receive even a modicum of sympathy from readers.[17]

When Miss Wade stumbles upon the extremely upset maid, Tattycoram, her words are actually kind and sympathetic. And yet the narrator again chooses to cast her in an entirely negative and suspect light:

> 'My poor girl, what is the matter?'
>
> She looked up suddenly, with reddened eyes … 'It's nothing to you what's the matter. It don't signify to any one.'
>
> 'O yes it does; I am sorry to see you so.'
>
> 'You are not sorry,' said the girl. 'You are glad. You know you are glad. I never was like this but twice over in the quarantine yonder; and both times you found me. I am afraid of you.'
>
> 'Afraid of me?'
>
> 'Yes. You seem to come like my own anger, my own malice, my own — whatever it is — I don't know what it is. But I am ill-used, I am ill-used, I am ill-used!' …
>
> The visitor stood looking at her with a strange attentive smile. It was wonderful to see the fury of the contest in the girl, and the bodily struggle she made as if she were rent by the Demons of old. (64-5; bk 1, ch. 2)

Miss Wade's smile here could be quite involuntary but the narrator interprets it as fascination with the way that Tattycoram's body manifests its extreme mental disquiet. Following this, Miss Wade advises Tattycoram to have patience with her employers:

> 'If they take much care of themselves, and little or none of you, you must not mind it.'
>
> 'I will mind it.'
>
> 'Hush! Be more prudent. You forget your dependent position.'
>
> 'I don't care for that. I'll run away. I'll do some mischief. I won't bear it; I can't bear it; I shall die if I try to bear it!'
>
> The observer stood with her hand upon her own bosom, looking at the girl, as one afflicted with a diseased part might curiously watch the dissection and exposition of an analogous case. (65; bk 1, ch. 2)

---

17   Carol A. Bock makes the point that Dickens's 'heavily ironic presentation' of Miss Wade prevents the reader from sympathising with her (115).

Miss Wade gives Tattycoram probably the best advice under the circumstances but the narrator interposes with his own interpretation of her actions and this interpretation significantly conflates voyeuristic sexuality ('the observer stood with her hand upon her own bosom') with pathology ('one afflicted with a diseased part'). Jagose has skilfully drawn attention to the novel's 'potent framing of same-sex desire within the medical discourses of disease and contamination ... [which] has resonance for a later figuration of female homosexuality' (429). Perhaps one of the best examples of the association of Miss Wade with contamination is when Tattycoram casually admits to having come in contact with Miss Wade:

> 'And Miss Wade,' said Mr Meagles, after they had recalled a number of fellow-travellers. 'Has anybody seen Miss Wade?'
>
> 'I have,' said Tattycoram.
>
> She had brought a little mantle which her young mistress had sent for, and was bending over her, putting it on, when she lifted up her dark eyes and made this unexpected answer.
>
> 'Tatty!' her young mistress exclaimed. 'You seen Miss Wade? — where?' ...
>
> 'I met her near the church.'
>
> 'What was she doing there I wonder!' said Mr Meagles. 'Not going to it, I should think.'
>
> 'She had written to me first,' said Tattycoram.
>
> 'Oh, Tatty!' murmured her mistress, 'take your hands away. I feel as if some one [*sic*] else was touching me!' (240; bk 1, ch. 16)

Here, Miss Wade is indirectly represented as being unwholesome, godless, polluting and repulsive. It is also important to mention that her affliction is represented as extremely far-reaching to the point where her contaminating hands cut across temporal and physical boundaries. This implicitly negative approach to Miss Wade is repeated again and again throughout the novel. After Tattycoram runs away from the Meagleses and goes to live with Miss Wade, there is the scene where Arthur Clennam and Meagles go on an expedition to find where Miss Wade lives. In the lead-up to finding her, the narrator spends an inordinate amount of time describing the derelict and deathly nature of the streets within the general vicinity of her house. There are 'wildernesses of corner houses, with barbarous old porticoes ... horrors that came into existence under some wrong-headed person in some wrong-headed time' (373; bk 1, ch. 27); there are 'parasite little tenements, with the cramp in their whole frame ... commanding the dunghills in the Mews' (373; bk 1, ch. 27); there are 'rickety dwellings of undoubted fashion, but of a capacity to hold nothing comfortably except a dismal smell' (373; bk 1, ch. 27); and there are shops with very little in their windows because 'popular opinion was as nothing to them' (373; bk 1, ch. 27).

Finally, Mr Clennam and Mr Meagles find Miss Wade's street, which is described as being 'one of the parasite streets; long, regular, narrow, dull and gloomy; like a brick and mortar funeral' (374; bk 1, ch. 27) and the house that she lives in is described as looking 'dingy' and 'empty' with bills in the windows announcing that the house is for lease. Even the bills are described in funereal terms: 'The bills, as a variety in the funeral procession, almost amounted to a decoration' (374; bk 1, ch. 27). Rather than an embarrassment of riches, this is an embarrassment of evils. It is as if the narrator cannot help himself and it is impossible for him not to 'go to town' with noxious, parasitic and deathly allusions to Miss Wade. The Meagles/Clennam underworld expedition is, however, to no avail because despite their efforts Tattycoram refuses to leave Miss Wade.

Much later, Arthur Clennam, on a solo expedition, tracks Miss Wade and Tattycoram down in France and here again readers are treated to an entirely negative description of her new abode:

> A dead sort of house, with a dead wall over the way and a dead gateway at the side, where a pendant bell-handle produced two dead tinkles, and a knocker produced a dead, flat, surface-tapping, that seemed not to have depth enough in it to penetrate even the cracked door. However, the door jarred open on a dead sort of spring; and he closed it behind him as he entered a dull yard, soon brought to a close by another dead wall, where an attempt had been made to train some creeping shrubs, which were dead; and to make a little fountain in a grotto, which was dry; and to decorate that with a little statue, which was gone. (716; bk 2, ch. 20)

The descriptions of Miss Wade's dwellings as lifeless are worth examining. There are two points to make about these descriptions. The first is that they illustrate Terry Castle's 'apparitional lesbian' thesis. According to this thesis, the Western literary imagination has since the early eighteenth century sought to deny the carnality of lesbian existence by engaging in a process of 'derealization'

(Castle 6). Castle defines 'derealization' as the cultural act of 'ghosting' a lesbian or making her seem invisible (4). Through this process, the lesbian is drained 'of any sensual or moral authority' (Castle 6) and then exorcised from the text 'as if vaporized by the forces of heterosexual propriety' (Castle 7). As Castle puts it:

> Given the threat that sexual love between women inevitably poses to the workings of the patriarchal arrangement, it has often been felt necessary to deny the carnal *bravada* of lesbian existence. The hoary misogynistic challenge, 'But what do lesbians do?' insinuates as much: *This cannot be. There is no place for this.* It is perhaps not so surprising that at least until around 1900 lesbianism manifests itself in the Western literary imagination primarily as an absence, as chimera or *amor impossibilia* — a kind of love that, by definition, cannot exist. Even when 'there' ... it is 'not there': inhabiting only a recessive, indeterminate, misted-over space in the collective literary psyche. (30-1, emphasis in original)

By depicting Miss Wade's dwellings as dead, Dickens effectively seeks to deny Miss Wade a valid place wherein she can express and explore her same-sex desire or, in other words, he forecloses the possibility of a lesbian love nest. In addition, he actively seeks to drain her of the 'sensual authority' that Terry Castle speaks of. Miss Wade may be a highly attractive woman but she inhabits an emphatically dead space which cannot possibly serve to engender, support or enhance life or desire. The equation therefore is: Miss Wade's lifestyle amounts to death. Moreover, if one takes into account Andrea Kaston Tange's premise that the Victorian house 'metonymically stood for its inhabitants' (6) then there is good reason to suggest that Dickens actually sought to depict Miss Wade as an apparition. Rather than being an 'angel in the house', Miss Wade is instead a 'ghost in the house'.

The second point to make about the depiction of Miss Wade's dwellings is that a woman's traditional realm at this time was the home but in the case of the unmarried Miss Wade, the homes that she inhabits are nothing short of dead. The implication thereby is that she is not fulfilling her traditional womanly function or that she has rejected heteronormative prescriptions. Certainly, this makes sense in the context of Freud's theory of an atrophied female desiring only to be fulfilled by the phallus or the penis substitute, a baby. Freudian theory postulated that 'the vagina is ... valued as a place of shelter for the penis' (Freud 312). Miss Wade's apparently dead 'shelter' means that she makes no sense or signifies the end of meaning within the heteronormative economy. Notably, too, just after the lone hero Clennam has *entered* the dead house, Tattycoram begins to reject Miss Wade by revealing that she had at one point slipped away from Miss Wade to go and look at her former employers' abode because it had been associated in her mind with the kindness that the Meagles family had once extended to her.

The scene with Clennam effectively marks 'the beginning of the end' in terms of Tattycoram's relationship with Miss Wade and the dismantling of her same-sex household. Not long thereafter Tattycoram frees herself and returns to Mr Meagles thoroughly repentant:

> I am bad enough, but not so bad as I was indeed. I have had Miss Wade before me all this time, as if it was my own self grown ripe — turning everything the wrong way, and twisting all good into evil. I have had her before me all this time, finding no pleasure in anything but keeping me as miserable, suspicious, and tormenting as herself … I only mean to say, that, after what I have gone through, I hope I shall never be quite so bad again, and that I shall get better by very slow degrees. (880; bk 2, ch. 33)

Mr Meagles is naturally pleased with Tattycoram's return and wastes no time in setting her straight by pontificating to her about the importance of feminine duty and pointing to Little Dorrit as a role model:

> 'You see that young lady who was here just now — that little, quiet, fragile figure passing along there, Tatty? Look. The people stand out of the way to let her go by. The men — see the poor, shabby fellows — pull off their hats to her quite politely, and now she glides in at that doorway. See her, Tattycoram?'
>
> 'Yes, sir.'
>
> 'I have heard tell, Tatty, that she was once regularly called the child of this place. She was born here, and lived here many years. I can't breathe here. A doleful place to be born and bred in, Tattycoram?'
>
> 'Yes indeed, sir!'
>
> 'If she had constantly thought of herself, and settled with herself that everybody visited this place upon her, turned it against her, and cast it at her, she would have led an irritable and probably an useless existence [*sic*]. Yet I have heard tell, Tattycoram, that her young life has been one of active resignation, goodness, and noble service. Shall I tell you what I

consider those eyes of hers, that were here just now, to have always looked at, to get that expression?'

'Yes, if you please, sir.'

'Duty, Tattycoram. Begin it early, and do it well; and there is no antecedent to it, in any origin or station, that will tell against us with the Almighty, or with ourselves.' (881-2; bk 2, ch. 33)

Miss Wade's questioning and rebellious nature is therefore implicitly negated and her existence is made to appear useless. However, the wholesale rejection of Miss Wade within the novel is finally effected by her own hand. For the quite implausible reason of wanting to show Mr Clennam what she means when she talks of hating someone, Miss Wade gives him a document containing the story of her life.[18] The document, only a few pages long, is called 'The History of a Self-Tormentor' and, significantly, readers are not provided with Mr Clennam's reaction to it. Presumably, in terms of the overall narrative strategy of the novel, the document is meant to stand on its own as the best means to indict Miss Wade — and, certainly, it does this very well.[19] As Janet Retseck writes: 'The purpose of Miss Wade's narrative is to establish that Miss Wade is and has always been a misreader of people's kind intentions towards her and that her anger and defiance are rooted in her personality, not reality' (223).

Furthermore, Carol A. Bock claims that Miss Wade's narrative serves as an exemplum: 'her history is a cautionary tale which dramatizes the destructive consequences of imprisoning oneself within the narrow confines of an egocentric vision imposed upon life through a perverse assertion of personal will' (116). Miss Wade is then left so entirely exposed as a psychologically disturbed woman that the narrator does not have to spend much more time making her look problematic and fairly soon thereafter she fades out of the novel. In the end,

---

18 Barbara Black asserts that Miss Wade engages in an 'embarrassing, purposeless self-exposure to Arthur Clennam' (102). Moreover, Anna Wilson claims that this document is 'narratively problematic' and 'under-motivated' (188).

19 Mary A. Armstrong points out the ideological and cultural work performed by this document: 'The ostensible purpose of the narrative is Miss Wade's own gratification …. But the more pointed function is to reorient her toward the medical discourses of the new homosexuality and to pathologize her emotional life, her perceptions, and her desires. Indeed, Dicken's working notes for *Little Dorrit* make the medical framework of Miss Wade's story explicit: his first notation for this chapter simply reads, "Dissect it"' (72).

readers are left to suppose that she lives out the rest of her days in France, presumably alone.[20]

Dickens manifestly uses every rhetorical weapon at his disposal to foreclose Miss Wade's identity, including using Miss Wade's own narrative to work against her. Interestingly, however, an examination of the Dickens oeuvre shows that he was fascinated by same-sex intimacy between women. In fact, he was so fascinated that one of the most passionate scenes in his fiction is between two women rather than a man and a woman. This scene occurs in *Bleak House* when, after having been ravaged by smallpox, the protagonist, Esther Summerson, finally comes face to face with her dear friend Ada. As Esther writes:

> I stood trembling, even when I heard my darling calling as she came upstairs, 'Esther, my dear, my love, where are you? Little woman, dear Dame Durden!'
>
> She ran in, and was running out again when she saw me. Ah, my angel girl! The old dear look, all love, all fondness, all affection. Nothing else in it — no, nothing, nothing!
>
> O how happy I was, down upon the floor, with my sweet beautiful girl down upon the floor too, holding my scarred face to her lovely cheek, bathing it with tears and kisses, rocking me to and fro like a child, calling me by every tender name that she could think of, and pressing me to her faithful heart. (537; ch. 34)

This episode, in terms of its intensity[21], makes all of the other love scenes between women and men in Dickens's fiction pale into insignificance. There really is no scene between a man and a woman in his fiction that displays anywhere near this level of intimacy and joyous connection. It is useful here

---

20 As Deidre David writes: 'Miss Wade fades away into some kind of French obscurity' (251).

21 Mary A. Armstrong writes of this passage: 'Female homoerotic desire seems unmistakeable … the confrontation is suggestive of nothing less than a reunion of lovers' (62-3). Patricia Ingham also notes the glaring disjunction between Esther's explicit passion for Ada and the decided lack of passion that she displays toward Allan Woodcourt: 'The measure of excess in the feeling that Esther shows for Ada is the absence of any similar expression of emotion for Woodcourt with whom she is supposed to be deeply in love' (127). Finally, Kim Edwards Keates claims that Esther and Ada 'enjoy an intensely passionate bond throughout the novel' and that their intimacy is 'excessive' (174).

to recall John Carey's thoughts on Dickens and sexuality. According to Carey, Dickens's writing 'leaves us to infer that even normal sexuality is guilty or unclean' (160). Carey supports his argument by referring to what he describes as 'a particularly sickening' passage in *Sketches by Boz*. The passage concerns the love of a little boy and a little girl. This love, as Carey writes, 'is offered to the reader as inherently preferable to the love which comes after puberty' (160):

> They have dreamt of each other in their quiet dreams, these children, and their little hearts have been nearly broken when the absent one has been dispraised in jest. When will there come in after life a passion so earnest, generous, and true as theirs; what, even in its gentlest realities, can have the grace and charm that hover round such fairy lovers! (Carey 160-1)

Admittedly, this rather infantile conception of passion would appear to reveal a deep-seated fear of sexuality or a conviction that sexuality is fundamentally impure. However, whilst Dickens may have struggled to reconcile and represent physical intimacy between men and women, he didn't appear to have any difficulties when it came to conveying physical intimacy between women. This is more than evident if we examine two other passages by Dickens. The first passage is from the historical novel *Barnaby Rudge*, which is set in the late eighteenth-century period of the Gordon riots. During the course of the novel, two young women, Dolly Varden and Emma Haredale, are kidnapped by insurgents. Ironically, this scene is made memorable not because of the trials that the women undergo but rather because of the 'lip-smacking' relish that the omniscient narrator indulges in. Indeed, the narrator registers nothing less than the utmost titillation at Dolly's agonies and her concomitant efforts to console her friend:

> Poor Dolly! Do what she would, she only looked the better for it, and tempted them the more. When her eyes flashed angrily, and her ripe lips slightly parted, to give her rapid breathing vent, who could resist it? When she wept and sobbed as though her heart would break, and bemoaned her miseries in the sweetest voice that ever fell upon a listener's ear, who could be insensible to the little winning pettishness which now and then displayed itself, even in the sincerity and earnestness of her grief? When, forgetful for a moment of herself, as she was now, she fell on her knees beside her friend, and bent over her, and laid her cheek to hers, and put her arms about her, what mortal eyes could have avoided wandering to the delicate

> bodice, the streaming hair, the neglected dress, the perfect abandonment and unconsciousness of the blooming little beauty? Who could look on and see her lavish caresses and endearments, and not desire to be in Emma Haredale's place; to be either her or Dolly; either the hugging or the hugged? (541; ch. 59)

This extract is particularly significant because the clearly male narrator is so excited by the intimacy that these women display that he actually voices the wish to foreclose his identity as a man in order to actively participate in such eroticism.

The second passage appears in Dickens's unfinished novel, *The Mystery of Edwin Drood*. In this erotically charged scene, Helena Landless who has previously been described as 'an unusually handsome lithe girl … of almost the gypsy type' (44) seeks to protect the terrified Rosa Bud from the sexually predatory John Jaspers:

> The lustrous gipsy-face drooped over the clinging arms and bosom, and the wild black hair fell down protectingly over the childish form. There was a slumbering gleam of fire in the intense dark eyes, though they were often softened with compassion and admiration. Let whomsoever it most concerned, look well to it! (54)

There is a strong degree of voyeuristic luxuriation in the way that this episode is related. Set alongside the *Barnaby Rudge* scene, it usefully serves to highlight Dickens's intense interest in exploring intimacy between women.

It would appear that at least a part of Dickens knew that intimate relations between women could be extremely intense, loving, caring, protective and pleasurable but when he chose to depict a woman who, in all probability, engaged in these intimate relations to the point where it became part of her identity or her orientation, he was compelled to depict her as tormented, sick, vengeful, predatory, deathly and devoid of sense or meaning. Added to this, he was compelled to depict her intimate same-sex relations in an abhorrent light.[22] The following passage where Miss Wade describes her youthful love for another girl could not be more antithetical to the scenes in *Bleak House*, *Barnaby Rudge* and *The Mystery of Edwin Drood*:

---

22 Dickens's profoundly negative rendering of Miss Wade's intimate same-sex relations conveys an overdetermined need to protect the Victorian social order. This need would have, in large part, been driven by a desire to satisfy his audience's values and beliefs but also by his own particular prejudices, beliefs, and sexual desires (as I argue here).

> When we were left alone in our bedroom at night, I would reproach her with my perfect knowledge of her baseness; and then she would cry and cry and say I was cruel, and then I would hold her in my arms till morning; loving her as much as ever, and often feeling as if, rather than suffer so, I could so hold her in my arms and plunge to the bottom of the river — where I would still hold her after we were both dead. (726-7; bk 2, ch. 21)

The character of Miss Wade in *Little Dorrit* represents a powerful figuration of emergent female sexual subjectivity within the Victorian era. Had the word 'lesbian' been available, it seems likely that the censorial and self-righteous Mr Meagles would not have hesitated to use it against Miss Wade. Nevertheless, in terms of the overall scheme of the novel there was little need for Mr Meagles to label Miss Wade because the omniscient narrator deployed every rhetorical technique in his repertoire to ensure that she was depicted as loathsome and lethal. Accordingly, there was next to no chance that she would ever be taken up by lesbians as one of the 'prestigious historical models' that Sarah Waters talks of.

A number of queer readings have sought to explore the ways in which Dickens's pathological representation of Miss Wade anticipates late nineteenth-century and early twentieth-century sexological accounts of lesbianism and inversion.[23] The contaminating, diseased and deathly depiction of Miss Wade, however, probably owes just as much to the author's voyeuristic and vicariously driven erotic proclivities as it does to his anticipation of medical models of female homoerotic desire. For Dickens, it would seem that it was fine for women to be physically intimate with other women provided that this intimacy was either in full view of men or did not amount to an ongoing orientation that precluded emotional and sexual bonds with men.

It may be possible, as Holly Furneaux contends in *Queer Dickens: Erotics, Families, Masculinities*[24], to claim 'a central position for Dickens in queer literary history' (8) by 'arguing that this eminent Victorian can direct us to the ways in which his culture could, and did, comfortably accommodate homoeroticism

---

23 See, in particular, the readings by Mary A. Armstrong and Annamarie Jagose.

24 Furneaux's *Queer Dickens: Erotics, Families, Masculinities* as its title suggests primarily focuses on masculinities. See the introduction of her book for the reasons behind the scope of the work (18).

and forms of family founded on neither marriage nor blood' (3). However, if we choose to remember Dickens's dubious representation of Miss Wade, it is open to question whether this eminent Victorian can direct us to the ways that his culture comfortably accommodated *female* homoeroticism. The beautiful and intelligent Miss Wade may be one of Dickens's 'queer travellers' (Furneaux 21) but she is a traveller who should, by the perverse terms of his narrative, be kept in strict isolation.

Works Cited

Anderson, Nancy Fix. 'Eliza Lynn Linton, Dickens, and the Woman Question.' *Victorian Periodicals Review* 22.4 (Winter, 1989): 134-41.

Armstrong, Mary A. 'Multiplicities Of Longing: The Queer Desires Of *Bleak House* and *Little Dorrit*.' *Nineteenth Century Studies* 18 (2004): 59-79.

Barrett, Edwin B. '*Little Dorrit* and the Disease of Modern Life.' *Nineteenth-Century Fiction* 25.2 (1970): 199-215.

'BBC2 dips into the sexy side of Victorian England: *Tipping the Velvet* author Sarah Waters.' *Moviepie.com*. 2002. http://www.moviepie.com/index.php/blog-moviepie/moviepie-musings/item/3089-bbc2-dips-into-the-sexy-side-of-victorian-england-tipping-the-velvet-author-sarah-waters, accessed 23 March 2014.

Black, Barbara. 'A Sisterhood of Rage and Beauty: Dickens' Rosa Dartle, Miss Wade, and Madame Defarge.' *Dickens Studies Annual* 26 (1998): 91-106.

Bock, Carol A. 'Miss Wade and George Silverman: The Forms of Fictional Monologue.' *Dickens Studies Annual* 16 (1987): 113-26.

Carey, John. *The Violent Effigy: A Study of Dickens' Imagination*. London: Faber and Faber, 1979.

Carter, Geoffrey. 'Sexuality and the Victorian Artist: Dickens and Swinburne.' *Tennessee Studies in Literature* 27 (1984): 141-60.

Castle, Terry. *The Apparitional Lesbian: Female Homosexuality and Modern Culture*. New York: Columbia UP, 1993.

Christmas, Peter. '*Little Dorrit*: The End of Good and Evil.' *Dickens Studies Annual* 6 (1977): 134-53.

David, Deidre. '*Little Dorrit*'s Theatre of Rage.' *Contemporary Dickens*. Ed. Eileen Gillooly and Deidre David. Columbus: Ohio State UP, 2009. 245-63.

'Desire, betrayal and "lesbo Victorian romps"'. *Guardian.co.uk*. 5 November 2002. http://www.guardian.co.uk/books/2002/nov/05/fiction, accessed 9 February 2011.

Dickens, Charles. *Barnaby Rudge*. 1841. Ed. Gordon Spence. Harmondsworth: Penguin, 1982.

———. *Little Dorrit*. 1855-1857. Ed. John Holloway. Harmondsworth: Penguin, 1985.

———. *The Mystery of Edwin Drood*. 1870. Ed. Margaret Cardwell. Clarendon Press, Oxford, 1972.

———. *Bleak House*. 1852-1853. Ed. Norman Page. Harmondsworth: Penguin, 1985.

Dingley, Robert. '"It was now mistress and maid no longer; woman and woman only". The Lesbian Menace in Victorian Popular Fiction.' *Victorian Turns, NeoVictorian Returns: Essays on Fiction and Culture*. Ed. Penny Gay, Judith Johnston, and Catherine Waters. Newcastle upon Tyne: Cambridge Scholars Publishing, 2008. 102-12.

Freud, Sigmund. 'The Infantile Genital Organization (An Interpolation into the Theory of Sexuality).' 1923. *On Sexuality*. Ed. Angela Richards. Vol. 7. Pelican Freud Library. Harmondsworth: Penguin, 1977.

Furneaux, Holly. *Queer Dickens: Erotics, Families, Masculinities*. Oxford: Oxford UP, 2009.

'Hot Waters,' *Guardian.co.uk*. 26 September 2002. http://www.guardian.co.uk/books/2002/sep/26/artsfeatures.bookerprize2002?INTCMP=SRCH, accessed 9 February 2011.

Ingham, Patricia. *Dickens, Women and Language*. Hemel Hempstead: Harvester Wheatsheaf, 1992.

Jagose, Annamarie. 'Remembering Miss Wade: *Little Dorrit* and the Historicizing of Female Perversity.' *GLQ: A Journal of Lesbian and Gay Studies* 4:3 (1998): 423-51.

——. *Inconsequence: Lesbian Representation and the Logic of Sexual Sequence.* Ithaca and London: Cornell UP, 2002.

Jennings, Rebecca. *A Lesbian History of Britain: Love and Sex between Women since 1500.* Oxford/Westport, Connecticut: Greenwood World, 2007.

Keates, Kim Edwards, '"Wow! She's a lesbian. Got to be!": Re-reading/Re-viewing Dickens and Neo-Victorianism on the BBC.' *Dickens and Modernity.* Ed. Juliet John. Woodbridge: Boydell & Brewer, 2012. 171-92.

Lapinski, Piya Pal. 'Dickens's Miss Wade and J.S. LeFanu's Carmilla: The Female Vampire in *Little Dorrit*.' *Dickens Quarterly* 11.2 (1994): 81-7.

Linton, Eliza Lynn. *The Rebel of the Family.* Ed. Deborah Meem. Peterborough, Ontario: Broadview, 2002.

'*Little Dorrit* — Miss Wade and Tattycoram.' *Afterellen.com.* 26 October 2008. http://www.afterellen.com/node/39358, accessed 24 February 2011.

Morgentaler, Goldie. *Dickens and Heredity: When Like Begets Like.* London and Basingstoke: Macmillan, 2000.

Retseck, Janet. 'Sexing Miss Wade.' *Dickens Quarterly* 15.4 (1998): 217-25.

Slater, Michael. *Dickens and Women.* Stanford: Stanford UP, 1983.

Smith, Patricia Juliana. *Lesbian Panic: Homoeroticism in Modern British Women's Fiction.* New York: Columbia UP, 1997.

Tange, Andrea Kaston. *Architectural Identities: Domesticity, Literature, and the Victorian Middle Class.* Toronto: University of Toronto Press, 2010.

Tew, Philip and Leigh Wilson. Introduction. *Writers Talk: Conversations with Contemporary British Novelists.* Ed. Philip Tew, Fiona Tolan and Leigh Wilson. London: Continuum, 2008.

Waters, Sarah. *Affinity.* London: Virago, 2000.

——. '"The Most Famous Fairy in History": Antinous and Homosexual Fantasy.' *Journal of the History of Sexuality* 6.2 October (1995): 194-230.

Whitbread, Helena. Ed. *The Secret Diaries of Miss Anne Lister 1791-1840.* London: Virago, 2010.

Williams, Merryn. *Women in the English Novel 1800-1900.* London and Basingstoke: Macmillan, 1984.

Wilson, Anna. 'On History, Case History, and Deviance: Miss Wade's Symptoms and Their Interpretation.' *Dickens Studies Annual* 26 (1998): 187-201.

Winterson, Jeanette. *Oranges Are Not the Only Fruit.* London: Vintage, 1991.

12

'All the world is blind': unveiling same-sex desire in the poetry of Amy Levy

Carolyn Lake

Amy Levy was a late-nineteenth-century British writer whose short life produced three novels, three collections of poetry, and numerous short stories and essays. She was active in the 1880s intellectual culture of Bloomsbury and acquainted with such figures as Olive Schreiner, Vernon Lee, the Black sisters, Eleanor Marx and Grant Allen. Levy's scholarly and creative writings reflect a keen awareness of contemporary literary and cultural movements, often prefiguring discussions regarding feminism and modernism which would not take place until after her death in 1889. In 1883, Levy published an essay in *The Cambridge Review* on the writings of James 'B.V.' Thomson, author of epic poem 'The City of Dreadful Night' (1874-1880).[1] Levy observed of Thomson that

> [h]e is distinctly what in our loose phraseology we call a minor poet; no prophet, standing above and outside things, to whom all sides of a truth (more or less foreshortened, certainly) are visible; but a passionately subjective being, with intense eyes fixed on one side of the solid polygon

---

1 'The City of Dreadful Night' was first published serially in Charles Bradlaugh's atheist *National Reformer* in 1874 and, later, in the 1880 book, *The City of Dreadful Night and Other Poems*.

of truth, and realizing that one side with a fervour and intensity to which the philosopher with his birdseye view rarely attains. (501)²

The narrative perspective that Levy alludes to here, a literary mode that eschews omniscience and distanced objectivity in favour of a 'passionate' partiality, is a technique she would later adopt in her third and final collection of poetry published in 1889 shortly after her death, *A London Plane-Tree and Other Verse*. Levy, however, would more explicitly reference Thomson in her second collection of poetry, *A Minor Poet and Other Verse*, from 1884, of which the title poem, a dramatic monologue following the final contemplations of a male poet, is an homage to Thomson. Yet her literary appraisal of Thomson is also an indication of Levy's wide literary and cultural knowledge. Compare Levy's assertion on Thomson above to the second paragraph of Charles Baudelaire's 'The Painter of Modern Life':

> Happily from time to time knights errant step into the lists — critics, art collectors, lovers of the arts, curious-minded idlers — who assert that neither Raphael nor Racine has every secret, that minor poets have something to be said for them, substantial and delightful things to their credit, and finally that, however much we may like general beauty, which is expressed by the classical poets and artists, we nonetheless make a mistake to neglect particular beauty, the beauty of circumstance, the description of manners. (1)

Levy's reading of Thomson as a 'passionately subjective' minor poet echoes Baudelaire's call to recognise the minor poet whose work expresses 'particular beauty'. It is impossible to know whether the allusion to Baudelaire here is intentional or incidental, yet Levy was fluent enough in French to perform paid translations (Beckman, 'Urban' 208) and references to Baudelaire and the French symbolists abound in her work, not least through her intense literary preoccupation with the city. This scholastic interest in the particular rather than the universal, and the recognition of minor or marginal feelings and behaviours, is performed in Levy's Saphhic poetry, functioning as politically queer.

---

2   All references to Levy's Thomson essay and poetry are taken from Melvyn New's *The Complete Novels and Selected Writings of Amy Levy 1861-1889*.

Although Levy's work fell into obscurity shortly after her death[3], it was brought back to critical attention in the 1980s by scholars profiling her as a Jewish woman writer. Prominent and first among these works was Edward Wagenknecht's 1983 collection, *Daughters of the Covenant: Portraits of Six Jewish Women*. She was then resituated in 1990 as a New Woman novelist with Deborah Epstein Nord's article in *Signs*, '"Neither pairs nor odd": Female community in late nineteenth-century London'. It is in these early analyses of Levy as a minority figure (as woman or Jew) where much scholarship has stayed. In her review of criticism about Levy, Sarah Minsloff observes that 'Minority identity was the reason for Levy's exile into literary obscurity; it was the means by which she was recovered to critical attention, and it has remained the crux of critical work on Levy's writing' (1318).

This interest in Levy's minor status is unsurprising, as what we know of her life indicates that she herself was interested in theorising, perhaps embracing, the minor as an epistemological frame. However, the overwhelming focus on Levy to date as a minority figure has tended to eschew the extent to which Levy actively worked against stable notions of identity. She did not embrace what we would now call 'identity politics' and worked against the universalising tendencies of canonical Victorian poetry. Rather, Levy uses the minor as a literary technique to represent, or acknowledge the impossibility of representation for, ontologies and epistemologies which have historically been denied and erased. The early focus on Levy as representing minority identity as woman or Jew has foreclosed queer readings of her work which do not, and cannot, align with identity paradigms. Her essay on Thomson, as I shall discuss, most explicitly articulates her opinions and arguments on the role and condition of the minor, but it is through her poetry, particularly her lyric poetry, that the minor is most effectively performed.

Amy Levy was born in 1861, the second of seven children to Isabelle and Lewis Levy (Bernstein 13). The middle-class Levy family resided at Clapham Road in what is now South Lambeth (Pullen 14). While it is difficult to clearly ascertain the Levy family's commitment to, or opinion of, Judaism, it is clear from Levy's life that her family had progressive views in relation to women's

---

[3] Melvyn New's 1993 publication of *The Complete Novels and Selected Writings of Amy Levy* brought a significant portion of Levy's work back into print and circulation for the first time in nearly a century.

education, and were not afraid to expose their children to non-Jewish religion, culture and sociality. As a young teenager in 1875, Levy won the 'junior prize' in *Kind Words Magazine for Boys and Girls* for her essay on Elizabeth Barrett Browning's *Aurora Leigh* (Bernstein 43). That same year Levy published her first poem, 'The Ballade of Ida Grey' in the feminist magazine *The Pelican* (Bernstein 43). Levy's feminist consciousness would be further developed when, in 1876, she was sent to the progressively-run (and secular) Brighton High School for Girls, founded by Emily and Maria Shirreff five years earlier and managed during Levy's time by Miss Edith Creak (Bernstein 14). The Brighton school was part of the Girl's Public Day School Company belonging to the Shirreffs, which was formed in 1871 to provide high-standard and rigorous secondary education for female students. In addition to a more conventional curriculum of geography, history, higher mathematics, French and German, Brighton offered female students studies in Latin — a significant requisite for classical studies and a subject traditionally denied to female students (Beckman, 'Amy Levy' 30). It was during this time at Brighton that Levy wrote what is now likely her most highly regarded poem, 'Xantippe', the dramatic monologue from the perspective of Socrates's wife (Bernstein 14).

Letters from Levy to her sister Katie during her years at Brighton show Levy with developed, romantic attachments to other women. Levy does not mark these desires as particularly extraordinary or deviant; indeed there is reference to Katie (who was by all evidence heterosexual) having had at least one such same-sex crush herself in years past (Beckman, 'Amy Levy' 221). Nevertheless, Levy does describe an attempt to visit her Brighton crush, Edith Creak, as 'bold' (Beckman, 'Amy Levy' 220) and Levy remarks many times on the difference between her feelings of same-sex desire and Katie's. One letter opens with Levy writing 'I utterly despise you! I never did think your passion" [*sic*] (?) worth much and now my suspicions of its spuriousness are confirmed' (Beckman, 'Amy Levy' 221). Without the corresponding letter from Katie to which this is a reply, it is impossible to determine the context of Levy's outpouring, yet it is clear that she feels a sense of betrayal in Katie's dwindled same-sex interest. In a later letter, Levy appears to tease Katie about her opposite-sex desires, when she writes of a man who is an 'awful fool & ignoramus' and tells Katie that because 'he was a real man so *you* wd. have honored him' (Beckman, 'Amy Levy' 224, emphasis in original). Perhaps the most significant letter, however, is the one in which Levy tells Katie that she envisions they will now have very different futures to one another. This admission comes after reflecting on time spent with Miss Creak ('that blessed woman'):

> Today that blessed woman mounted guard for 4 hours — so you may imagine my eyes were not bent solely on my paper — She did look sweet — just working mathematics contentedly to Herself. She has flung out minute crumbs of sweetness lately to her wormy adorer, who bagged a divine passion-inspiring — whenever I think-of-it — embrace today at the sanctum door. Frankly I'm more in love with her than ever — isn't it grim? I don't believe it will go for ages; and I can never care for anyone or anything else while it lasts. Don't you like these egotistic outpourings? Of course this is quite confident-like. I make such different future pictures to what I used to-you married maternal, prudent & [illegible] with a tendency to laugh at the plain High School Mistress sister who grinds, lodges with chums and adores 'without return'. (Beckman, 'Amy Levy' 224)

Here Levy positions her future outside of the ideological domain of the patriarchal family by contrasting it with Katie's hypothetical 'married maternal' one. That this prediction comes after an extended recount of her feelings for Miss Creak indicates that Levy's potential future as a single, working-woman is motivated not merely or even primarily by a desire for independence, education and professional growth. Rather, Levy here is positioning the family as synonymous with heterosexuality. It is also notable how Levy recognises that her romantic desires contrast with opposite-sex desires, and identifies from them that a 'new' future, with new prospects must therefore follow.[4] Though Levy at no point in any of her other remaining letters *explicitly* constructs herself with an alternate 'lesbian' sexual identity, in the 'pre-lesbian' era in which she lived and wrote, this account can be read as an attempt to construct a realisable alternative to heterosexuality out of the discourses available to her in London in the late nineteenth century.

In October 1879 Levy enrolled at Newnham College, Cambridge, where she was the first Jewish student to attend (Bernstein 43, 15). Women had been allowed to enrol in Cambridge for only ten years at this time, with the first

---

4   Emma Francis also makes this observation (196).

women's college, Girton College, having opened in 1869 and Newnham itself in 1871. Levy never completed her studies at Cambridge, leaving after two years, though her literary output during this time was great — publishing two short stories in 1880 ('Euphemia: A Sketch' in *Victoria* Magazine and 'Mrs. Pierrepoint: A Sketch in Two Parts' in *Temple Bar*) and having her first collection of poetry, *Xantippe and Other Verse*, published in 1881 during her final year. Letters from this period continue to recount romantic interests in other women; being helped by one such woman in gym class is described as 'bliss' (Beckman, 'Amy Levy' 229).

After leaving Cambridge, Levy travelled throughout the Continent. In 1886 she met Vernon Lee (Violet Paget) in Florence (Beckman, 'Amy Levy' 254-5). She appears to have developed some romantic feelings for Lee though they were never reciprocated (Goody, 'Murder' 464; Beckman, 'Amy Levy'; Newman 53). Letters certainly show strong feelings for Lee, with Levy writing in one, for example, that 'You are something of an electric battery to me (this doesn't sound polite) & I am getting faint fr. want of contact!' (261). Becoming acquainted with Lee brought Levy into contact with new social circles, which included fellow artists and probable homosexuals (Beckman, 'Amy Levy' 132). One such new acquaintance, Dorothy Bloomfield, was likely romantically engaged to Levy for a time (Beckman, 'Amy Levy' 152). Levy clearly relished her relationship with Lee and her time spent in Florence, as references to both are peppered throughout her late poetry.

Despite the queer desires clearly expressed in Levy's letters and, as I shall argue, her poetry, the only full-length queer reading of Levy to date is Emma Francis's astute 'Amy Levy: Contradictions? Feminism and Semitic Discourse', which, to necessarily over-simplify, analyses the (dis)junctions between Levy's radical sexual politics and her comparatively conservative racial politics. Francis reads a collection of Levy's 'queer' poems from *A London Plane-Tree and Other Verse* through the ghosting theory Terry Castle formulates in *The Apparitional Lesbian*. Yet, even here, Francis is forced to conclude:

> I hesitate to call the poems in the 'Love, Dreams and Death' sequence 'lesbian' because they work to interrogate rather than affirm sexuality and sexual identity … [H]er later poetry interrogates the process by

which mythic, symbolic and identificatory structures are produced. Levy's later poetry studies subjectivities and forms of experience which become increasingly less locatable, less intelligible within conventional accounts of sexual and social identification. Her explorations of same-sex desire invoke some disquieting images and associations which concentrate more on pain than on pleasure, more on conflict than on consensus. (196)

Francis goes on to write that her reservations in deeming this collection of poems 'lesbian' stems from their anarchic relationship to sexuality (201). I disagree with Francis's conclusion that Levy's poems are not lesbian *because* they interrogate sexuality and sexual identity. Sexual identity, as distinct from sex acts or desires, is a relatively new phenomenon and not one applicable to many same-sex attracted women prior to the twentieth century. A paradigm not centred on identity is required for lesbian historiography. Monique Wittig's observation that to be a lesbian inherently produces an opposition to not only the category of 'woman' but to the ideological institutions that define and produce 'woman' (13) renders lesbian ontology — especially in the nineteenth century — less locatable, less intelligible, more conflicted and, indeed, sometimes painful. 'Conventional' accounts of sexual and social identification were, indeed largely still are, heterosexual. A woman's role was defined in relation to the home and the family. The process of subjectification for women in the nineteenth century was, therefore, predicated on heterosexuality. Without a widespread discourse of lesbianism that creates opportunities for lesbian subject-hood, a dismantling of 'conventional' (heterosexual) sexual and social identification is one path towards realising a queer existence. Levy's poetry is strategically queer in this regard. It is actively navigating how to represent an existence that is almost entirely denied by cultural, legal and linguistic institutions, resulting in a near symbolic annihilation. Levy's poetics and her politics of the minor engage lyrical modes that give voice to a pre-lesbian subject.

Two poems in particular from *A London Plane-Tree* represent the symbolic exclusion of lesbian desire. The first is 'A Wall Flower', the title of which already positions the speaker as 'outside' the represented cultural milieu. This exclusion is heightened by the poem's epigraph:

> I lounge in the doorway and languish in vain
> While Tom, Dick and Harry are dancing with Jane.

Read queerly, the speaker is looking at a love-interest as she dances. The issue is not that the speaker's love-interest ('Jane') is dancing with a specific lover but that the speaker's love-interest is dancing with 'man' as a category. The use of 'Tom, Dick and Harry' colloquially refers to men, all men. It implies, when read queerly, that the speaker is watching Jane enmeshed in the sociality of heterosexuality. The four stanzas of the poem proper then read:

> My spirit rises to the music's beat;
> There is a leaden fiend lurks in my feet!
> To move unto your motion, Love, were sweet.
>
> Somewhere, I think, some other where, not here,
> In other ages, on another sphere,
> I danced with you, and you with me, my dear.
>
> In perfect motion did our bodies sway,
> To perfect music that was heard always;
> Woe's me, that am so dull of foot to-day!
>
> To move unto your motion, Love, were sweet;
> My spirit rises to the music's beat —
> But, ah, the leaden demon in my feet! (399)

Dancing, a cultural activity of heterosexual courtship, is used here as a stand-in for what the speaker is unable to intelligibly do — love a woman. In a letter written by Levy to Dollie Maitland Radford in 1884, she describes a piece of prose she is working on and what narrative tropes she is employing. Taking jest, Levy sarcastically refers to the machinations of her heterosexual romance plot as 'subtle' (Beckman, 'Amy Levy' 244). Beckman notes that this demonstrates Levy's self-awareness of the 'formulaic nature of popular fiction' (244), but it also demonstrates an awareness of the performativity of heterosexual courtship. The cynicism present in this letter is presented in 'A Wall Flower' without the humour, as the consequences for the speaker of heterosexual scripts are obliquely manifest, excluding her from participation. The second stanza points to a utopia — 'some other where, not here. / In other ages, on another sphere' — where such desires can be realised, where both their bodies would move together and where the music would play with perfection. While, as Francis notes, there is a tragedy to Levy's 'queer' poems, some, like 'A Wall Flower', also envision, even if momentarily, utopic otherworlds where same-sex desire could exist and signify.

Writing of prose (rather than poetry), Castle has noted of lesbian fiction that it often exhibits an otherworldliness. She writes:

> By its very nature lesbian fiction has — and can only have — a profoundly attenuated relationship with what we think of, stereotypically, as narrative verisimilitude, plausibility, or 'truth to life'. Precisely because it is motivated by a yearning for that which is, in a cultural sense, implausible — the subversion of male homosocial desire — lesbian fiction characteristically exhibits, even as it masquerades as 'realistic' in surface detail, a strongly fantastical, allegorical, or utopian tendency. (88)

'A Wall Flower' exhibits these queer tendencies when its desires are fulfilled only in the speculative otherworld. The 'leaden fiend/demon' (also an otherworldly reference) is that which figuratively renders the speaker immobile, holding her down and foreclosing her realisation of same-sex desire. Read as an exploration of queer symbolics, the leaden fiend/demon is the cultural impossibility of representing lesbian desire in the late nineteenth century.

Levy's posthumously published poem 'A Ballad of Religion and Marriage' also creates a utopic otherworld. It foresees a time when women's lives and identities will not be determined by their marriage-status. The final stanza of the poem reads:

> Grant, in a million years at most,
>   Folks shall be neither pairs nor odd —
> Alas! we sha'n't be there to boast
>   "Marriage has gone the way of God!" (404)

While 'odd' is often conceptualised in relation to the 'problem' of 'surplus women' identified in the 1851 census which led to the title of George Gissing's 1893 novel *The Odd Women*, Castle also notes that 'odd' had been used by same-sex attracted women to describe themselves and their alternate sexualities as early as Anne Lister in the 1820s (10). The critique of marriage here, while most obviously occurring from a critique of gendered relations, also implicitly critiques a powerful structure and symbol of heterosexuality.

Another tactic Levy employs is to do away with gender altogether, as in the poem 'Philosophy' in which the speaker recalls a summer spent with a 'dear friend', when they would stay up 'talking half the night' on the 'stairway's topmost height' gazing 'on the crowd below', the 'philistine and flippant throng'

(401). Here, in youth, they were 'Scarce friends, not lovers (each avers), / But sexless, safe Philosophers' (401). Sharing here a relationship that is 'above' gender, the speaker also notes that not only does gender dissolve between the pair but their individuated subjectivities do as well: 'For, you and I, we did eschew / The egoistic "I" and "you"' (401). Joseph Bristow notes that the sex of both speaker and friend is 'teasingly obscure' and he proposes a resistant reading to the poem's 'structures of denial', suggesting that 'Their scornful pride — setting themselves above the Philistines — may well have masked their amorous interest in each other' (85).

The quest in 'Philosophy' for a sexless society performs the same symbolic refusal of patriarchy that the existence of the lesbian does (Castle 5). 'A Wall Flower', however, concedes its social reality by positioning its speaker as barred from the social situation in which she finds herself, removed from the activities and desires displayed before her. She has set herself apart and is unable or unwilling to engage in the heterosexual cultural practices before her, but with no other social reality available, she is left to languish in a doorway, itself a liminal 'between-space'.

The second poem that explores the symbolic impossibility of lesbian desire is 'At a Dinner Party'. Its two stanzas read:

> With fruit and flowers the board is deckt,
> The wine and laughter flow;
> I'll not complain — could one expect
> So dull a world to know?
>
> You look across the fruit and flowers,
> My glance your glances find. —
> It is our secret, only ours,
> Since all the world is blind. (400)

Here the scene describes same-sex love not expected or acknowledged by the wider world. Indeed, the world is 'blind' to their love which is 'secret'. While like Levy's other Sapphic poems, 'At a Dinner Party' conspicuously eludes gendering the speaker (and additionally here, naming the gender of the love interest), a queer reading of this poem is supported by the doubled reference to fruit and flowers over which the loving glances are exchanged, both objects being commonly gendered as feminine. The invocation of the 'secret', particularly the love which is secret, is also coded as queer. Eve Kosofsky Sedgwick has noted the importance of secrecy and disclosure, of demarcations between the public and the private, to understandings of modern sexualities (71-2). 'At a Dinner Party' performs these pleasures and perils of the queer closet. Though the lovers are separated their shared glances are erotically charged. This ambivalence is a common feature of popular understandings of queer subjectivity. That the speaker pities the world too dull to recognise queer love shows how queer 'identity' is often 'experienced as a stigmatizing mark as well as a form of romantic exceptionalism' (Love 3).

A poem from Levy's earlier collection of poetry, *A Minor Poet and Other Verse*, also includes references to love which is secret and which eludes literal physical intimacy. This is 'Sinfonia Eroica', dedicated in brackets to Sylvia. The title references Ludwig van Beethoven's Symphony No.3 of the same name, which is renowned for the funeral march of the second movement. Levy was obviously aware of the cultural valency of this funeral march, referring in the poem to a 'mystic melody of death' (377). The poem opens 'My lover, my lover' as the speaker recalls an evening in June when both persons happened to frequent the same music hall, where a 'high magician' can 'draw the dreams from out the secret breast' (377). Soon after arriving the speaker sees her love interest:

> I, with the rest,
> Sat there athirst, atremble for the sound;
> And as my aimless glances wandered round,
> Far off, across the hush'd, expectant throng,
> I saw your face that fac'd mine. (377)

As in 'At a Dinner Party', the soon-to-be object of the speaker's love is encountered from a distance — space and people are between them, and they are unable to be or converse together openly. The poem continues:

> Clear and strong
> Rush'd forth the sound, a mighty mountain stream;
> Across the clust'ring heads mine eyes did seem
> By subtle forces drawn, your eyes to meet.
> Mingled in all my blood and made it wine.
> Straight I forgot the world's great woe and mine;
> My spirit's murky lead grew molten fire;
> Despair itself was rapture.

> Ever higher,
> Stronger and clearer rose the mighty strain;
> Then sudden fell; then all was still again,
> And I sank back, quivering as one in pain. (377)

Here, unlike the two poems examined earlier, there is a form of consummation. As in the connected poem that follows in *A Minor Poet*, 'To Sylvia', this poem conflates bodily experiences with music. As the speaker's spirit grows hot as 'molten fire', her despair becomes rapturous and 'the strain' becomes stronger and clearer, before ending suddenly leaving her 'quivering as one in pain'. The 'problem' of pre-1900 lesbian representation is also partially eclipsed here through associating it with, and exploring it through, music — a form of expression that avoids the representational constraints of linguistic signification. It is difficult to read these lines without a sexual, orgasmic subtext. Yet, again, not only is the object and source of the desire out of reach, but the desire itself is associated with a larger despair than *le petite mort* suggests. Here are the beginnings of what would come to dominate Levy's Sapphic poems in *A London Plane-Tree*: her preoccupation with death. While the music allows Levy opportunity to explore sexual desire in 'Sinfonia Eroica', her particular choice of symphony also associates the desire with not only heroism but also with despair and death.

If we turn back to the Sapphic poems from *A London Plane-Tree*, it is evident that many of the poems concern themselves with death, loss and pain, as Francis notes. As previously mentioned, Castle has noted the long history of literary 'lesbian ghosts' but it is also evident that Levy explores states of liminality other than those between life and death, finding in these inarticulate times and spaces opportunities for transgressive feelings and behaviours.

Interested in this liminality in Levy's late poetry, Alex Goody argues that while Levy seeks ontology outside or between identity categories, such a project is inevitably fraught:

> Poems such as 'In the Mile End Road' reveal the double-edged nature of Levy's writing/passing, of her celebration of the space between. The articulation of transgressive racial and sexual identities — of being neither one nor an other — leads to a splitting of subjectivity into disparate fragments. The text is enunciated in the action of traversing and thereby delineating the liminal space between the posed fragments of identity, but

the becoming-subject cannot keep circulating, keep passing between; at some point, the self is sacrificed, destroyed as the Other. The idealized 'smooth' space that Deleuze and Guattari describe in *A Thousand Plateaus* and elsewhere, which does not have separation, capture, territorialisation, or designation, is perhaps what Levy's *A London Plane-Tree and Other Verse* is seeking, but what the poems show is that this ideal is a figuration that cannot be maintained. ('Passing' 175)

The unintelligibility and non-recognition of female same-sex desire, the unwillingness to 'separate', 'capture', 'territorialise' or 'designate', though, can also be read as a queer strategy of representation. There is, as Goody notes, a refusal to submit to the (heterosexual) subjectifying structures of late-nineteenth-century London, but there is also a frustration, such as in 'Philosophy' and 'A Dinner Party', that late-nineteenth-century London fails to recognise the lesbian as a subject. Where Goody reads the themes of death and loss in Levy's 'Sapphic' poems as a psychoanalytically narcissistic dissolution of the self, in a beloved-as-self model, they can also be read as politically queer, as acknowledging that which socially, culturally, legally and politically could not be acknowledged, represented or brought into discursive being. Castle has noted that due to its challenge to patriarchal paradigms, 'it is perhaps not surprising that at least until around 1900 lesbianism manifests itself in the Western literary imagination primarily as an absence, as chimera or *amor impossibilia* — a kind of love that, by definition, cannot exist' (30-1). While Goody concedes this representational impossibility and acknowledges the liberatory potential of a Deleuzian refusal of identity politics, by reading through a psychoanalytical model of narcissism he does not capture the creative potential of the simultaneously impossible yet omnipresent 'lesbian ghost'. That is, to be haunted by loss is to be constantly surrounded by that which is lost. To quote Castle at some length:

A ghost, according to *Webster's Ninth*, is a spirit believed to appear in a 'bodily likeness.' To haunt, we find, is 'to visit often,' or 'to recur constantly and spontaneously,' 'to stay around or persist,' or 'to reappear continually.' The ghost, in other words, is a paradox. Though nonexistent, it nonetheless *appears*. Indeed, so vividly does it appear — if only in the 'mind's eye' — one feels unable to get away from it. ... What of the spectral metaphor and the lesbian writer? For her, one suspects, 'seeing ghosts' may be a matter — not so much of derealisation — but of rhapsodical embodiment: a ritual calling up, or *apophrades*, in the old mythical sense. The dead are indeed brought back to life; the absent loved one returns. For the spectral vernacular, it turns out, continues its own powerful and perverse magic. Used imaginatively — repossessed, so to speak — the very trope that evaporates can also solidify. In the strangest turn of all, perhaps, the lesbian body itself returns: and the feeble, elegiac waving off — the gesture of would-be exorcism — becomes instead a new and passionate beckoning. (46-7)

In much of Levy's Sapphic poetry there is a literal or metaphorical absence attached to the love-interest, whether it be in the form of a dead love, a lost love or a love that literally cannot be reached. Yet there is also a deep carnality to Levy's Sapphic poetry. Take, for instance, 'Borderland', where, as the speaker lies in bed unsure whether she is waking or sleeping, she is 'aware / Of an unseen presence hovering' that 'is she', 'sweet as love, as soft as death':

> Am I waking, am I sleeping?
> As the first faint dawn comes creeping
> Thro' the pane, I am aware
> Of an unseen presence hovering,
> Round, above, in the dusky air:
> A downy bird, with an odorous wing,
> That fans my forehead, and sheds perfume,
> As sweet as love, as soft as death,
> Drowsy-slow through the summer-gloom.
> My heart in some dream-rapture saith,
> *It is she.* Half in a swoon,
> I spread my arms in slow delight. —
> O prolong, prolong the night,
> For the nights are short in June! (391)

'Borderland' takes place in the early hours of the morning between night and day, when only faint light pierces the darkness, making shapes visible only in uncertain fluidity. The opening line also positions the speaker between sleeping and wakefulness, in an indeterminate space between the unconscious desires of dreams and their circumscription in reality. Here, in the pre-dawn hours, the speaker's love — 'It is she' — appears to her, swooning. Again the presence of desire conjures death explicitly — 'As sweet as love, as soft as death'. Unlike in 'Sinfonia Eroica', where sexual intimacy is represented orgasmically through music, here an 'em' dash signifies the failure to represent climax.

These literary techniques, like those performed by the symbolists, operate to represent facets of life previously (or continuously) denied by hegemonic discourse. In the introduction to this chapter I suggested that Baudelaire's 'The Painter of Modern Life' can be read as an intertext to Levy's essay on Thomson. Indeed, Levy's essay positions Thomson as a poet of modern life. She writes that 'James Thomson is essentially the poet of mood; he has symbolised, as no poet has done before him, a certain phase of modern feeling, I was going to say modern pessimism, but the word scarcely covers the sense' (502). The city that Thomson conjures 'rises before us, a picture distinct, real in itself, real in the force of its symbolic meaning' (503). Clearly inspired by the Symbolist movement, and pondering how to value and give authority to minor works and poets, Levy proposes that

> [t]he value of the poem does not lie in isolated passages, in pregnant lines which catch the ear and eye and linger in the memory; it is as a complete conception, as a marvellously truthful expression of what it is almost impossible to express at all, that we must value it. And the truthfulness is none the less that it has been expressed to a great extent by means of symbols; the nature of the subject is such that it is only by resorting to such means that it can be adequately represented. Mood, seen through the medium of such draughtsmanship and painter's skill, is no longer a dream, a shadow which the sunbeams shall disperse, but one side of a truth. (505)

Levy is writing here of Thomson's representation of what she called 'grey pain' — major depression, a state of being that continues to elide representation. Yet, in the late nineteenth century, female same-sex desire also resisted representation. Levy captures the incoherent pleasures of same-sex desire in 'A Wall Flower' and 'Borderland'. Most forcefully rendered through the musical climax in 'Sinfonia Eroica', symbolism allows Levy to represent desires which have been largely denied by language and law.

Levy notes of Thomson's epic poem that for those who have not wandered the City of Dreadful Night and felt its pain, the poem may have little meaning. Appreciating the power of cultural and intersubjective recognition, she writes that 'he dwells on a view of things which is morbid, nay false, which does not exist for the perfectly healthy human being'. Nonetheless, she goes on, 'The fact that a state of mind exists is enough; it is one of the phenomena of our world, as true, as false, as worthy, as unworthy of consideration as any other' (502). It is this impossibility of recognition from the wider public of Levy's same-sex orientated erotic desires that causes, as Goody phrased it, 'a splitting of subjectivity into disparate fragments' ('Passing' 175).

Scholars have often focused upon the 'triple marginalisation' of Levy: her female gender, her Jewishness, and her non-heterosexuality, and though here she references the self-experience or recognition of depression required to develop meaning from Thomson's poetry, her critique of the universal can be applied to many aspects of her work which explored culturally incoherent identities, desires and subjectivities. Read queerly, it is the failure of society to recognise female same-sex desire in 'At a Dinner Party' that gives the poem its erotic politics and performs the cultural critique of the type evidenced in the Thomson essay. As Judith Butler has explored, this incoherence and unintelligibility continues to be an attribute of the queer subject today. The queer is still the minor. Subjective coherence enables a speaking position through which an effective form of agency can be wrought. To be recognised is to be allowed to speak. Yet this coherence also has its limits. Identity is created through discourse and is a normalising, disciplining form of production. It forecloses possibilities for change. Writing in a proto-lesbian era, Levy's work is valuable for its attempts to negotiate and theorise agency and change despite, or even through, a poetics of misrecognition. It is here, in its poetics and its politics, that Amy Levy produced fine queer work.

Works Cited

Baudelaire, Charles. *The Painter of Modern Life*. Penguin Great Ideas. London: Penguin, 2010.

Beckman, Linda Hunt. 'Amy Levy: Urban Poetry, Poetic Innovation, and the Fin-De-Siècle Woman Poet.' *The Fin-de-Siècle Poem: English Literary Culture and the 1890s*. Ed Joseph Bristow. Athens: Ohio UP, 2005. 207-30.

———. *Amy Levy: Her Life and Letters*. Athens: Ohio State UP, 2000.

Bernstein, Susan David. Ed. *The Romance of a Shop/Amy Levy*. Ontario: Broadview, 2006.

Bristow, Joseph. '"All out of Tune in This World's Instrument": The "Minor" Poetry of Amy Levy.' *Journal of Victorian Culture* 4.1 (1999): 76-103.

Castle, Terry. *The Apparitional Lesbian: Female Homosexuality and Modern Culture.* New York: Columbia UP, 1993.

Francis, Emma. 'Amy Levy: Contradictions? Feminism and Semitic Discourse.' *Women's Poetry, Late Romantic to Late Victorian: Gender and Genre, 1830-1900.* Eds Virginia Blain and Isobel Armstrong. New York: St Martin's, 1999.

Goody, Alex. 'Passing in the City: The Liminal Spaces of Amy Levy's Late Work.' *Amy Levy: Critical Essays.* Ed. Naomi Hetherington and Nadia Valman. Athens: Ohio UP, 2010. 157-79.

Goody, Alex. 'Murder in Mile End: Amy Levy, Jewishness, and the City.' *Victorian Literature and Culture* 34.2 (2006): 461-79.

Love, Heather. *Feeling Backward: Loss and the Politics of Queer History.* Cambridge, MA: Harvard UP, 2007.

Minsloff, Sarah. 'Amy Levy and Identity Criticism: A Review of Recent Work.' *Literature Compass* 4.4 (2007): 1318-29.

New, Melvyn. *The Complete Novels and Selected Writings of Amy Levy 1861-1889.* Gainesville: University Press of Florida, 1993.

Newman, Sally. 'The Archival Traces of Desire: Vernon Lee's Failed Sexuality and the Interpretation of Letters in Lesbian History.' *Journal of the History of Sexuality* 14.1-2 (2005): 51-75.

Nord, Deborah Epstein. '"Neither Pairs nor Odd": Female Community in Late Nineteenth-Century London.' *Signs* 15.4 (1990): 733-54.

Pullen, Christine. *The Woman Who Dared: A Biography of Amy Levy.* Surrey, UK: Kingston UP, 2010.

Sedgwick, Eve Kosofsky. *Epistemology of the Closet.* Berkeley and Los Angeles: University of California Press, 1990.

Wagenknecht, Edward. *Daughters of the Covenant: Portraits of Six Jewish Women.* Amherst: University of Massachusetts Press, 1983.

Wittig, Monique. *The Straight Mind and Other Essays.* Boston: Beacon Press, 1992.

13

From 'Peter Panic' to proto-Modernism: the case of J.M. Barrie

Maggie Tonkin

The author may be dead as far as Roland Barthes is concerned, but the news is yet to hit the street. Probably nothing speaks more loudly of the gap between academic literary criticism and the culture of reading outside the academy than the latter's continuing obsession with the author. Barthes's claim that the author is neither the originator nor the final determiner of textual meaning has assumed the status of orthodoxy in scholarly poetics. Whilst the early austerity has faded somewhat, such that discussion of the historical specificity of the author is no longer scorned in literary studies, the Romantic privileging of the author as the 'fully intentional, fully sentient source of the literary text, as authority for and limitation on the "proliferating" meanings of the text', as Andrew Bennett puts it (55), has never regained its former currency. Yet outside the academy, public fixation on the figure of the author has never been greater: the author is now a communal fetish.

J.M. Barrie, famed for his authorship of *Peter Pan*, is a case in point. *Peter Pan* has long been neglected within the academy, but recently the tide has turned and it has become the focus of renewed scholarly attention. However, as Peter Hollindale notes, there are 'two co-existent stories' about *Peter Pan*, 'each with the capacity to distort or confuse our understanding of the other' ('A Hundred

Years' 199), for alongside the renewed scholarly attention to Barrie's best-known work has emerged a public fixation on his life, which is manifest in popular cultural forms such as biography, film, popular science books and websites. These depictions range from those that stick to known facts about Barrie's life to those that Hollindale dubs a 'speculative psycho-sexual cocktail' ('A Hundred Years' 201). Defamatory claims about Barrie's purported perversions multiply willy-nilly in popular culture, fed by the anxiety about paedophilia ubiquitous in the late twentieth century. Indeed, Richard Morrison has tagged the popular association of Barrie and his most famous text with paedophilia as 'Peter Panic'. The problem with this fetishisation of Barrie the author is not simply that it is largely based on unsubstantiated speculation and moral panic, but rather that it generates a mass of author-based criticism that obscures, rather than illuminates, his singularity *as an author*. In this chapter, I will scrutinise some of the allegations made about Barrie, and then change the subject from the author to the *authored*. In particular, I want to see what happens when we consider Barrie not as a subject of perversion but as a subject of literary history. When we separate the text from the life — in contradistinction to the many critics who read *Peter Pan* psycho-biographically — and situate it at the moment of its production, it becomes apparent that Barrie's most famous work ought to be considered in the light of early Modernism.

The mythology around Barrie, which rivals that of his most famous creation, has its roots in the disjunction between his highly successful public career and his unusual personal life. In public, Barrie had a relentlessly upward trajectory. Born in 1860 as the ninth child of a humble handloom weaver in rural Scotland, James Mathew Barrie gained admittance to Edinburgh University from where he graduated with a B.A. He then moved south to England where he carved out a journalistic career before becoming one of the most celebrated authors of the *fin de siècle*, writing critically and commercially successful novels and plays, and, of course, creating *Peter Pan*. Writing enabled Barrie's transformation from a lower-class Scottish outsider into a member of the British establishment: he mingled with famous artistic figures of the period; hobnobbed with royalty; became a Baronet in 1913; was awarded the Order of Merit in 1922; and was appointed Rector of St Andrews University, and later Chancellor of Edinburgh University. Furthermore, his writing earned enormous sums of money both during his lifetime and after his death: his bequest of the *Peter Pan* royalties to the Great Ormond Street Hospital for Sick Children has helped keep that institution afloat through the intervening century. His death in 1937 was the occasion of national mourning, with condolences sent to his family by the King and a service at St Paul's Cathedral led by the Archbishop of Canterbury.[1]

Yet this public success masked a private life that included many tribulations. The first of these, which is the origin of much of the Barrie mythology, was the death of his fourteen-year-old brother David in a skating accident when Barrie was six. As Barrie recounts in his memoir of his mother, *Margaret Ogilvy*, David's death had a profound effect on the family. His mother never recovered from her grief over the death of her favourite son, and it seems that Barrie, more urgently than the six other surviving children, felt that he had to console her by assuming the role David had occupied in her affections. Margaret Ogilvy's subsequent possessiveness, and Barrie's mother-fixation, would provide a goldmine to later biographers. A later source of grief for Barrie came from the failure of his thirteen-year marriage to actress Mary Ansell. In the divorce proceedings, Ansell claimed that their marriage had never been consummated, which Barrie never publicly refuted. Barrie's failure to 'perform' Edwardian masculinity in his marriage, coupled with his unconventional interest in children, lies at the heart of many of the accusations later made about him.

Furthermore, his love of play for its own sake, indeed of games of all types, especially cricket, is yet another indication of how far at odds Barrie was with the glorification of masculinity, work and Empire that dominated the Edwardian period. Kevin Telfer's *Peter Pan's First XI: the Extraordinary Story of J.M. Barrie's Cricket Team*, gives an intriguing account of Barrie's obsession with play. Telfer argues that play, rather than winning, was Barrie's main preoccupation. Hence he ensured that his cricket team always contained a fair proportion of 'duffers' (non-skilled players, amongst whom he included himself), so that the game remained fun rather than a contest of skill. Banter, larking about, teasing, wordplay, and the construction of fanciful narratives were essential to Barrie's notion of 'playing the game'. Barrie's reverence for both games and storytelling is a manifestation of his desire to contest the devaluation of play consequent on

---

1   For the biographical information in this chapter I am indebted to Lisa Chaney's excellent *Hide-and-Seek with Angels: A Life of J.M. Barrie*.

instrumental reason and the social mores of late Victorian England, and comes through strongly in his most famous text.

Finally, Barrie's deep attachment to the five sons of his friends Sylvia and Arthur Llewelyn Davies, whom he unofficially adopted and raised after the early death of their parents, was the source of both happiness and grief, since two of the boys died tragically young. Barrie publicly acknowledged that the make-believe adventures he shared with the boys were the inspiration for *Peter Pan*. What he could not have foreseen were the sinister terms in which this relationship would be depicted after his death.

During his lifetime, his literary peers showered him with praise. As R.D.S. Jack points out, the most common descriptor was that of 'genius': Robert Louis Stevenson hailed him as 'a man of genius'; the drama critic James Agate called him an 'irritating genius'; and William Archer described him as 'a humourist of original and delightful genius' (qtd in Jack, *Never land 3*).[2] J.A. Hammerton's *J.M. Barrie: the Story of a Genius* (1929), in which Barrie is hailed as 'the finest embodiment of Scotland's national genius' (338), exemplifies the hagiographic approach that generally prevailed. However, after Barrie's death in 1939 interest in his work waned. He was increasingly seen as old-fashioned and sentimental and dismissed as a late-Victorian or, even worse, an Edwardian writer — the kiss of death since Woolf's attack in her essay, 'Mr Bennett and Mrs Brown'. Since Barrie's death, his plays — with the exception of *Peter Pan* — have rarely been performed on the professional stage, his novels have remained out of print, and, until very recently, critical monographs on his oeuvre have been few and far between. As Jack notes, Barrie appears to have fallen 'from a position above criticism to one below it' (*Never land* 6).

But as interest in Barrie's work declined, fascination with his life increased. The BBC documentary drama, *The Lost Boys* (1978), written by Andrew Birkin, and the subsequent publication of Birkin's book, *J.M. Barrie and the Lost Boys* (1979), marked a turning point in public perceptions of Barrie. Birkin had unprecedented access to Barrie's letters, journals and notebooks. Particularly significant, though, was the input of the last surviving Llewelyn Davies boy,

---

2   Whilst Barrie writes NeverLand as a single word in the *Peter Pan* texts, critics have sometimes chosen to write it as two words, as Jack does here. In this chapter I have duplicated the individual usage of each writer.

Nico, who gave Birkin access to his family's private letters and papers, and was himself interviewed. Whilst Birkin's book was by no means the first Barrie biography, it was the first to focus so extensively on his family trauma, and on his relationship with the Llewellyn Davies boys. Birkin's approach is scrupulously evidence-based and, unlike many who followed, he does not reduce *Peter Pan* to being merely a fictionalised account of Barrie's psychological complexes. Birkin is also at pains to repudiate the claims of paedophilia which had begun to circulate after the showing of his TV series. In his Introduction to the 1979 edition, he addresses the 'speculation that has arisen in the last decade over Barrie's sexuality' by saying:

> Several psychiatrists have classified him as a paedophile, while a number of critics and viewers jumped to the same conclusion on watching *The Lost Boys*. It would seem that sexual categories, like so many judgments, lie in the eye of the beholder, and some readers will inevitably behold similar ambiguities in this book. As Barrie's sole surviving son, perhaps Nico is better placed for determining the truth; and so, while thanking him profoundly for having allowed me to trespass so freely on his past and present, I give him the last word: 'Of all the men I have ever known, Barrie was the wittiest, and the best company. He was also the least interested in sex. He was a darling man. He was an innocent; which is why he could write *Peter Pan*.'('Introduction' 1979 n.p.)

But, as Birkin predicted, those predisposed to find Barrie a paedophile did so regardless, and in the wake of *The Lost Boys* accusations continued to proliferate. In the Introduction to the 2003 edition, Birkin cited Nico again in a further attempt to hose down such claims: 'As Nico so delightfully remarked, "I don't believe that Uncle Jim ever experienced what one might call a stirring in the undergrowth for anyone — man, woman, or child. He was an innocent …"' ('Introduction to the Yale Edition' n.p.). Birkin has subsequently made his archival material on Barrie available online to other scholars, and in yet another letter, posted on the website, Nico reiterates:

> All I can say is that I, who lived with him off and on for more than 20 years: who lived alone with him in his flat for five of these years: never heard one word or saw one glimmer of anything approaching homosexuality or paedophiliacy — had he had either of these leanings in however slight a symptom I would have been aware. (JMBarrie n.p.)

In a 2001 television interview, Barrie's great-niece Margaret Sweeton described Barrie's asexuality in rather more blunt terms, stating, 'He was a runt' (qtd in Hollindale, 'A Hundred Years' 201). Yet these repeated denials from the persons most likely to know Barrie's sexual proclivities have had little effect, to judge by Barrie's listing on a site celebrating paedophilia, 'Famous British Paedophiles' (n.p.).

Another unsubstantiated claim about Barrie comes from the pen of Robert Sapolsky, in his book *Why Zebras Don't Get Ulcers: a Guide to Stress, Stress-Related Diseases, and Coping* (1994), which, as the title indicates, is a work of popular science. Sapolsky claims that Barrie suffered from stress dwarfism — a condition in which a child stops growing in response to extreme emotional trauma and in the absence of physical causes — as a result of trying to take the place of his dead brother in his mother's affections:

> The younger boy, ignored ... seizes upon this idea; by remaining a boy forever, by not growing up, he will at least have some chance of pleasing his mother, winning her love. Although there is no evidence of disease or malnutrition in his well-to-do family, he ceases growing. As an adult, he is just barely five feet in height, and his marriage is unconsummated. The forlorn boy became the author of the much-beloved children's classic, *Peter Pan*. J.M. Barrie's plays and novels are filled with children who didn't grow up ... (Sapolsky, *Zebras* 91-2)

Here, Sapolsky underscores the link between what he regards as Barrie's psychopathology and his most famous character. To wit, Barrie himself could not grow up, *ipso facto*, his texts in true Freudian fashion are inscriptions of his unconscious conflicts: the life determines and explains the text.

More contentiously, though, Sapolsky asserts that Barrie had a 'lifelong obsession with young boys, and his private writing includes passages of sadomasochism and pedophilia' (*Zebras* 308). He makes further claims in an online article dated 2002, in which he describes Barrie as 'the creepiest example of Stress dwarfism that I have encountered' (Sapolsky, *Thought Leader Forum* n.p.). However, Sapolsky's argument is undermined by his cavalier attitude to facts, which lead him to give not only an incorrect height for Barrie but also an incorrect date and place of birth and an incorrect age at death.[3] Far more egregious than his cavalier attitude to factual accuracy, however, is Sapolsky's claim that Barrie was 'repeatedly in trouble for sadomasochistic relationships with young boys. He spent half of his fortune keeping these stories out of the newspapers. He spent his entire life unsuccessfully dealing with his Stress Dwarfism' (Sapolsky, *Thought Leader Forum* n.p.).

It is difficult to reconcile Sapolsky's position as Professor of Biological and Neurosciences at Stanford University with such factual inaccuracies and unsubstantiated claims, to say nothing of his failure to consider an alternative diagnosis for Barrie's problems.[4] Barrie scholar Jason A. Quest dismisses Sapolsky's theory as 'a complete fiction' that 'besmirched Barrie's reputation, misrepresented his medical history' and 'utterly fabricated a legal record', concocted in order to 'spice up' his lecture on stress dwarfism (*Neverpedia* n.p.). Yet no matter how vigorously Sapolsky's theory is refuted by Barrie scholars such as Quest, it continues to be cited in the media and in undergraduate essays as if it were irrefutable fact.

A less defamatory author-based reading of Barrie is presented in the *Handbook of Psychobiography*, published by Oxford University Press in 2005. In the Introduction, William Todd Schultz avers that the aim of psychobiography is 'the understanding of persons', adding that psychobiography is an attempt to

---

[3] Sapolsky claims that Barrie 'lived to be 60 years old and 4'10". It was confirmed in his autopsy that he never reached puberty. This is a perfect example of Stress Dwarfism' (Sapolsky, *Thought Leader Forum*). In fact, according to his passport, Barrie was substantially taller than this, and, according to Jason A. Quest, photographic records show that his adult height fell within the normal range for his family (*Neverpedia*). Furthermore, Barrie was 77 when he died. Additionally, in all his adult photos he sports a bushy moustache, which is a sign of at least some degree of sexual maturity, although it may be incomplete. No biography of Barrie mentions him having an autopsy, nor is there any obvious medical or legal reason why he should have been given one.

[4] It is, for instance, possible that Barrie suffered from an endocrine disorder such as Kallmann's Syndrome (or Hypogonadotropic Hypogonadism), a disorder caused by underdeveloped testicles that fail to produce sufficient testosterone, leading to short stature and sexual dysfunction. Depending on the degree of testosterone insufficiency, some patients with this condition may attain partial sexual maturity, which would account for Barrie's abundant moustache. Kallmann's Syndrome is now recognised and treatable, but such was not the case in Barrie's day.

solve a 'tantalizing incoherence' in the subject's life (9). Schultz argues that the psychobiographer should be alert to a 'supersaliency': a 'single scene encapsulating all the core parameters of a life story' which will unlock the 'tantalizing mystery' of the person (48). This he refers to as 'striking paydirt'. Artists, he claims, are exemplary subjects for psychoanalysis because they are 'prototypical outsiders' (136). Schultz disagrees with the notion that the art can or ought to be separated from the life, asking rhetorically — as if the answer were self-evident — 'Does one get more out of *Peter Pan* after learning of Barrie's brother's death and his relationship with his mother in its wake?' (140)

In his chapter on Barrie in the *Handbook*, Daniel M. Ogilvie's answer to this question is never in doubt. Whilst Ogilvie dismisses Sapolsky's theory of Stress dwarfism as lacking in evidence (182), his own analysis simply recycles the scene presented in Barrie's memoir which recounts how the young James crept into his mother's affections by pretending to be his dead brother. Far from offering us any new insight, the psychobiographical analysis simply affirms the story that Barrie himself advances as the explanation to understanding his life and that is central to almost every biography of him. The notion that this scene might itself be a fiction from the pen of a writer given to almost compulsive storytelling does not occur to Ogilvie. The perfect recall of dialogue, for instance, seems unlikely if we consider that the recalling subject was only six at the time. But this failure to acknowledge the possible fictionality of Barrie's account, alongside the reductive interpretation to his text that it gives rise to, is symptomatic of the project of psychobiography articulated in the *Handbook*, which disregards the historical context in which art is created, is blind to the aesthetic choices an author might make and is wilfully ignorant of the textuality of writing. As Jack argues, the Freudian or psychobiographical approach is little more than 'a dogged attempt to reduce all Barrie's extremely varied output to the unity of this pre-ordained premise', in which 'only the discovery of the prototype is important' (*Never land* 9). 'Striking paydirt' turns out to be merely stirring up weary old dust.

No such complaint can be laid at the door of Piers Dudgeon, whose recent book *Captivated: J.M. Barrie, Daphne Du Maurier & the Dark Side of Neverland*, contains the most bizarre claims ever made about Barrie. Dudgeon accuses Barrie not only of illicit sexual possession, but a crime more dastardly still: Satanic possession of the mind. Dudgeon argues that Barrie, through his Svengali-like powers, exercised a 'malign power' (35) over successive generations of the du Maurier family, including Sylvia Llewellyn Davies and her sons. The fact that none of his so-called victims had a bad word to say about Barrie simply proves his point. According to Dudgeon: 'most of the victims of possession when they are told to name their controller; they cannot see that they are being controlled. None of Jim's victims ever had anything bad to say about him. Nor do victims of possession in the many cases that come before the courts today' (271).

Dudgeon recycles the previous accusations of paedophilia, but his claims about Satanic 'possession' go well beyond this to accusations that Barrie continued to hold sway over his victims posthumously: 'a piece of him — a little live spark of individual consciousness — lodged in a corner of their minds until the end' (175). Because of his diabolical powers, Barrie is held responsible for every untoward event in the Llewellyn Davies and du Maurier families, including those that occurred after his death. Even his friendship with the Antarctic explorer Captain Scott is cast as an act of psychic possession; Dudgeon blames Barrie's mind control for transforming Scott into a fantasist, and thereby causing him to embark on a foolhardy expedition in the Antarctic which resulted in his death (182). More bizarre still is Dudgeon's attempt to frame the six-year-old Barrie for his brother David's death:

> Suppose Jamie had travelled to Bothwell Academy with Alick and David at the end of the Christmas holiday in order to celebrate David's birthday with him, in particular to go skating with him, taking a brand new pair of birthday skates to Rothesay. Suppose Jamie had been the 'friend [who] set off on the one pair of skates which they shared', he goes on, and 'accidentally' knocked David down and was the one who 'fractured his skull'. It is of course highly speculative, but it explains the emotional dynamic between mother and son, Margaret's alienation from Jamie, and why Jamie continued, throughout his life, to make reparation. Moreover this worrying emotional dynamic between mother and son turns out to be replicated in the story of Peter Pan. (73)

Never mind that this wildly speculative scenario, scaffolded upon a tottering tower of 'supposes', does not fit with any of the established facts, such as the inconvenient fact that the six-year-old Barrie was hundreds of miles away at the time of David's death.

Condemnation of Dudgeon's work has been universal amongst Barrie scholars. Andrew Birkin, for instance, describes 'Dudgeon's ridiculous book' as 'so full of errors, distortions, half-truths, and his own opinions passed off as fact, that I personally regard it as worthless' (JMBarrie, n.p.). Nico Llewellyn Davies's daughter Laura adds, 'I personally think Dudgeon is more or less raving mad and lives in a world of wildest fantasy'. (JMBarrie, n.p.). Craig Brown, reviewing the book in the *Daily Mail Online*, scoffs that 'conspiracy theories don't come much loopier than this' (1). Yet the book has sold well and has been endorsed, at least according to the cover blurb, by respected literary critics such as Nina Auerbach and David Lodge, so it is perhaps not surprising that Dudgeon's preposterous theory is recycled uncritically in undergraduate essays.

Jacqueline Rose's *The Case of Peter Pan: Or, the Impossibility of Children's Fiction* is work of an entirely different order. Rose's book is a landmark text in children's literary studies. Its central thesis — that the child as addressed by and presented in children's fiction is a fantasy construct of innocence and purity that does the ideological work of masking the nostalgia and incompleteness of adults — is now so widely accepted as to seem self-evident, although it was a paradigm-shifting assertion at the time of publication in 1984. However, it is not her central thesis but rather her use of *Peter Pan* as primary exemplar that I focus on here. Rose is a highly regarded post-Structuralist literary critic, yet arguably even she is not immune to conflating the author, with all his purported frailties, with his text.

The Case of Peter Pan was first published shortly after Birkin's work on Barrie appeared, and Rose explicitly acknowledges the influence of Birkin's revelations:

> This is to describe children's fiction, quite deliberately, as something of a soliciting, a chase, or even a seduction. *Peter Pan* is certainly all of these. Recently we have been made at least partly aware of aware of this, as J.M. Barrie's story has been told and retold, as the story of a man and five small boys, whom he picked up, stole and possessed (Dunbar, 1970; Birkin, 1979). Barrie eventually adopted the Llewelyn Davies boys around whom he built the story of *Peter Pan*, staking a claim to them which he had already acted out symbolically by drawing them into his tale. (Rose 2-3)

Rose compares Barrie's purported seduction of the Llewelyn Davies boys to Charles Dodgson's sexual fixation on Alice Meynell, which gave rise to another children's classic, *Alice in Wonderland* (3). Yet despite casting these aspersions on Barrie — that he was sexually obsessed with the Llewelyn Davies boys, whom he 'stole' and 'possessed' — Rose insists that her critique of Barrie's text is not dependent upon proving that Barrie was a paedophile: 'It is not relevant, therefore, to insist that nothing ever happened, or that Barrie was innocent of any interest in sex' (3). Here Rose is occupying the same ambivalent position with regards to Barrie and paedophilia as Morrison, who, as Hollindale points out, manages to simultaneously 'convict and acquit Barrie of paedophilia' ('A Hundred Years' 201). But Rose's disavowal notwithstanding, her argument is haunted by the notion that there is something sinister about the author and the genesis of his text: 'Behind *Peter Pan* lies the desire of a man for a little boy (or boys), a fantasy or drama which has only recently caught the public eye' (3). In her argument, then, the life seeps into the work: *Peter Pan* has its origin in Barrie's unspeakable desires, which it both conceals and unconsciously reveals.

But although Rose distances herself from populist claims of Barrie having acted on his paedophiliac desires, the imbrication of *Peter Pan* with the violation of children runs through her book. This is particularly apparent in her introductory essay to the 1992 edition, 'The Return of Peter Pan', which situates a House of Lords debate on the play's unique copyright status in relation to the decline in government services to children and the prevalence of paedophilia. Without delineating the *actual* relationship between *Peter Pan*, perversion and child abuse, Rose repeatedly juxtaposes them in her prose. Thus, '*Peter Pan* lays bare a basic social and psychic structure — that so-called perversion resides in the house of innocence' ('Return' xii); and '*Peter Pan* offers virtuality and openness with such insistence that it seems to call attention to the trouble and murkiness not so much hidden underneath as running all along the seams' (xii). She continues:

> *Peter Pan* is a front — a cover not as concealer but as vehicle — for what is most unsettling and uncertain about the relationship between adult and child. It shows innocence not as a property of childhood but as a portion of adult desire. In this context, the eruptions in the 1980s, as they relate

to *Peter Pan* and to childhood more generally, can be read as the return of the repressed. (xii)

As her reference to the 1980s suggests, Rose is writing at the historical moment when anxiety about paedophilia was becoming an abiding obsession in Britain, and which has since given rise to such a level of panic that even the most well-intentioned of interactions between man and child is viewed with suspicion. As Hollindale and others have noted, this linking of Barrie's text with paedophila speaks more about the cultural moment from which Rose is writing than about the text itself. Hollindale describes Britain as now enduring 'a period when justified terror of paedophile assault has been seen to mutate into witch-hunts aimed at the innocent and proscription of harmless contacts between male adults and children' ('A Hundred Years' 201).

Much recent work on *Peter Pan* has taken issue with this aspect of Rose's argument. For instance, Alison B. Kavey argues that Rose 'conflates the sexual abuse of children with the literary text of *Peter Pan* … The tale is not the author and the author is not the tale' ('Introduction' 4). And, significantly, recent scholarship has turned away from the author-based criticism that I have outlined above towards an examination of how the Peter Pan texts reflect their historical moment of production.[5] Of the two collections published in the past eight years, *J.M. Barrie's Peter Pan in and Out of Time: a Children's Classic at 100* and *Second Star to the Right: Peter Pan in the Popular Imagination*, the former in particular has concerned itself with reinstating Peter Pan in history. Essays in that collection read the various *Pan* texts productively in relation to Edwardian discourses of childhood, gender, race and Empire, and *fin-de-siècle* discourses of Decadence and aestheticism.

Other recent scholarship has read Peter Pan as a response to modernity itself. Wilson, for example, argues that the representation of Mr Darling speaks of middle-class anxieties about work in the climate of increasing technological change in the workplace: '*Peter Pan* is a fable of modernity, anxiously negotiating industrial technologies that produced a middle class predicated on instability and which encoded impossible roles for men and women'(Wilson 8). The text's deliberate creation of nostalgia, she argues, is a way of managing anxiety about

---

5 I use the unitalicised Peter Pan to refer to the whole body of Pan texts, and the italicised *Peter Pan* to refer to the stage play of that name.

modernity, in which NeverLand functions as an idealisation of what never was: 'nostalgia for a (mis)remembered past now gone' (Wilson 9). R.D.S. Jack discusses Barrie's dramatic works as responses to modernity in his book, *The Road to the Never Land: A Reassessment of J.M. Barrie's Dramatic Art*, which is an ambitious examination of Barrie's engagement with significant modern thinkers, most notably Darwin, Nieztsche and Roget. Jack's study is a serious attempt to reinstate Barrie as a modern dramatist alongside Ibsen, Shaw and Wilde, who were considered his equals during his lifetime.

By and large, though, these recent attempts at finding Barrie a place in literary history have privileged thematics over stylistics. As yet, little consideration has been given to where Barrie's prose works sit on the greater historical continuum from Victorianism to Modernism in *stylistic* terms. Interestingly, despite her apparent reservations about Barrie, Rose is almost the only critic who comments on his prose style in relation to literary history. If we disregard the aspect of her argument which is haunted by 'Peter Panic', and turn to her discussion of Barrie's prose style, Rose hints at a productive line of inquiry that merits further consideration. Here I refer to the radical instability of tone and narrative address that is so striking in the novels *Peter Pan in Kensington Gardens* and *Peter and Wendy*.

A little textual history is in order here, for the Peter Pan texts have a long and complicated history. The first published text in the *Peter Pan* corpus is a novel for adults, *The Little White Bird* (1902). This novel recounts its narrator's obsessive relationship with a poor couple and their baby Peter, who flies out of his nursery at one week of age to live with the birds on an island. This was the genesis of the eternal boy in the play, *Peter Pan*, which was first performed in 1904, and published as a play script in 1928.[6] The novel, *Peter Pan in Kensington Gardens*, which came out as a children's book in 1906, contains the Peter Pan sections of *The Little White Bird*. In 1911, Barrie published *Peter and Wendy*, which is usually described as the novelised version of the play, but which contains more characterisation, adds several scenes (most notably a new ending) and provides a great deal of authorial commentary. Confusingly, its name was changed to *Peter Pan and Wendy* in 1924, and even more confusingly later became simply

---

6   Barrie continued to revise the play for performance until his death in 1937, so there are multiple versions of the play script extant.

Peter Pan, usurping the name of the play. Currently, the novel is published under the name *Peter and Wendy*. To complicate matters further, there are innumerable bowdlerised and simplified versions of both play and novel not authored by Barrie in existence, which are marketed under the name of *Peter Pan*.

The most notable difference between the novels, *Peter Pan in Kensington Gardens* and *Peter and Wendy*, and the play *Peter Pan*, is the presence of narrative commentary in the novels. To some extent, this replaces the extensive stage directions characteristic of Barrie's play scripts, but it goes much further, creating rapid and bewildering changes of tone and narrative address. Take the opening paragraph of *Peter and Wendy*:

> All children, except one, grow up. They soon know that they will grow up, and the way Wendy knew was this. One day when she was two years old she was playing in a garden, and she plucked another flower and ran with it to her mother. I suppose she must have looked rather delightful, for Mrs. Darling put her hand to her heart and cried, 'Oh, why can't you remain like this forever!' This was all that passed between them on the subject, but henceforth Wendy knew that she must grow up. You always know after you are two. Two is the beginning of the end. (69)

This passage is marked by slippage from a universalising statement, to the external description of the scene by the omniscient narrator, to the intrusion of the unidentified narrator in the 'I' of 'I suppose', to the assumption of the child's point of view, 'you always know after you are two', back to an universalising statement: 'Two is the beginning of the end'. The tone ranges from neutral observation, identification with the mother's sentiments, to parody of the tragi-comic grandiosity of the concluding statement. The question of who is speaking and who is being addressed is left open.

Throughout the novel, this same refusal to occupy any stable position of enunciation is evident. The following passage, which depicts the grieving Mrs Darling sleeping in the nursery just as the children are about to return home from Neverland, is a further illustration of how shifts in narrative voice and address produce an ambivalent tone:

> You see, the woman had no proper spirit. I had meant to say extraordinarily nice things about her; but I despise her, and not one of them will I say now. She does not really need to be told to have things ready, for they are ready.

> All the beds are aired, and she never leaves the house, and observe, the window is open. For all the use we are to her, we might go back to the ship. However, as we are here we may as well stay and look on. That is all we are, lookers-on. Nobody really wants us. So let us watch and say jaggy things, in the hope that some of them will hurt. (*Peter and Wendy* 208)

Two pages on, readers are told, 'Now that we look at her closely and remember the gaiety of her in the old days, all gone now just because she has lost her babes, I find I won't be able to say nasty things about her after all. If she was too fond of her rubbishy children she couldn't help it' (*Peter and Wendy* 210). Here the narrative voice moves from scorn to self-pity back to scorn: the phrases 'say jaggy things, in the hope some of them will hurt' and 'rubbishy children' are redolent of the spiteful speech of an adolescent. Is this, as some have assumed, Peter Pan himself speaking? At other times, the narrative voice seems to speak from the position of a child, only to slip into the alternately indulgent and moralising perspective of an adult describing children:

> Everything just as it should be, you see. Off we skip like the most heartless things in the world, which is what children are, but so attractive; and we have an entirely selfish time; and then when we have need of special attention we nobly return for it, confident that we shall be embraced instead of smacked. (*Peter and Wendy* 166)

In this passage, children are both the subjects — 'we' — and the objects — 'so attractive', and this oscillation between child, adolescent and adult perspectives, in which each is savagely satirised, this refusal to occupy any stable position of enunciation, combined with the constantly shifting tone, underscores the deeply ambiguous nature of Barrie's depiction of both child and adult.

In his Introduction to the Oxford World Classics edition of *Peter Pan in Kensington Gardens* and *Peter and Wendy*, Hollindale comments on the effects of the unstable tone and narrative voice in the novels:

> Again it is comedy which gives Barrie permission to enter territory where children's literature did not at that time usually go. Arbitrary, comic-serious, sudden changes in the narrative voice give the comedy its characteristic tone. Its remarkable achievement is to bring satire within children's compass, without forfeiting the more straightforward lures of fairy story, fantasy, and adventure. In both the stories, however, a Chinese-boxes narrative is at work, and below the surface another narrative voice

> is speaking which is likely to be audible only to grown-ups ... Under the surface of the children's book is a sharp and sometimes ferocious dialectic, exploring the collision and relation of the child and adult worlds. (xxi)

For Hollindale, this 'disconcerting and destabilizing narrative intrusion' is for the most part masterly, at least for the adult reader, and he argues that the complexity of their narrative procedures renders the prose texts of *Peter Pan* 'very complex works which we are still learning how to read' (xxv). Rudd similarly celebrates the narrative plurality of the novel, arguing that the prose versions of *Peter Pan* are heteroglossic in the Bakhtinian sense of containing multiple discourses collaboratively made (298).

Rose alone relates Barrie's sport with narrative voice and enunciation to literary Modernism, albeit obliquely. Her argument rests on a distinction between the myth of Peter Pan as emblematic of childish innocence as it circulates in culture, and the actual texts that Barrie penned. She relates that Barrie was reluctant to write the novels: 'Barrie persistently refused to write a prose version of the play, and when he did, it was a failure, almost incomprehensible, and later had to be completely rewritten' (6). For the most part, it is the sanitised rewritings of the novel by others which have been made available to children, and have formed the basis of versions in other media; the original is rarely read. Barrie's originals were considered to be 'almost incomprehensible' failures because they did not adhere to the dominant aesthetic of children's literature: realism. According to Rose, 'Realism — in the sense in which we have seen it defined here for children — is that form of writing which attempts to reduce to an absolute minimum our awareness of the language in which a story is written in order that we will take it for real' (65). In her view, *Peter and Wendy* is a 'dual travesty — a travesty of the basic rules of literary representation for children, and a mixing of genres' (83). Rose argues that the books of the 'Golden Age' of children's fiction, amongst which the Peter Pan texts are usually included, were largely untouched by the linguistic and formal experimentation of Modernism (65).

Rose's assertions about Barrie are part of a larger argument about the question of address in classic children's fiction, which she views as a body of texts that rest on a rupture between writer and addressee. This is in contradistinction to the concomitant developments in adult fiction, which was increasingly foregrounding narrative voice and interrogating the rupture between writer and reader. In contrast, according to Rose, the children's book 'works precisely to the extent that any question of who is talking to whom, and why, is totally erased' (2). With this assertion Rose conveniently ignores a whole tradition of children's literature, from the limerick and nonsense rhyme to Edward Lear, Lewis Carroll, Astrid Lundgren, Norman Lindsey and Dr Seuss, which insistently foregrounds language and, to varying degrees, plays with tone, address and point of view, as Rudd points out (292-3). Disavowing this tradition of linguistic play in children's literature enables Rose's assertion that *Peter Pan*, ostensibly a book *for* children which foregrounds language and constantly calls into question narrative address, must be a failure. Rose paraphrases the traditional view of children's fiction thus:

> The demand for better and more cohesive writing in children's fiction ... carries with it a plea that certain psychic barriers should go undisturbed, the most important of which is the barrier between adult and child. When children's fiction touches on that barrier, it becomes not experiment ... but *molestation*. Thus the writer for children must keep his or her narrative hands clean and stay in his or her place. (Rose 70, emphasis in original)

Barrie's narrative hands are dirty because his prose transgresses boundaries that critics regard as sacrosanct: those between narrator and characters, and adult and child. That Rose couches a textual or generic 'offence' in sexual terms — *molestation* — hints at the residual 'Peter Panic' underpinning her argument.

However, the claim that Barrie's prose style in the *Peter Pan* novels is a form of textual molestation of children is undermined by even a cursory reading of Barrie's other novels, all of which were written for an adult market. From the very first page of his most successful novel *Sentimental Tommy* (1896), the narrative voice calls attention to the compact between reader and writer to mutually create and sustain the fiction: 'The celebrated Tommy first comes into view on a dirty London stair, and he was in sexless garments, which were all he had, and he was five, and so though we are looking at him, we must do it sideways, lest he sit down hurriedly to hide them' (*Sentimental Tommy* 1). In both *Sentimental Tommy* and its sequel, *Tommy and Grizel* (1900), commentary from the unidentified narrator frequently intrudes upon the action, so that the illusion of verisimilitude is fatally undermined. For example:

> Oh, who by striving could make himself a boy again as Tommy could! I tell you he was always irresistible then. What is genius? It is the power to be a boy again at will. When I think of him flinging off the years and whistling childhood back, not to himself only, but to all who heard, distributing it among them gaily, imperiously calling on them to dance ... I cannot wonder that Grizel loved him. I am his slave myself ... (*Tommy and Grizel* 214)

The self-conscious narration of this passage, in which the narrative voice calls attention to itself and, by calling itself the protagonist's 'slave', broaches boundaries between narrator and characters, is typical of Barrie's prose style. Furthermore, Barrie's narrator frequently addresses the reader directly — almost conspiratorially — in a manner that verges on the metafictional: 'She is not so broken-hearted, after all, you may be saying, and I had promised to break her heart. But, honestly, I don't know how to do it more thoroughly, and you must remember that we have not seen her alone yet' (*Tommy and Grizel* 287).

Far from being evidence of his 'molestation' of the child through the medium of the book, Barrie's *Tommy* novels demonstrates that the foregrounding of narrative voice and the broaching of boundaries between narrator and characters constitute Barrie's habitual procedure, whether his prose is aimed at children or at adults.

Indeed, there is considerable doubt as to whether the *Peter Pan* texts were ever intended for children. Barrie never otherwise wrote for children; out of his large body of work only the *Peter Pan* texts have come to be regarded as children's literature. Yet this may be by accident rather than design, as many commentators have pointed out. Not a single child was invited to the opening night of the play *Peter Pan*; it was not until children attended a later matinee that its enormous appeal for them became apparent, and it was subsequently marketed as a work for children (see Chaney 225-40). The question of the text's intended audience has exercised many critics, including Rose herself, who argues — somewhat paradoxically, given her claim that it is a failure as a children's book — that '*Peter Pan* has never ... been a book for children at all' (1).

When read through the lens of textuality rather than sexuality, cultural history rather than pathology, Barrie's prose style seems neither a failure nor incomprehensible, but rather an early manifestation of those representational practices that we have come to call Modernist. That Barrie's *Tommy* novels ought to be considered precursors to, or early manifestations of, Modernism has already been mooted. Andrew Nash cites a review of *Sentimental Tommy* in *The Nation* in 1897 that suggests the novel's focus on the interior life of the artist would herald a 'new dawn' in the literary representation of the mind of the writer. He also mentions that T.S. Eliot and D.H. Lawrence were readers of the novel. Lawrence was impressed enough to write that it had helped him understand his own predicament, which supports the notion that it be viewed as an 'unacknowledged precursor to modernism' (Nash, 'A Phenomenally Slow Producer' 53). Nash goes on to argue that the *Tommy* novels' emphasis on the emotional or 'sentimental' as an aspect of masculinity is particularly *avant-garde*:

> Barrie's work can be identified as an important contribution to one of the most forward-looking idioms of his age. Anxiety over male sexuality and its relationship with creativity was to become a commonplace of modernism and it is perhaps not surprising that a young D.H. Lawrence responded to the *Tommy* novels with great enthusiasm, suggesting, in a letter to Jessie Chambers, that they helped to define the way he felt about himself. ('Trying to be a Man' 125)

However, Michelle Ann Abate argues that in its depiction of the relation between masculinity and sentiment, *Sentimental Tommy* models 'emerging modernist forms of queer sexuality' rather than new masculine identities:

> With his sexual impotence and his inability to engage in "normal" heterosexual relations, the book's title character can most accurately be described as a modern queer figure, and one whose queerness is, paradoxically, the source of both his personal pain and his professional creativity. (476)[7]

For both Nash and Abate, the *Tommy* novels herald new modernist subjectivities. This same claim can be made about the *Peter Pan* texts, in which Barrie destabilises the boundaries between adult and child, interpellating sequentially or simultaneously the child in the adult and the adult in the child. Thus, Paul D. Fox argues that Neverland is a 'repudiation of the impositional strictures

---

7 Abate notes that the novels have often been read as biographically revealing of Barrie's own sexual difficulties, but from her perspective Barrie's asexuality is an instance of 'queer sexuality' rather than evidence of latent paedophilia (474). She seems to suggest here that it is not just Barrie's texts but Barrie himself who models a new kind of subject.

of Edwardian discourse that equally determine adult and child' (254), and that Barrie attempts to undermine any such boundaries or fixed identities. Rather, he requires his readers 'to imagine, to fictively produce, new ways of conceiving the world, and its patterns of relationships' (259), including those between adults and children. Although Rose notes that '*Peter Pan* was written at the time of Freud' (10), the implication of her study is that Barrie himself was unaware of Freud's ideas. However, it could be argued that, with his postulation of the child and adult as coterminous — with the child always telescoped within the adult — Barrie underscores Freud's notion that childhood experiences and fantasies are pivotal to the formation of adult psychic life.

In fact, Barrie's position is closer to the Freud of *Civilization and Its Discontents* than to his theories of psycho-sexual development; the brief description of John in the final chapter of *Peter and Wendy* is a tragic indictment of the cost of growing up and assuming a fixed adult identity, of the dead hand of 'civilization' which Barrie so abhorred: 'The bearded man who doesn't know any story to tell his children was once John' (220). Telling stories is the verbal equivalent of play in the Barrie pantheon: Peter may be the embodiment of play, but Wendy is the embodiment of story. That adulthood entails the end of play and the end of stories equates it with the death of the imaginary and creativity: adulthood is thus the antithesis of NeverLand because it entails a fixed and hence diminished subjectivity. With the loss of play and story, the subject is lost to her or himself: the man who 'was once John' is reduced to a nameless fossil.

Through its ambivalent tone and linguistic play, its destabilisation of narrative voice and narrative address, its broaching of boundaries between narrators, characters and readers, and its modelling of new forms of subjectivity, Barrie's prose fiction, such as *Peter and Wendy*, is a harbinger of the experimentation in literary representation which emerged at the end of the Victorian age and gathered pace after World War I. In situating Barrie's novels in relation to Modernism, I am not making grand claims; his narrative and linguistic experimentation is clearly not of the same order as that of Joyce or Woolfe. But if, as Peter Childs claims, '[t]he tendency towards narrative relativity, before and after Einstein, is perhaps the most striking aspect of Modernist fiction, from Conrad and James to Proust and Woolf, in its use of perspective, unreliability, anti-absolutism, instability, individuality and subjective perceptions' (66), then

Barrie's play with enunciation, his rapid-fire shifts in narrative perspective and the remarkable instability of tone that characterises all his later novels, including the *Peter Pan* texts, surely qualify him to be considered, if not as a fully-fledged Modernist, then as a proto-Modernist. If we turn our attention from Barrie's purported perversions to his prose, it is clear, I suggest, that Barrie himself was challenging the fixities of the Victorian subject through formal experimentation and the interpellation of new subjectivities. Surely, a detailed consideration of Barrie's work in relation to Modernism is long overdue.

Works Cited

Abate, Michelle Ann. 'Constructing Modern Lesbian Affect from Late Victorian Emotionalism: Willa Cather's "Tommy, the Unsentimental" and J.M. Barrie's *Sentimental Tommy*.' *Women's Writing* 18.4 (November 2011): 468-85.

Barrie, J.M. *Peter Pan in Kensington Gardens* and *Peter and Wendy*. Oxford: Oxford World's Classic, 1991.

——. *Margaret Ogilvy*. The Uniform Edition of the Works of J.M. Barrie. 1922. London: Hodder and Stoughton, 1932.

——. *Sentimental Tommy: the Story of His Boyhood*. The Uniform Edition of the Works of J.M. Barrie. 1896. London: Cassell and Company, Ltd., 1932.

——. *Tommy and Grizel*. The Uniform Edition of the Works of J.M. Barrie. 1900. London: Cassell and Company, Ltd., 1932.

Bennett, Andrew. *The Author*. The New Critical Idiom. Ed. John Drakakis. London and New York: Routledge, 2005.

Birkin, Andrew. *J.M. Barrie and the Lost Boys: the Real Story Behind Peter Pan*. 1979. New Haven and London: Yale UP, 2003.

——. *The Lost Boys*. 3 episodes. Dir. Rodney Bennett. BBC, 1978.

Brown, Craig. 'Peter Pan and the Serial Killer.' MailOnline. 22 July 2008. http://www.dailymail.co.uk./home/books/article-1037275/Peter-Pan-, accessed 7 December 2012.

Chaney, Lisa. *Hide-and-Seek with Angels: a Life of J.M. Barrie*. New York: St Martin's Press, 2005.

Childs, Peter. *Modernism*. The New Critical Idiom. John Drakakis. Ed. London and New York: Routledge, 2000.

Dudgeon, Piers. *Captivated: J.M. Barrie, Daphne du Maurier & the Dark Side of Neverland*. London: Vintage, 2008.

'Famous British Paedophiles.' http://www.glgarden.org/ocg/archive1/barrie.html, accessed 8 June 2012.

Fox, Paul D. 'Other Maps showing through: the Liminal Identities of Neverland.' *Children's Literature Association Quarterly* 32.3 (Fall 2007): 252-68.

Hammerton J.A. *J.M. Barrie: the Story of a Genius*. London: Sampson Low Marston, 1929.

Hollindale, Peter. 'A Hundred Years of Peter Pan.' *Children's Literature in Education* 36.3 (September 2005): 197-215.

——. 'Introduction'. J.M. Barrie. *Peter Pan in Kensington Gardens* and *Peter and Wendy*. Oxford: Oxford's World's Classic, 1991. vii-xxviii.

Jack, R.D.S. *The Road to the Never Land: A Reassessment of J.M. Barrie's Dramatic Art*. Aberdeen: Aberdeen UP, 1991. Glasglow: humming earth, 2010.

——. 'The Manuscript of Peter Pan.' *Children's Literature* 18. Ed. Francleia Butler, Margaret R. Higonnet and Barbara Rosen. Yale: Yale UP, 1990.

JMBarrie. www.jmbarrie.co.uk/, accessed 30 October 2012.

Kavey, Alison B. 'Introduction: from Peanut Butter to the Silver screen.' *Second Star to the Right: Peter Pan in the Popular Imagination*. Ed. Alison B. Kavey and Lester D. Friedman. New Brunswick, NJ: Rutgers UP, 2008. 1-12.

Morrison, Richard. 'Peter Panic: Is It a Paedophile Nightmare or an Innocent Tale?' *The Times* (29 December 2004).

Nash, Andrew. '"Trying to Be a Man": J.M. Barrie and Sentimental Masculinity.' *Forum for Modern Language Studies* 35.2 (April 1999): 113-25.

——. '"A Phenomenally Slow Producer": J.M. Barrie, Scribner's and the Publication of *Sentimental Tommy*.' *The Yale University Library Gazette* 74.1-2 (November 1999): 41-53.

Ogilvie, Daniel M. 'Margaret's Smile.' *Handbook of Psychobiography*. William Todd Schultz. Ed. Oxford: Oxford UP, 2005. 175-87.

Quest, Jason A. *Neverpedia*. http://neverpedia.com/pan/Why_Zebras_Don%27t_Get_Ulcers, accessed 30 October 2012.

Rose, Jacqueline. *The Case of Peter Pan, or the Impossibility of Children's Fiction.* 1984. Philadelphia: University of Pennsylvania Press, 1992.

———.'The Return of Peter Pan.' *The Case of Peter Pan, or the Impossibility of Children's Fiction.* Introductory essay to 1992 edition.

Rudd, David. 'Children's Literature and the Return to Rose.' *Children's Literature Association Quarterly* 35:3 (Fall 2010): 290-310.

Sapolsky, Robert A. *Why Zebras Don't Get Ulcers: a Guide to Stress, Stress-related Diseases and Coping.* New York: W.H. Freeman and Company, 1994.

———. 'Why Zebras Don't Get Ulcers: Stress, Disease & Coping' *Thought Leader Forum.* http://www.capatcolumbia.com/CSFB%20TLF/2002/sapolsky_sidecolumn.pdf, accessed 5 August 2012.

Schultz, William Todd. Ed. 'Introduction' *Handbook of Psychobiography.* Oxford: Oxford UP, 2005. 3-18.

———. 'How to Strike Psychological Pay Dirt in Biographical Data' *Handbook of Psychobiography.* Oxford: Oxford UP, 2005. 42-63.

Telfer, Kevin. *Peter Pan's First X1: the Extraordinary Story of J.M. Barrie's Cricket Team.* London: Sceptre, 2010.

White, Donna R. and C. Anita Tarr. Ed. *J.M. Barrie's Peter Pan In and Out of Time: a Children's Classic at 100.* Children's Literature Association Centennial Studies Series, no. 4. Lanham, Maryland: The Scarecrow Press, 2006.

Wilson, Ann. 'Hauntings, Anxiety, Technology and Gender in *Peter Pan.*' *Modern Drama* 43.4 (Winter 2000): 595+. *Expanded Academic ASAP*, accessed 11 January 2012.

This book is available as a free fully-searchable ebook from
www.adelaide.edu.au/press

www.ingramcontent.com/pod-product-compliance
Lightning Source LLC
Chambersburg PA
CBHW081131080526
44587CB00021B/3830